Soldiers' League
The story of Army Rugby League

Sean Fanning

London League Publications Ltd

Soldiers' League
The story of Army Rugby League

Front cover: Danny Hunter in action for Army RL; Sean Fanning on active service; 2006 Combined Services team after winning series in Australia; Army 2010 Inter-Services Champions (Photo: Peter Lush). Back cover: From top: 2012 Army Academy team; 2012 Ladies team with Inter-Services trophy; 2010 Army Vets team (all photos Peter Lush)

A CIP catalogue record for this book is available from the British Library.

First published in Great Britain in October 2013 by:
London League Publications Ltd, P.O. Box 65784, London NW2 9NS

ISBN: 978-1903659-69-4

Cover design by: Stephen McCarthy Graphic Design
                                46, Clarence Road, London N15 5BB

Layout and research: Peter Lush

Printed and bound in Great Britain by Charlesworth Press, Wakefield

This book does not represent the views of The Army, Army Rugby League or Soldiers' League.

Forewords

Andy Gregory

I got involved with Army Rugby League through Jimmy Aspinall, who is a good mate of mine, and has been in the Army for over 20 years.

I found the team easy to coach. They were disciplined, fit and listened to the coaches and other players. They showed me the utmost respect. The hardest job I had was when we were playing the Royal Navy in the Inter-Services competition. I had to try to keep them calm! I didn't realise there was such a rivalry between the Army and the Navy, I was a bit naïve. I built up some great ties with the team; they didn't like losing at all, especially against the Royal Navy. They felt that the Navy boys got all the perks. The players were very determined; they played the game hard and always gave 110 per cent.

I remember going to a barracks in Yorkshire to coach the team. At the gate, the sentry asked me who I was. "Coach of the British Army rugby league team" I replied. "But what are you?" he asked me. I was a bit confused, so I replied "A Great Britain international". "No", he said, "Are you a civvy?" "Yes" I said, so after that I was "Andy Gregory, British Army coach and 'Civvy'".

When I was staying in a barracks they would always put me in the Officers' Mess, and looked after me. I had a great time.

One of the problems we had, which was also true for the RAF and the Royal Navy, was that we never knew what team we would have. We needed a regular team, to develop some fluency. But we would have players flying in a day or two before the game, then some more would turn up the next day. If we could have played regularly, with a consistent side, we would have matched the best amateur teams.

When we played in the Inter-Services tournament, the captain gave a really good speech. He explained what we were here for, what the Army means, and to go out and do battle, show determination and team spirit. They always backed each other up. They had a real team spirit, a camaraderie, based on their Army life.

Jimmy organised for me to go to Germany, to Munster, to do presentations there for one of their tournaments. I had a great time, we had a German meal, and the food and hospitality were absolutely superb. And I went in a tank – Jimmy has the photos!

I have no links with the Army, but my granddad fought in the Second World War, and was a Prisoner-of-War in Burma. He raised me with my mum, and helped me on my way. He had died by the time I coached the Army team, but I think he would have been very proud of me.

July 2013

Andy Gregory was one of the best British scrum-halves in the post-war period. He won every honour in the game, played for Widnes, Warrington, Wigan, Leeds and Salford, and played 26 times for Great Britain.

Lieutenant-Colonel Jeremy Bethell

I am delighted to be able to write the forward to *Soldiers' League, The Story of Army Rugby League,* as it is a story that needs to be told and then preserved. There are soldiers joining the Army today that have no idea of the birth pangs of this sport within the Services, indeed there are still many serving today who joined when Rugby League just did not figure in the military sporting bible *Games & Sports in the Army,* so playing this great game could only be undertaken when not on duty. I am so pleased that this heritage has been assembled in such an easily read and digestible way.

I am also delighted because the idea behind this book and the biggest contribution is from Sean Fanning, who, leading by example, has managed to elicit contributions from most of those who have been influential in the game's development within the Army. Their input, and particularly the editing by Peter Lush, has made this book come to life. Sean is a very modest man, and although there is passing reference within the text, many initiatives, such as the formation of the Soldiers League - "a members club, using the profile of Army Rugby League to raise money for service charities" have been at his instigation, hence the full title of this book.

Rugby league in the Army is a sport played by soldiers for soldiers. The ethos of the game and the military ethos are both intertwined and complimentary. "Stand up for your mates, and be counted" seen in 13 players in a line on the field of play in Aldershot, is reflected in the patrols around the fields of Helmand Province, and vice versa. This is the story of the first two decades of Army Rugby League, the setting of its foundations and how it has developed. I commend it to you all.

July 2013
Lieutenant-Colonel (retired) Jeremy Bethell is the Vice President and former Chairman of Army Rugby League and the President of Soldiers League.

Army Rugby League: Presidents and Chairmen

Presidents
Lieutenant-General Sir Scott Grant
Major-General David Judd
Major-General Michael Huntley
Major-General Ian Dale CBE
Major-General Carew Wilks CBE

Chairmen
Major Martin Morris – Founding Chairman
Lieutenant-Colonel Mike Bowman 1995 to March 2002
Lieutenant-Colonel Jeremy Bethell March 2002 to September 2007
Brigadier Frank Noble September 2007 to present

Introduction

In 2000, London League Publications Ltd published a book by David Hinchliffe MP, *Rugby's Class War*. It was about the work of the All-Party Parliamentary Rugby League Group. An important part of the book was the work the Group had done to help establish that rugby league should become a recognised sport in the Armed Forces.

It was a campaign that was finally successful in April 1994. We did not cover in that book the development of the sport in the Armed Forces, and I must admit that until starting work on this book, it was an area of the sport that I knew little about.

Having now been working on this book with Sean for almost three years, I now am aware that the progress the sport has made is fantastic. This is particularly true given the demands there have been on the Armed Forces over the past 10 years. One point that Sean has stressed to me regularly is that this is a book about rugby league players who are in the Army, and are serving soldiers. I hope that we have made that clear. It is also important to show the difficulties that rugby league in the Army, and the other Armed Forces, face. Anyone who has run an amateur team in any sport has faced the problem of players not turning up, often for a variety of reasons, from work commitments to – for a Sunday morning team – a heavy night out on a Saturday! But forces teams lose players for six months or more because they are on active service on the other side of the world. Having said that, there is universal agreement among everyone we have interviewed that sport is very important in the Armed Forces, and that rugby league matches very well the qualities necessary to be a good soldier.

Another area covered in the book was the importance of building structures for what was a new sport in the Army. One of the strengths of Army RL is having people to draw on whose jobs involve organisation of activities, and they can transfer these skills to the sporting arena. I do not believe it is a coincidence that the first Army RL Secretary, Martin Coyd, now is heavily involved with one of the biggest and best organised amateur clubs in the south of England. The structures in Army Rugby League that were put in place in the early years, allowing players to play at different levels, have lasted.

I suspect that many rugby league fans are not really aware of the strength of the sport in the Armed Forces. Hopefully the recent Armed Forces World Cup will make more supporters aware of the sport in the forces, as will this book, but it is frustrating that often the trade press does not cover the Inter-Services matches. Something that could be considered is to again try playing some matches in the north of England, allowing rugby league fans to watch the matches live, especially in communities that have strong links with the Armed Forces.

Finally, a massive 'thank you' to everyone who has contributed to this book through providing photos, programmes and reports, being interviewed and reading drafts. My only previous connection with the military was working with my dad on his book on the history of our family. He was in the Royal Engineers in the Second World War, and his memories of that time were an important part of that book and his life. He died in 2011, but I think would have been very proud at me being involved with a book about the Army. It has been an absolute privilege to work with Sean and everyone else in Army RL who has been involved in this book. I hope it helps give the sport a higher profile and raises plenty of money for Soldiers' League.

Peter Lush
July 2013

Thank you

Sean Fanning and London League Publications Ltd would like to thank everyone who contributed to the book, agreed to be interviewed, lent us photographs, match reports, programmes and other documents. A special thank you to Jeremy Bethell, Martin Coyd, Mick Scholes, Richard Naivalurua, Jason Grant, Dave Groce, Jimmy Aspinall and Julie Hulatt for help and support well beyond the call of duty! Our thanks to Brigadier Frank Noble, chairman of Army RL, who does a great job for the sport.

Thank you to Richard 'Sponge' Beattie and Julie Hulatt for providing photos; to Graham Williams for writing chapter 10, and the profile of Lee Innes; to David Ballheimer for writing the report on the 2013 Armed Forces World Cup Final; to Steve McCarthy for designing the cover and the staff of Charlesworth Press for printing the book.

Many thanks to the families of David Monkhouse, Tom Sephton and Craig Hopson for their support, and Alan Boyle and Jason Grant for their help with Chapter 1.

About the author

Staff Sergeant Sean Fanning played professional rugby league for Leigh and Highfield. He has served as a medic in the Army for over 22 years. He has been on four operational tours overseas, including Northern Ireland, Operation Granby, Iraq and Afghanistan in 2012. He has played for and coached the Army and Combined Services rugby league teams. He also captained the Great Britain Armed Forces team on two tours of Australia, including winning the 2008 Defence Forces World Cup.

Danny Hunter

Danny kindly consented to us using his photo on the cover. He told us a bit about himself: "I was born in Hull on 11 September 1990. Mum got me into rugby at the age of four to try and get rid of some of my energy. I played for Myton Warriors which is a great family club and great for introducing young boys and girls into the game, I then moved to West Hull to progress as a young player and develop my skills because at the time West Hull was probably the best club in the city. I then got selected to represent Hull FC's youth from the age of 12 to 17. I then was given the chance to sign professional at Hull Kingston Rovers in 2009, aged 19. I only played in three games throughout the year, got released, joined up in 2010 and haven't looked back since. I am in the Light Dragoons, Royal Armoured Corps.

About this book

During the time this book was written, Sean Fanning was a serving soldier in the Army. This included a six month tour in Afghanistan in 2012. Research for the book, and interviews for the profile section were therefore done by Peter Lush.

As well as being the author, Sean was also a participant in many of the matches in this book. Therefore, in certain sections, his memories and views are quoted, rather than being put in the first person.

Our apologies for any spelling mistakes or inconsistencies in names. We have done our best to be consistent and accurate, but verification has been difficult at times. Also, in some cases nick-names have been used. We have based our team line ups and match reports on what was in the media at the time. The same applies to photo captions.

We have done our best to source all photos, but if we have not done this, no breach of copyright was intended. Please contact London League Publications Ltd if you believe this to be the case.

Contents

Chapter 10 was written by Graham Williams.
The 2013 report in Chapter 7 was written by Peter Lush, referring to reports written by David Lawrenson on behalf of the RFL.

Above: The Soldiers' League stall at Chorley in June 2013, with some of the Vets players. (Photo: Julie Hulatt). Below: Jeremy Bethell and Julie Hulatt present a cheque to Denise Edgar from the Royal British Legion in 2012. (Photo: Peter Lush)

Soldiers' League is a members' club which uses the profile of Army Rugby League to raise money for service charities, including the Royal British Legion, BLESMA and Combat Stress. Members give regular donations and Soldiers' League also has a stall at many Army matches – such as at Chorley in the top photo. The organisation is completely run by volunteers.

Soldiers' League also has an annual dinner on the eve of the Challenge Cup Final. To support Soldiers' League, visit the website: http://www.pitchero.com/clubs/soldiersleague

Sean in action for The Army against BARLA.

Sean Fanning would like to dedicate this book:

In memory of my mum, Catherine Fanning who died of cancer on 18 June 1996; to my wife Clare and children Jack and Scarlett; also to my dad Tony, brother Anthony and my sister Sara.

and

To all those in the British Army who have lost their lives or had their lives changed through involvement in conflict around the world.

1. Not forgotten

Jack Harrison VC

John (Jack) Harrison was a school teacher and star winger with Hull FC in the Northern Union, the forerunner to Rugby League, in the period before the First World War. He was a regular first team player and a top try scorer. During the battle for Arras in 1917 he charged an enemy machine gun position alone. He was awarded the Victoria Cross posthumously, missing believed killed. He had already won the Military Cross for earlier bravery.

Harrison is rightly remembered as the only professional player who was playing the sport when he enlisted. However, it is important to mention two other professional rugby league players who also won the VC. Thomas Steele played briefly for Broughton Rangers after the War; and Thomas Bryan played for the original Castleford club in 1906–07. (See chapter 10 for further information)

To honour this extraordinary soldier and player, the Army Rugby League presented the Jack Harrison VC Memorial Trophy to the Combined Services Rugby League in 2000, to be contested for annually in the Inter Services fixture between the Army and the Royal Navy.

He joined the Army as a volunteer and a private in November 1915. He was sent for officer training at the Inns of Court OTC, and on 5 August 1916 was commissioned as a temporary 2nd Lieutenant in the 11th Battalion of the East Yorkshire Regiment. He was posted to active service on 19 September. In October 1916, when the Hull Brigade was sent back from the front for 'rest and recuperation', his Battalion won the Brigade Rugby tournament.

On 20 February 1917, his Battalion was involved in an attack on the German lines. For his leadership, he was awarded the Military Cross. The *London Gazette* outlined on 17 April 1917 that this was for "Conspicuous gallantry and devotion to duty. He handled his platoon with great courage and skill, reached his objective under the most trying conditions and captured a prisoner. He set a splendid example throughout."

The Hull Brigade then moved to Ecurie, north of Arras. On the night of 2 and 3 May, he was leading 'B' Company in an attack on the German lines. His men were under constant attack from a German machine gun post. The *London Gazette* reported the following which led to the award of the Victoria Cross, for "most conspicuous bravery and self-sacrifice in attack": "Owing to darkness and to smoke from the enemy barrage and from our own and to the fact that our objective was in a dark wood, it was impossible to see when our barrage lifted off the enemy front line. Nevertheless, 2nd Lieut. Harrison led his company against the

1

enemy trench under heavy rifle and machine gun fire but was repulsed. Re-organising his command as best he could in no-man's land, he again attacked in darkness, but with no success. Then, turning round, this gallant officer single-handedly made a dash at the enemy machine gun, hoping to knock out the gun and so save the lives of many of his company. His self-sacrifice and absolute disregard of danger was an inspiring example to all. (He is reported missing, believed killed.)". He was 26 years old.

Harrison had been married in September 1914, and had a son, also named John, but known as Jackie. A plaque was displayed at Lime Street School where he had been a teacher. A fund was set up to pay for the education of his son, who later played rugby union and cricket, and also joined the Army. He was commissioned into the Duke of Wellington's (West Riding) Regiment, and was killed at Dunkirk on 1 June 1940.

In Hull, a block of flats was named in Jack Harrison's honour in 1986, and a memorial to him at the KC Stadium was unveiled before the Great Britain versus Australia test match on 15 November 2003.

Jack Harrison was born in East Hull on 12 November 1891. He attended Craven Street School, and then did a teacher training course at St John's College in York. He was a very good sportsman, and played five matches as an amateur for York NUFC, scoring three tries. He made his debut for York on 30 March 1912, and kept his place for the rest of the season.

In 1912 he returned to Hull to teach at Lime Street Boys School and joined Hull FC. He played 101 first team matches for Hull, scored 91 tries and kicked two goals. In his last season for the club, 1914–15, he twice scored six tries in a match, against Bradford Northern and Wakefield Trinity. This record stood until Clive Sullivan broke it in 1968. His 52 tries that season is still a club record.

He scored the second try in Hull's 6–0 win over Wakefield Trinity in the 1914 Challenge Cup Final and played in the 1914–15 Yorkshire Cup Final when Hull were beaten by Huddersfield. Had it not been for the War, he would almost certainly have won representative honours.

His widow, Lillian Harrison, was presented with his Victoria Cross at Buckingham Palace by King George V in March 1918. His body was never found and he is commemorated on the Commonwealth War Graves Commission Arras Memorial. Lillian Harrison died in December 1977; her husband's medals were donated to the East Yorkshire Regiment Museum in Beverley.

(Photo: Roger Pugh)

Bombardier Craig Hopson
40th Regiment, The Royal Artillery

In 2009, Castleford was devastated by the loss of two soldiers from the town in Afghanistan. As the funeral for another young soldier was being held, news came through that Bombardier Craig Hopson had been killed in action in Helmand province on 25 July. The *Yorkshire Post* reported: "A tribute from his family, who include mum Lynn, his partner Eleanor and three-month-old daughter Amelia, said: "Craig was the light in so very many lives. The light has now gone out. His family and many, many friends will love him and miss him forever. Craig the legend. Our Craig has left a hole in our lives that no one else can ever fill. He was loved so much."

Bombardier Hopson was killed when the Jackal vehicle in which he was travelling struck an explosive device while taking part in Operation Panchai Palang. He was part of a patrol in the Babaji area of Helmand province looking for an area for a polling station in the forthcoming Afghan Presidential elections.

The former Castleford High Technology College pupil joined 40th Regiment Royal Artillery, the Lowland Gunners, in 2002. Lieutenant Colonel Owen Adams, Commanding Officer of 40th Regiment Royal Artillery said: "Bombardier Hopson was part of the fabric of my regiment, known to everyone as a man with an enormous personality and a huge heart. He had that rare quality of being able to inject his own brand of gruff Northern humour into any situation, always at ear splitting volume, generally at the expense of his superiors in the Regiment, but always in good spirit.

"A talented sportsman, he gave no quarter on the rugby field and expected none in return and this characterised his approach to life and conduct of operations in Afghanistan, yet, for all his tenacity and uncompromising nature, he displayed a humility and compassion that only served to endear him further to those who were privileged to know him."

He added: "The quality of a man's life cannot be measured in days or years, but by the memories left when they are gone. Those touched by the life of Bombardier Hopson are left with the anguish of his loss but are consoled by their memories of him."

Bombardier Hopson had previously completed operational tours in Iraq and Cyprus. He was deployed to Kandahar in March 2009 as Second in Command of a Fire Support Team, attached, with his Battery, to The Black Watch, 3rd Battalion the Royal Regiment of Scotland. Lieutenant Colonel Stephen Cartwright, Commanding Officer, The Black Watch, 3 SCOTS Battle Group, said: "'Hoppo' was so proud of his new born daughter and we cannot begin to imagine the hole that has been left in Eleanor's and Amelia's lives. Amelia will never know her father; our lives have been made richer by him in every way and I hope they can take some comfort from our thoughts and prayers at this most tragic time."

Thousand lined the streets of Castleford for his funeral, which received national press coverage. His family wore black and yellow, the colours of the local Castleford Tigers team, which Craig supported. There were also tributes from local councillors, and the Secretary of State for Defence, Bob Ainsworth MP.

Since 2010, an annual match has been played in Craig's memory. The Royal Artillery Corps RL website outlined that: "The Hopson Trophy is dedicated to one of our players Bombardier Craig Hopson from 40th Regiment RA who tragically died during the summer of 2009 whilst on operations in Afghanistan. Craig known as "Hoppo' to colleagues was a larger than life character whose sense of humour was legendary. He was an excellent soldier both determined and committed who was always willing to help those in need of guidance. This proud steadfast Yorkshireman was the light in so very many lives.

On the field Craig was a talented sportsman representing the Army at Rugby League on several occasions. In tribute to Craig the memorial match between the Royal Artillery and Castleford District Select is played annually. This fixture not only enables his legacy to live on in the rugby league community but it also allows funds to be raised for a worthy charity nominated by Craig's family. The 2010 fixture was on Tuesday 16 February in Castleford. The game was a great advert for rugby league producing at times some real quality play from both sides, which we know Craig would have approved of. The game was won 18–16 by the Royal Artillery in front of over 800 people who had turned up to pay their respects.

The 2011 fixture was played at The Stoop as the curtain raiser to the Harlequins versus Castleford Tigers Super League match. The game finished with a nail biting penalty kick as the Royal Artillery won the game 22–20. The 2012 fixture saw the match return to the heartland of rugby league at Cutsyke in Castleford, Craig's home town. The match finished with a 28–20 victory for the Royal Artillery team as they retained the trophy for a third consecutive year. Craig would have been proud of the rugby played in his remembrance.

The 2013 fixture saw the match get played again at the Castleford RU ground. The match finished with a 26–18 victory for the Royal Artillery team as they retained the trophy for a fourth year. Once again hundreds of spectators turned up to pay their respects.

Craig we will never forget."

The Nottingham Outlaws club were also involved in organising a charity match in 2010 against the Royal Artillery Gunners in Craig's memory, which raised almost £2,000 for Help for Heroes. There is also the Craig Hopson Memorial Fund, a Facebook page in his memory, and a website, www.craighopsonrl.co.uk which all support fundraising efforts for service charities through sales of kit and publicising other fundraising activities.

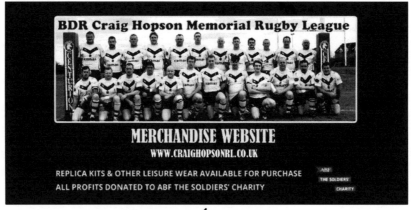

4

Sergeant David Thomas 'Bob' Monkhouse
Mechanized Brigade Reconnaissance Force
The Royal Dragoon Guards, The Royal Armoured Corps

In July 2010, Army Rugby League lost one of its founder members. Sergeant David Thomas Monkhouse, known as 'Bob' to everyone in his Regiment and Army Rugby League, was 35 years old. He was born in 1974 in Carlisle and raised in Aspatria. On leaving school aged 16, he joined the Junior Leaders' Regiment in Bovington. On 31 July 1992 he joined The 5th Royal Inniskilling Dragoon Guards as a Chieftan Gunner, shortly before it was amalgamated into The Royal Dragoon Guards.

Throughout his colourful career he served on four tours in Northern Ireland and in Iraq in 2007. He qualified as a Regimental Combat Medical Technician Class 1. He was the stalwart of the Regimental Medical Centre, providing enthusiasm and initiative in keeping the Regiment medically fit.

On Saturday 17 July 2010, the Brigade Reconnaissance Force (BRF) was conducting an influence patrol, searching likely insurgent compounds to reduce the intimidation of the local population of Adinzai. At 4.45am, while moving into a cordon position, Sergeant Monkhouse was struck by an Improvised Explosive Device (IED) and killed in action. He left behind his mother, Bobby; his sister Deborah; and the love of his life, his daughter, Daisy-Twinkle.

He was one of the earliest strappers and kitmen for Army Rugby League and served the sport loyally for many years. He was instrumental in its early success in the Army and its development within the Royal Dragoon Guards. The Army RL match programme for the game against the Royal Navy in September 2010 said that "We hope you will spare a thought to him, whilst enjoying the match, he loved this sport and will be sadly missed by all members of the Armed Forces Rugby League Community."

Jason Grant from the RDG worked with Bob in Army Rugby League for a long time and knew him well: "As a fellow Cumbrian Bob and I always got on. In terms of Regimental rugby league, Bob didn't join us until about 1998 by which time he was firmly embedded as the Regimental Medic and wished to help out as the physio. In true Bob fashion, he paid for his own courses and got straight into it. He wasn't a rugby league man by heart and therefore there were a lot of tricks of the trade we required him to pick up in a relatively short space of time. By the time we had our most successful season, in 2001, he was absolutely first rate. He could get on the pitch and, as the coach, I would know almost straightaway whether the player was coming off or staying on. If the team was under pressure and needing to reorganise Bob could provide that for us, a calming word in the ear of the injured player would ensure he stayed down for that extra minute or two while momentum was taken out of the opposition' attack and we could sort ourselves out.

Cheating, no; bending the rules, most definitely. As a man who could get players quickly back into the action, he was also first rate. I liked to deal with the 'now' and not what we could be doing in the next game. He helped me do that and get players back on the field.

5

At Royal Armoured Corps level, we wouldn't have got through the 2006 tour to Australia without him. We were battered in the first match by Parramatta's 3rd team, and picked up several injuries. Two of the players did not take to the field again on the tour. He somehow managed to keep everyone else patched up and moving for the rest of the trip.

On that tour Bob decided it would be funny to swipe the Corps flag as a souvenir – RDG always had a 'property manager', no matter whose company we were in. As per usual, his timing couldn't have been worse because it was required for a photo shoot with the England team who were there prepping for the Three Nations tournament. Major Port went ballistic, but calmed down after it mysteriously reappeared outside his room some hours later.

Having fallen victim to his sense of humour once too often, those who knew him were aware of the signs that Bob was about to get up to no good. In Australia this backfired on him superbly on a walk around Darling Harbour. With a glint in his eye the lads just knew he was angling for something and decided to strike first. As Bob tried to coax lads to the water's edge, Eddie Edwards sneaked up behind him and launched him seawards off the pier. It was at least a 15 feet drop and Bob was none too pleased as the lads, tourists and locals alike roared with laughter."

Private Tom Sephton
Battalion The Mercian Regiment (Cheshire)
The Prince of Wales's Division

Tom Sephton was from Warrington, and joined the Army in July 2008. After initial training, he joined the 1st Battalion The Mercian Regiment (Cheshire) [1 MERCIAN] in January 2009, He joined Mortar Platoon and served in the United Kingdom, The Falkland Islands and Kenya, and on operations in Afghanistan.

On the morning of Sunday 4 July 2010, operating in a Rifle Platoon, Private Sephton deployed to provide flank protection to an IED clearance operation. While clearing a route for his section, he was caught in an IED blast and seriously wounded. He was taken by helicopter to hospital at Camp Bastion, and then flown to the UK. Tragically he died of his wounds on the afternoon of 5 July 2010, with his family present. Only days earlier, a school friend of his had also been killed while on duty in Afghanistan. Both had been classmates, had played at Crosfields (his friend had played football) and had joined up together.

Lieutenant Colonel Andrew Hadfield, Commanding Officer 1 MERCIAN, said: "Private Tom Sephton had been enthused by the nature of the Platoon, and he fitted in well from the very start, training with them in the Falkland Islands and Kenya, before deploying to Afghanistan. He was a hardworking man, always ready to volunteer for additional work or responsibility in order to improve the lot of others.

He is remembered by his friends as a man who never complained, who just got on with the job, however difficult or unpleasant it was. This is probably the reason that he was often to be found at the head of patrols, searching for IEDs that would threaten them.

He was courageous and selfless to the last, placing himself in harm's way to save others. When he was mortally injured he was alongside his best friend Private Charlie Emina, and among his mates whom he did so much to help.

Tom Sephton was not a particularly big man in terms of size, but he had a big heart, and was full of fun and energy. He was a keen rugby player and enjoyed playing on the wing for his Company, where his fitness and speed were more than a match for most.

He punched above his weight in every way, whether militarily, in sporting activities or by just being a great friend and comrade. His obvious ability had been spotted, and he was due to attend a promotion course on return from Afghanistan.

If any man lived the motto, 'Stand Firm Strike Hard', it was Tom Sephton. He will be missed deeply by the Mortar Platoon, and by the men of C Company to whom he was attached. The thoughts and prayers of the entire Battalion are with his family and friends at this most difficult of times."

Tom never got the opportunity to play for the full Army Rugby League team. But the sport was very important to him. Some of the tributes from his fellow soldiers commented on his enthusiasm for the game and ability at playing it.

Lieutenant Richard Sawyer, Officer Commanding 9 Platoon, C Company, 1 MERCIAN, said: "Private Tom Sephton was a mature soldier. His courage was unflinching regardless of danger. His natural size meant that he did not look like a rugby player but his speed and love for playing the game ensured that he was a talented player."

Lieutenant David Payne, C Company, 1 MERCIAN, commented: "He was also a great rugby league player who ran rings round me on more than one occasion when on the training field. His enthusiasm for the game reflects his attitude to all things in life."

Warrant Officer Class 2 Paul Morley, Mortar Platoon Second in Command, on behalf of the Mortar Platoon, 1 MERCIAN, said: "[Tom was] a keen sportsman, he represented his Company at rugby, subsequently playing a key role within Support Company's trophy winning effort. At times he left a few Battalion rugby players a little red faced and more than surprised with his pace and skill."

In September 2010, a memorial match in Tom Sephton's memory was held. The publicity for it outlined his background in the sport: "Tom started playing rugby league in 2000, working his way up through the ranks of Crosfields ARLFC and went on to represent Warrington schoolboys (although for some bizarre reason Tom was a St Helens fan! Even going so far as to wear a St Helens shirt underneath his Warrington shirt!)

Tom was never going to be the biggest lad, so he made his game revolve around his natural pace. A county level sprinter, he could be seen burning down the wing with the ball tucked safely under his arm. He was a key and influential part of the 2006 under-16s squad that swept all before them winning the league championship and making the national cup semi-final, losing only three games that year.

The manager of that team, John Griffin, commented: 'He was never one to shy away from a situation, and put his body on the line for the team. He tackled well above his weight, and had an ability that cannot be coached, in that he had "situational awareness", usually making the right choice when the game got tough.

Tom would do anything asked of him by and for coaches and teammates, indeed was ready to do extras at any time. It was a privilege to be involved with such a man. Tom was a pleasure to be with on and off the pitch, a young man of honour with a wry sense of humour and a sharp wit, a man with a courage that belied his stature and loyalty beyond measure.'"

Warrington Wolves versus Castleford Tigers 11 July 2010

The above match was played six days after Tom died. His parents were guests of the Warrington Wolves at the game, along with 12 1 MERCIAN soldiers who were recovering from injuries sustained on operations in Afghanistan.

Before the match, the families, soldiers and players from both teams took to the pitch and held – at the parents' request – a minute's applause. The applause from the crowd continued, with the players delaying the kick-off of the match, until the family members and soldiers were sat in their seats in the stand.

After the match, Warrington forward Ben Westwood, the man-of-the-match, joined the soldiers and bereaved families, which was greatly appreciated. Both the Warrington Wolves and Castleford Tigers clubs have produced special or commemorative shirts to help raise funds for military charities as a tribute to the soldiers from the towns who were killed in action.

The Sephton Trophy

On 18 September 2010, the first memorial match was staged at Crosfields ARLFC, between a Crosfields Select XIII and an Army Select XIII. Nearly 2,000 people attended the match, and £7788.03 was raised for Help for Heroes. The Crosfields ARLFC Select team was be made up of players who played alongside Tom in his playing days with the club, in particular the under-16s side from 2006. An impressive number of these players have gone on to achieve great things in their young rugby careers, playing first team rugby league with Super League clubs, Warrington Wolves, St Helens and Salford Reds. More played for Championship clubs and in Super League under-20 sides. Others have had a change of code and are playing Rugby Union for teams in Bath, New Zealand and France. It was these young men who first came up with the idea for a charity memorial game for Tom.

The Army won 32–30, having conceded three tries in the first 20 minutes. Paul Riley was outstanding as skipper of the Army team, and Brigadier Andrew Sharpe OBE (Late CHESHIRE) Regimental Colonel of the MERCIAN Regiment played at prop for the last 20 minutes. He became the oldest player to play for Army RL. At full-back was Private Tom Snooks, of 1 MERCIAN, who – aged 17 – was too young to be deployed on operations, and was outstanding as man-of-the-match.

A report on the match by Sergeant Alan Boyle said: "The game itself was indeed a full blooded affair – both sides were determined to do Tom's memory justice. Hard, physical rugby league played for all the right reasons in the very best of spirits."

The Army squad was: Stu Butters RE, Kuki Tamani REME, Rob Smart RAMC, Tim Tamani REME, Karl O'Doherty REME, Paul Riley (c) RA, Dancer Kenway RLC, Ginge Windle RE, Matt Pritchard RE, Rushi Naisau REME, Casey Shaw REME, Mags Marangon REME, Dale Burnley RE, Frenchie Debaughan KRH, Jordan Kerman REME, Ryan Swindale PARA, Tom Snooks MERCIAN, Andrew Sharpe (Late CHESHIRE), Rob Muir MERCIAN.

After the match, the trophies were presented by Tom's parents, Angela Horn and Ian Sephton, in the presence of the local MPs and Mayors. The Army XIII asked that 1 MERCIAN keep and display the Tom Sephton Challenge Trophy, and that it be awarded to the winners of the Battalion's annual inter-company rugby league competition.

Since 2010 further matches have been played. On 9 July 2011, A Crosfields Select XIII played against the 1 MERCIAN RL team. In 2012 – on Armed Forces Day, two matches were played. 1 MERCIAN RL played 1 LANCS RL, followed by Crosfields ARLFC against the then Army Corps Champions, Royal Engineers RL. In 2013 once again on ARMED FORCES DAY the Royal Engineers returned after requesting a rematch after their shock defeat in 2012 – they had only been beaten six times before. The fixture looks set to continue and it has become Warrington's focus on Armed Forces Day. It will continue to be played; to keep Tom's memory alive, and to raise funds for service charities. Mike Donnison, the chairman of Crosfields ARLFC outlines: "The Tom Sephton Memorial Trophy event has become the focal point for the people of Warrington, to show their support to the Armed Forces and I am delighted to once again welcome the two Warrington infantry regiments, The 1st Battalion The Mercian Regiment, 1 Mercian, and The 1st Battalion The Duke of Lancaster Regiment, 1 Lancs. We are honoured that the Army Rugby League Corps Champions, The Royal Engineers have asked to return and play a re-match of 2012 and take part today, in doing so commemorate the occasion in a way that Tom and his family would appreciate. The game of rugby league is a combative sport, which relies on bravery, team-work, camaraderie, skills and fitness to be a success; all the attributes required to be successful in the Armed Forces.

But, the forces are much, much more than that. It is one thing putting your body on the line in this great sport, but it is no longer a ball-game, when you are putting your life on the line as our men and women of the forces are called upon to do. The importance of the event and the interest it generates is evident from the number of people attending, the volunteers helping out and the sponsors, all of whom want to show their support and pay their respects, for which I thank them most graciously. People want to be involved, because it means so much to us. The debt we owe our servicemen and women can never be repaid, but on days like today, we can at our very least show them our support."

Tom Sephton Memorial match

Left: Army RL Select skipper Paul Riley with the Mayor and Mayoress of Warrington.
Right: Richard Naivalurua presents the Crosfield ARLFC secretary Anthony Parker with an Army RL shirt. All photos of the Tom Sephton Memorial match taken by Bob Brough.

The Army RL Select team, including Brigadier Andrew Sharpe, with the Challenge Cup.

A piper leads out the teams. The referee is Steve Abel, who was in the Grenadier Guards.

Left: Richard Naivalurua presenting an Army RL shirt to Tom's Dad, Ian Sephton.

Right: Richard Naivalurua presenting an Army RL shirt to Tom's Mum, Angela Horn.

Left: Paul Riley takes the ball up.

Right: Ginge Windle charges forward.

Bottom left: Brigadier Andrew Sharpe OBE, Mr Ian Sephton and Private Tom Snooks (Mercian)

Part 1: The development of Army Rugby League

2. Building Army Rugby League

On 11 May 1994, the Army beat the RAF 26–22 at Leigh RFC's Hilton Park in the first inter-services match. A try from Richard Rasa-Phillips six minutes from time saw the Army win the Combined Services Cup in a closely fought game.

In the *Daily Telegraph*, John Whalley reported that "Though the occasion was more important than the result, both sides can feel satisfied with their contribution to an attacking encounter which featured nine tries. The RAF made the more impressive start, leading 12–0 after 14 minutes with tries from Graham Thompson and Andy Bottomley, but though they enjoyed a narrow authority in the forwards, the Army had the livelier backs, with Sean Anders and Shaun Knott impressing at half-back.

Knott sent Simon Dickson over and Phil Marsh kept the Army in touch with a try after a 45-metre break. When Dave Marsh went over for the RAF's fourth try early in the second half, the Army looked out of contention."

However, a further touchdown by Phil Marsh was followed by Rasa-Phillips's try – he was knocked out in the act of scoring – which won the match. Brian Chambers from Warrington coached the team.

Army: M. Hughes, S. Dickson, P. Marsh, M. Buckingham, A. Sanger, S. Knott, S. Anders, K. Tunstall, D. Platt, J. Wilson, M. Airey, J. Corker, D. Clark (R Rasa-Phillips). Subs: C. Brown, P. Jones, S. Burton.

RAF: A. Prout, J. Rowson, S. Hicks, A. Bottomley. A. Pattie, P. Hillier, D. Clayton, A. Killeen, S. Hainsworth, P. Briggs, R. Marsden, D. Marsh, G. Thompson. Subs: P. Dorke, B. Ward.

Referee: F. Lindop (Wakefield)

Martin Coyd had been elected as secretary after a 7-a-side tournament in Chepstow the previous month. From the players in that tournament a squad had been selected and a training weekend held. Martin organised accommodation for the players, and recalls that the next problem was finding kit for the team: "The shirts arrived, red and white with 'Army' on them, but there were no proper shorts and socks. There was a bin liner of shorts from Army Apprentices rugby union, but they were very small, and the socks were blue and burgundy! And Sky Sports were covering the game. Fortunately, Alan Rowley and Steve Simms from Leigh asked if we needed any help, and the Leigh kitman lent us socks, tie ups and shorts. I was very grateful for the goodwill of the Leigh club. We looked like a real rugby league team"

For the RAF, Damian Clayton recalled that: "It was the first time I met Martin Coyd. We had spoken on the phone a lot. It was a massive occasion for our overall development to get the game on.

We had played the French Army and Air Force, but this was playing the British Army, and was important for us. Things developed from that game, we were on the same page. I remember that we had some sponsorship from Isostar, and on the morning of the match I had to go to Dewsbury to collect all the free stuff we were getting and the banners to put up. It was a good game, and there was a match report in *The Times*, which was good for our self-esteem and recognition. The RAF had been supportive to us, as long as we did things properly. The RAF Sports Board were helpful, and liked grassroots development."

The match was well attended, including officials from the RFL and BARLA. Wigan and Great Britain stars Phil Clarke and Ian Lucas were the guests of honour.

The first Army Rugby League team who beat the RAF 26–22 at Hilton Park, Leigh in May 1994. The coach was Brian Chambers. (Photo: Courtesy Martin Coyd)

Training at Chatham for the first ever Army RL game against the RAF.
(Photo: Courtesy Martin Coyd)

Almost 100 years after the establishment of the Northern Union in Huddersfield on 29 August 1895, on 28 April 1994, Jeremy Hanley MP, the Armed Forces Minister in the then Conservative government, announced that rugby league could become a recognised sport in the Armed Forces.

As Martin Coyd outlines in his interview, there was still some work to do before recognition was to be granted by the Army Sports Control Board. In fact, the first match against the RAF took place before either sport was officially recognised in their service.

Army Rugby League had in fact been launched by Major Martin Morris, who was originally from Wigan, in October 1993. He was in command of 82 Training Squadron, and organised the first sevens competition which attracted players from 12 units and showed the potential for the game in the Army. The players from this competition formed the basis of the team that played the RAF. The RAF had been playing as the Blue Bombers since 1992, having been set up by Damian Clayton, a rugby league player from Halifax.

Before recognition, the game was being played in Germany. Jason Grant had managed to establish a team in his regiment and an 'ad-hoc cup tournament' in 1992, and regular matches were organised until the sport was officially recognised.

Much of the credit for the decision in Parliament must go to the All-Party Rugby League Parliamentary Group, led by David Hinchliffe MP, Ian McCartney MP and Geoff Lofthouse MP (later Lord Lofthouse). They had campaigned successfully on various issues, particularly over the issue of student and amateur rugby league players having the right to play rugby union. They had raised the issue of union receiving public funding while excluding amateur rugby league players. Hinchliffe himself had, in his younger days, been barred from playing union because of having played league.

Change was also happening in rugby union. With its World Cup, and cup and league competitions for clubs, the sport's much cherished concept of 'amateurism' throughout the game was systematically being undermined. Just over a year after the first rugby league inter-services match, and almost a day to the 100th anniversary of the formation of the Northern Union, rugby union declared itself to be an 'open' game. Professionalism was allowed, and after some teething troubles, players could play both codes, facilities could be shared and longstanding barriers started to come down.

All this has been covered in considerable detail elsewhere. Graham Williams shows in Part 3 of this book that there had always been links between rugby league and the Army, particularly in both World Wars and during the post-Second World war period of National Service.

Rugby league followers had always believed there was huge potential for their sport in the Armed Forces, and by and large their hopes have been fulfilled. The sport developed quickly. This was due in part to rugby league players and followers already in the Army getting involved, but also because of the ability of the sport's leadership. Martin Coyd gives much credit to the support he got from senior officers, who traditionally in Army sports take the roles of President and Chairman. However, the sport itself was also fortunate to have someone of Coyd's organisational ability and enthusiasm to develop a sport. It is no accident

15

that since leaving the Army he has been involved in developing one of the most successful amateur clubs outside the sport's traditional areas.

In 1994, the Army Rugby League Challenge Cup, subsequently called the Yeoman Cup, named after Major General Alan Yeoman, was set up for regiment teams. In 1995, the Lawson Cup, for Corps teams, was started. Both were crucial in developing the sport's grassroots. By now rugby league was also established in Germany, which was a strong base for British Forces at the time.

Martin Coyd's links with the game in his native Warrington were useful for the sport's development again when former New Zealand international Kevin Tamati became the Army's first team coach. Having someone of his stature involved helped raise the sport's profile and credibility, both within the Army and the wider rugby league community.

In 1996, an Army under–21 side played for the first time. This was subsequently changed to under–23, but has been a regular feature of Army RL since then, allowing younger and less experienced players a path into the Army first team.

The next couple of years saw three major developments. One followed the example of the professional game and the newly formed Rugby League Conference in switching to playing in summer. The RL Conference had been set up in 1997 to cater for teams in development areas, often playing on rugby union club grounds and often with union players. It opened up huge new geographical areas for the game, and avoided a head-on clash with union. There was still some resistance by union die-hards to league in the Army; this removed another barrier. Pitches and equipment would be more easily available, and players could play both codes. Some players had always played league and had no interest in union, but many others wanted to give league a try, and could now do so without putting at jeopardy their positions in union teams.

The second important development was the establishment of rugby league in the Royal Navy. This now meant that a full inter-services competition could be played, which was switched to September, so it came at the end of the season rather than the beginning. Again, this helped raise the sport's profile, both in and out of the Armed Forces.

The establishment of rugby league in the Royal Navy also meant that a Combined Services side could be formed. This also added to the sport's status, and later saw a marvellous win in the 2008 Defence Forces World Cup in Australia, when they played as Great Britain Armed Forces, with the approval of the RFL, and wearing Great Britain kit.

The third major breakthrough came in 1999, when the forces teams entered the Challenge Cup for the first time. Originally, the Rugby Football League had offered one place to the winners of the previous season's inter-services competition, but was persuaded that all three services should enter. Playing in the sport's oldest knock-out competition was a great boost for publicity and prestige. It has also brought problems – the matches are usually 'out of season' for the services teams, and operational demands have at times made team selection difficult. However, all the forces teams have beaten some of the country's top amateur sides on occasion, and have played the top semi-professional sides.

First ever Army RL Coach Education course.
Kevin Tamati and Ted McNamara (Steve's Dad) were the tutors.

The Army winners, Inter Services RL Challenge Cup 1996. General Simon
Lytle, Director Army Sport Control Board, sitting in the front row.

(Photos Courtesy Martin Coyd)

Army, winners, Inter Services RL Challenge Cup 1994.
Coached by David Ellis.

Major General Alan Yeoman presents Andy Sanger with the
Inter Services RL Challenge Cup.
Andy Sanger MBE later coached the Army RU and RL teams.

(Photos Courtesy Martin Coyd)

Left: Tim White and Richard Nelson take on BARLA.

Middle: David Ellis.

Bottom: Richard Nelson takes on the RAF.

(All photos Courtesy Martin Coyd)

Rugby League in Germany – 1 Royal Regiment of Wales, 1999 Nines winners.

Super League referee John Connolly with the other match officials in 2000.
John refereed the Grand Final at Barker Barracks in Paderborn.
(Both photos: Jimmy Aspinall)

1 Royal Regiment of Wales 2000 team with John Connolly and Wigan forward Mick Cassidy.
(Photo: Jimmy Aspinall)

Left: Sennelager Training Centre – winners, 1999 Inter-Unit Nines tournament.
(Photo: Jimmy Aspinall)

Below: Rugby league legend Andy Gregory in a Challenger 2 tank simulator while on a visit to Germany.

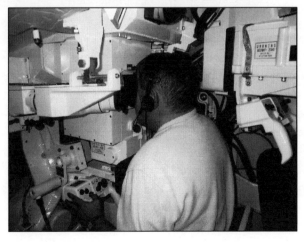

The Army team which defeated Great Britain Students for the first time, at Central Park in 1997.
(Photo: Courtesy Martin Coyd)

Another important development was the launch of the Public Services Cup, which gave the Army, along with the other two forces teams, more competitive matches during the season. Beating the Great Britain and Ireland students in the 1999 Final at Knowsley Road was a major achievement.

The redevelopment of the stadium in Aldershot as a rugby stadium, open to use by both codes, was also important. It gave the Army a well maintained accessible ground, with floodlights. Inter-services and challenge cup matches could be played there at a venue that could comfortably house supporters as well as the teams.

The development of the game also proceeded well on the international front. In 2000, the Army played Tonga in a warm-up match for the 2000 World Cup, and two Army players, Lee Innes and Darrell Cooper, played for the victorious BARLA side in the Emerging Nations World Cup competition. Darrell was awarded the BARLA 'Player of the Year', an amazing breakthrough achievement for a serviceman.

The selection of Darrell Cooper and Lee Innes marked an important change in the international amateur set-up. Martin Coyd recalls: "At the time, there was the beginning of the drive towards bringing BARLA back into the family as opposed to having two Rugby League governing bodies.

I asked the question 'How can a servicemen play for his country?' and Niel Wood, my contemporary at Student Rugby League likewise with students. We did this in BARLA meetings and were told that the players would have to play for one of three counties – Lancashire, Yorkshire or Cumbria. I challenged that the BARLA team should not be called Great Britain if it only represented that geographical area.

There was much debate and, pleasingly, the good of the wider game won the day. The BARLA team was shelved and a new 'Great Britain & Ireland' team was established for all those in the British Isles. The collars of the shirt were green!

A selection panel to appoint the head coach and team manager was formed: Terry Parle (BARLA Chair), Billy Gill (BARLA Vice-Chair – A deputy, hastily arranged on the day, as Jackie Reid MBE, BARLA International manager had broken down on route), Martin Coyd (Combined Services RL), Niel Wood (Student RL) and Joe Lydon (RFL Performance Director).

We chose Vinny Webby (GB Students) as head coach and Gordon Robb (Kells RLFC & Cumbria) as team manager. Vinny appointed Simon Tuffs as his assistant and Craig Twist as his strength & conditioning coach.

Trials were held at Blackbrook RLFC in St Helens featuring Lancashire, Yorkshire, Cumbria, Prison Service, Civil Service, GB Students, Combined Services and RL Conference.

Darrell Cooper and Lee Innes were the two players who made it through from outside of the BARLA establishment. It is worth noting that Innes was a prominent player for West Bowling in the National Conference League. Cooper had made a huge impact before the trials with an outstanding performance in the Scottish Courage Cup Final when The Army defeated Great Britain Students, at Knowsley Road, in front of a big crowd as it was a curtain raiser to Saints versus Castleford in Super League.

These events were critical in the evolution of the game. The Rugby League Joint Policy Board, the fore-runner of the current Community Board, was established and I was the Armed Forces Representative. There were huge strides taken breaking down the walls."

For any amateur side, international tours are important. The success of tours to New Zealand in 2001, Australia in 2004 and South Africa in 2009 added a new dimension for the players involved, and a new incentive for players to be involved in Army RL. The success of the Combined Services team in the 2008 Armed Forces World Cup in Australia, when they were unbeaten and beat the hosts twice, showed how far the sport had developed.

In 2003, the first ladies' match was played against the RAF. Ladies' teams are now established in all three services, although there is a lot of cross-over with the rugby union teams. And there are also now Veterans teams in place, allowing players who are past their peak to remain active in the game.

The Army's Veterans side, which was set up by Brian Stow, caters for players who are aged 35 or older, have played at Corps level for 2 years and be serving members of the Army. They are known as the RATS (Race Against Time and Senility) although the term RATS also has links with the Army dating back to the Second World War. Although the team plays against the Royal Navy and RAF teams, one of their main activities is to raise money for charity. They have played against Yorkshire Veterans sides including former international professional players, including Paul Newlove and Darryl Powell.

Brian Stow recalls that "The aim of the Vets (RATS) was to enable the ageing players to continue playing with a couple of eligibility clauses; first they must have played at least at

Corps level, be 35 or over and continue to put something back to the game within the Services. This could be in the shape of coaching, refereeing, managing or general admin support in the development of rugby league within the Services. Secondary aims were to raise money for charity and keep the Army, and eventually the RAF and Royal Navy, in the public eye positively. I must add that the name of the RATS (Race Against Time and Senility) was the brain child of Richard Naivalurua. The connection with the Desert Rats in the Second World War was a contributing factor. Ironically the first game in 2004 pitched the Army RATS against the Leeds RATS (Rhinos And Tykes Staff). The Leeds team evolved into a Yorkshire Vets side with a number of former internationals from both codes pitched against the Army/CS Vets including: Daryl Powell, Barrie McDermott, Terry O'Connor, Gary Mercer, Paul Newlove, Anthony Farrell, Darren Fleary, Lee Jackson, Dean Sampson, Jonathan Callard and Mick Cook (who was also their manager)."

In May 2003, as Army Rugby League was starting to plan celebrations of its 10th anniversary in 2004, it was proposed from within, that a team be raised at Sandhurst, the military academy for officer cadets in Surrey. Colour Sergeant Richard Turner of the 1st Battalion Parachute Regiment was the instructor at Sandhurst who set up the team, and around 50 officer cadets were interested in playing. He had arranged friendly matches against teams from the London Amateur Rugby League (London ARL). Ensuring that the all the necessary administrative issues involved in a new sport being recognised at Sandhurst was taking a long time and risked the season being missed altogether. This lead some commentators from outside the military to suggest that this was motivated by a vestige of the rivalry between rugby union and rugby league within the military; that had taken the intervention by Members of Parliament to resolve nearly 10 years before. Louis Turner, the chairman of the London ARL (no relation to the team's coach), commented to *League Express*: "It's very disappointing, and quite infuriating that interference from a senior officer should have led to this. It smacks of the bad old days. The senior officer who has vetoed the club has apparently said that he will now allow the officer cadets to play the game, giving the impression that rugby union is the only sport they should play, despite many of them wanting to play rugby league during the summer. We would hope that Sandhurst would reconsider its stance, however, because many people in very senior positions in the BA have commented on what a perfect sport rugby league is for soldiers and officers to play."

The Sandhurst side planned to field a team in the Middlesex Nines, organised by the London Skolars. Hector McNeil, their chairman, commented: "The Nines is going to have two or three union sides, like the [rugby union] Middlesex Sevens has league sides, and it gives union the chance to take revenge for their defeat last time. Sandhurst said they wanted to get involved and have a few practice games in advance. Their social committee, to be fair to them, have boxes to tick when new sports come on board – insurance, coaching and so on and he [Richard Turner] needed to go through that hoop and he's doing that at the moment."

The British Amateur Rugby League Association (BARLA) supplied match insurance for the players, which enabled them to play some games. Army RL chairman Jeremy Bethell also offered the team support. The chairman of the London Amateur Rugby League, Louis Turner helped arrange some fixtures for them. The Sandhurst team made their debut at St Albans on 14 June, and beat the club's second team 48–4. They were led by Wiganer Adam Birley, who had played for Wigan Warriors under–16s before joining the Army.

Richard Turner commented: "I knew we would be fit and strong, but I had no idea what standard we would be after only four or five training sessions in League", he admitted. "So I was chuffed to bits by that performance. I'd not seen any of the guys play a game, but those that I thought would shine, did. The lads are delighted. They loved it. The union guys thought it was superb, and are asking when the next game is!" The team played a few more matches, and did enter the Middlesex 9s competition, which was organised by the London Skolars RL club. At the Soldiers' League dinner in 2013, Richard Turner, who has since left the Army, was presented with an Army Rugby League cap in recognition of the pioneering work he had done at Sandhurst.

The first Sandhurst team who played a St Albans RLC XIII in June 2003. (Photo: Peter Lush)

The profile of Army RL within rugby league was also raised by teams entering various high-profile nine-a-side competitions, including the York 9s, Carnegie 9s and the Middlesex 9s. The Royal Engineers won the Middlesex 9s in 2003 and 2005, and were runners-up in 2004. Competitions such as the York 9s and Carnegie 9s were high profile tournaments, well covered in the game's publications, and gave the players a chance to compete with strong civilian sides.

Army RL players and coaches were also involved in various teams in the Rugby League Conference, which had been founded in 1998 to help spread the development of the game. It has played an important part in the sport's growth into a national game.

British Army (Germany) versus Scottish Students in 2002 at Paderborn.

British Army (Germany) before beating the English Students at Paderborn in 2002.
(Both photos courtesy Richard Naivalurua)

The Army team that beat the Great Britain Police side at Gosport in 2004.

The Army team that scored over 40 points in beating the BARLA Great Britain side on 27 July 2005; the Army's first win over a BARLA team, and there was a lively celebration afterwards. Team manager Richard Naivalurua says it was "One of the greatest Army RL performances I have witnessed."

The first Army Veterans (RATS) match against the (Leeds) Rhinos and Tykes Staff (RATS) at Morley RFC in 2004. Former Great Britain coach Mal Reilly coached the side.
(All photos courtesy Richard Naivalurua)

The 2007 York 9s competition

The Army squad.

Tyson El Wainiqolo charges forward for The Army.
(Both photos courtesy Richard Naivalurua)

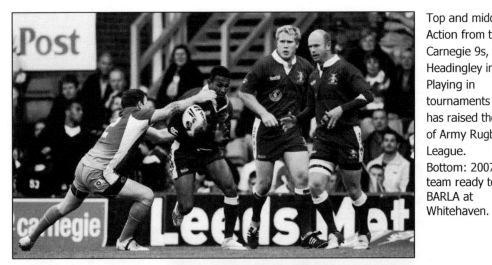

Top and middle:
Action from the
Carnegie 9s, at
Headingley in 2008.
Playing in
tournaments like this
has raised the profile
of Army Rugby
League.
Bottom: 2007 Vets
team ready to play
BARLA at
Whitehaven.

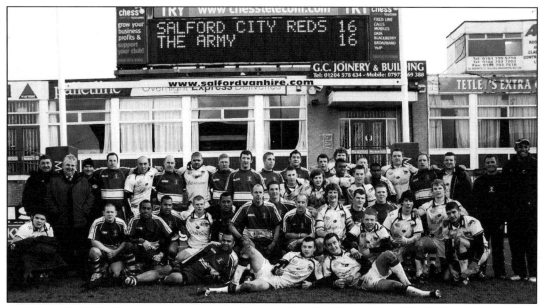

The Army RL Academy team that drew 16–16 with Salford City Reds Academy side in 2007. Richard Naivalurua remembers the match as "One of the best team performances I witnessed at any level, against a strong Super League Academy team. The Army were winning with five minutes left. The team was coached by Tony Cheadle from the Royal Engineers."

The Army RL Ladies team who won the Cheltenham 9s in April 2009.
(Both photos courtesy Richard Naivalurua)

A report from Major Richard Naivalurua, the director of Army community rugby league in 2011 shows the base the sport has maintained, despite all the operational demands of the past few years: "In 2011 we have attempted a number of innovations in the Community game, which overall have been successful. With much appreciated support from the RFL via the Armed Forces Development Officer George Taylor we negotiated a nil cost insurance premium for Unit Teams, with Army RL covering the reduced cost for insurance, which covered all RFL registered and Army RL affiliated soldiers who played in 2011.

The season opened with a fantastic festival of Rugby League at the Army RL 9s in Aldershot on Friday 6 May, the day before Army versus Navy rugby union game. 3 YORKS (The Dukes) were victorious, but it is indicative of the level of competition, that to win, the Dukes had to come back from being behind at half time in 3 of their 5 matches; versus 2 RTR in a pool game, in the semi-final versus 1 LANCS and the final versus 2 LANCS, which they won 10–8. The Yeoman Cup – Army Inter-Unit 13s competition was made a single day festival in the hope that any interested Unit should be able to make at least a single day commitment with the opportunity to become Army Unit Champions. 29 Regt RLC were crowned Yeoman Cup Champions in 2011. The single day event also saw the inaugural Women's Inter-Corps RL 9s games between the REME and AMS, who played two cracking exhibition games, the final game being decided by a golden point score by REME Women after a 4–4 score line at the end of normal time. There have also been various rugby league 9s events organised at Corps, Brigade and Divisional levels, as well as the bone crunching Trafalgar Cup game between the Paras and Marines.

The Army RL Lawson (Inter-Corps) Cup was set up as a two tier competition in 2011 to enable less established Corps teams to consolidate and develop their playing bases against similar level opposition, with the incentive that the winners of League 2 would replace the losers of League 1 in the 2012 season.

The Lawson Cup in 2011 has seen eight different Corps compete, compared with only 6 teams in 2010, with the Royal Engineers (RE), Royal Electrical and Mechanical Engineers (REME), Royal Artillery (RA), Royal Logistics Corps (RLC) in League 1 – a "group of death" and the Infantry (INF), Royal Signals (R SIGNALS), Royal Armoured Corps (RAC) and the Adjutant General's Corps (AGC) battling it out in League 2.

We kicked off with a single day festival where all eight Corps played in four matches at Andover RUFC on 18 May, which was a unanimous success. The Infantry won League 2 and will compete in League 1 in 2012. The Final was competed for by the RE and REME, the two most consistent Corps teams in the short history of the competition. The Sappers (RE) are the current Lawson Cup Champions after beating the REME; 22–10 at The Stoop in the Lawson Cup Final on Saturday 25th June as a curtain raiser for the Harlequins RL versus Hull KR Super League game. It is indicative of the strength of RE RL that they have been outright Corps champions in 13 out of the 16 Inter-Corps competitions played so far – an incredible record and level of consistency, by any team, in any sport. 2010 was only the first year that the Sappers have not been in the Lawson Cup Final, when the REME played the RA, with the

Gunners victorious. The Sappers finished another fantastic season with a very successful Tour to the South of France.

I would like to thank all the personnel who have led, managed and organised to get soldiers onto the field in 2011 as well as the small band of dedicated referees who punch well above their weight, without whom no matches could take place. I would also particularly like to thank; George Taylor from the RFL, WO2 (AQMS) Andy Franklin REME Secretary Yeoman Cup and Army 9s, Capt Si Oats MBE RE (who deployed on ops prior to Lawson Cup Final) Secretary Lawson Cup and SSgt Pat Patterson REME who stepped up to assist me in running the Lawson Cup Final event at the Stoop."

Above: Royal Engineers – 2011 Lawson Cup winners. The Royal Engineers have been the most successful team in Army competitions. Below: Programmes from the 2008 Yeoman Cup and the 2006 Skanska Cup Final.

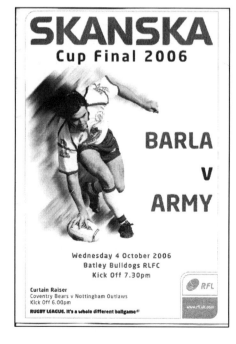

The 2001 Lawson Cup

Army Medical Service team 2001.

Infantry team 2001.

REME team 2001.

Royal Engineers team 2001.

Another strength of Army Rugby League has been encouraging players to stay involved in the game, on the coaching and administrative side. In 2012 a Level 2 coaching course was held, at the Army School of Physical Training which resulted in 19 new coaches, including two representatives of the Ladies team, Katie Garside and Rosie Haigh. All the 10 current rugby league corps teams were represented. The course was organised by Captain Eddie Williams from the Royal Army Physical Training Corps, and the coach educators were Andy Lindley from the Leeds Rhinos, with WO2 Chris Richards from the Royal Marines. The RFL has developed a four day course for the Armed Forces which will be important for the sport's development. There was support from George Taylor, then the RFL's Development Officer responsible for the Armed Forces, and from the Army Sports Control Board.

There have also been refereeing courses over the years, which have also been vital to spread the game. The latest was delivered in May 2013, and nine new Army RL referees qualified. Earlier in the week many had taken part in the coaching course outlined below.

Another Army Rugby League Level 2 Coaching Course was delivered in the Army School of Physical Training (ASPT) Aldershot during the week 20 to 23 May 2013, funded by the Army Sports Lottery. Another 19 Army RL coaches qualified. The course was again delivered by Andy Lindley and Chris Richards. The new Director of Army RL Coach Development and Education, Major Mark Bairstow MBE AGC (ETS), also briefed the candidates on the future Army RL/RFL Continual Personal Development (CPD) opportunities and the Army RL Coach Pathway. The courses could not have been run without the support of the Commanding Officer ASPT and the Secretary Army Sports Control Board. Captain Eddie Williams and Staff Sergeant Gareth-Slade-Jones were the Army RL reps in the ASPT, and were critical in making the courses happen.

The coaches had the chance to put theory into practice when they entered a team into the Army Rugby League 9s on Wednesday 22 May in Aldershot, playing as the ASPT. They won the Plate Competition against 27 Theatre Logistic Regiment RLC.

34

Left: Action from the 2011 Lawson Cup Final between REME and the Royal Engineers. The game was played at The Stoop, and was preceded by the Craig Hopson Memorial match, and followed by the Harlequins versus Castleford Tigers Super League match.

Middle: 24 July 2013 Yeoman Cup Winners 3 YORKS The Dukes at Aldershot. The Dukes are the most successful Army RL Unit side having won the Yeoman Cup six times as well as beating the UK winners of the Yeoman Cup twice as Champions of BA (G). A very poignant last victory as 3 YORKS played as the last time as 'The Dukes' because the day after the final, the renaming parade was held of the newly formed 1 YORKS. The famous Dukes rugby Regiment now no longer exists.

Bottom: Army RL Level 2 UKCC RL coaching course at ASPT, which included the first two women coaches in Army, Katie Garside and Rosie Haigh.

(All photos courtesy Richard Naivalurua).

Army RL 9s Cup competition was won by the Parachute Regiment who beat the current Army Cup champions, 3rd Battalion The Yorkshire Regiment, 3 YORKS (The Dukes) in a fitting Final which involved the two best teams in the competition. A bruising final game ended with the Paras winning 10–4. Over 140 soldiers played in the competition, which shows how the sport has continued to develop. The executive secretary of Army Rugby League, Major Dave Groce RLC, on behalf of the chairman Brigadier Frank Noble, presented the newly named Army Rugby League 9s Naivalurua Cup to the winners. It has been named in recognition of service to Army RL at all levels as a player, manager, coach, secretary and director since 1996 by the current Director Army Community Rugby League, Major Richard Naivalurua.

Finally, it is worth reflecting on the influence of the Armed Forces throughout the game. In 2012, Martin Coyd represented tier 4 clubs on the RFL's Community Board and RL Council, and Damian Clayton, now the RAF first team coach having played in the first match in 1994, represented the armed services. Jimmy Aspinall completed seven years as manager of the Great Britain and England community Lions team. Marc Donnelly from the Army played for the England Community Lions on their tour of Canada. And at the Super League Grand Final two players from each service take the Super League trophy onto the pitch, recognition of the development of the sport since that first match in 1994.

Organising sport in the Armed Forces will always be a challenge, with the operational requirements now on all the services. Rugby league looks forward to its 20th anniversary in 2014, after successfully hosting the Armed Forces World Cup in 2013. Much has been achieved since 1994, and the sport can look to the future with confidence.

The Vets team photographed below the statue of the Duke of Wellington in Aldershot.

The Level 2 coaching course in May 2013 at the Army School of Physical Training in Aldershot.
(Photo: Courtesy Richard Naivalurua)

The referees course in May 2013 at the Army School of Physical Training in Aldershot. The shield with
the crossed swords and Crown is that of the Royal Army Physical Training Corps.
(Photo: Courtesy Richard Naivalurua)

Army RL 9s May 2013 for the Naivalurua Cup

The Parachute Regiment team, who beat the 3rd Battalion The Yorkshire Regiment, 3 YORKS (The Dukes) in the final. (Photo: Courtesy Richard Naivalurua)

Theory into practice – the coaches team who as the ASPT won the Plate competition.
(Photo: Courtesy Richard Naivalurua)

The Vets team that beat Chorley Panthers 32–12 in June 2013,
pictured in front of the Soldiers' League Gazebo (Photo: Julie Hulatt)

The Ladies team that was beaten 30–22 by a Lancashire Select team.
The fixture was played as a double-header with the Vets match,
and raised £1,500 for Soldiers' League.
(Photo: Julie Hulatt)

**Army Rugby League
Team of the Decade 1994 to 2004**

1. Bob Hinton
2. Peci Nacamavuto
3. Sean Fanning
4. Darrell Cooper
5. Mark Denton
6. Richie Yeomans
7. Andy Sanger
8. Wayne Braddock (c)
9. Paul Roberts
10. Richard Nelson
11. Paul Jones
12. Dave Goddard
13. Dave Clark

14. Steve Fox
15. Lee Innes
16. Anthony Cowburn
17. Carl Shaw
18. Stuart (Sly) Silvester
19. Richard Naivalurua

Coach: Dave Ellis

Chosen by Martin Coyd, after consultation with Wayne Okell (Royal Navy) and Damian Clayton (RAF).

3. Inter-Services matches

One of the great attractions of any sport is local or traditional rivalries. In rugby league, the derby matches in Hull, or between Wigan and St Helens, Leeds and Bradford or between Wakefield, Castleford and Featherstone, all are eagerly anticipated by players and supporters alike. Traditional rivalries are also important; at a lower level of rugby league, the Varsity match between the Oxford and Cambridge University sides is always a tense affair with 100 per cent commitment on both sides.

In the forces, some traditional rivalries have come to the fore as rugby league became established – the annual battle between the Paras and the Marines for the Trafalgar Cup immediately comes to mind. But the Inter-Services competition, initially between the Army and the RAF and then from 1998 involving all three services has usually been the season's highlight, and deserves to take its place along with the sport's other traditional rivalries.

Former Army RL chairman Jeremy Bethell commented that "The Inter-Services is the pinnacle of the season; it is what everyone strives for; players to be selected and the team to win the Championship, preferably by whitewashing the other two services!"

Although rugby league had been established for longer in the RAF, it was the Army who had the better of the first clashes between the forces. After the match at Leigh in May 1994, the teams met again at Chatham on 13 December 1994, with the Army winning 18–12.

From an RAF perspective, Damian Clayton commented that "Inter-services matches were massive for us; especially after 1998, when all three services were involved. We first played the Navy at Collingwood, which was a fiery encounter. As a player, it was a bit like State of Origin; there were friendships with players from the other services; but those occasions were very competitive. And we didn't know who was going to win before the competition. The rugby league played was fierce, competitive and relentless."

Wayne Okell has been involved in the Royal Navy team from the beginning. He said: The Inter-Services Rugby League competition is the closest thing to combat on the sports field for the Armed Forces. The rivalry between the services is huge, it's a similar intensity and ferocity to State of Origin but at our level, we are absolutely willing to put everything on the line; safety is not a consideration, it simply goes out of the window."

The next clash between the Army and the RAF was at RAF Uxbridge on 28 April 1995. The report in *League Express* said that "Small nuggets of information occasionally sneak out about the tremendous developments for RL in the services, but if the standard of play in this robust and at times ferocious match is anything to go by, the progress made is nothing short of remarkable." The RAF took the lead with a try from Coco Hillier, with Hick converting. But two tries from Andy Sanger and Justin Thorpe, both converted by Hughes, gave the Army a half-time lead. In the second half the RAF were on top, and after Hick and Hughes had both kicked penalties, their winger Prout scored, with Hick converting to level the scores. Webster and Sanger, who won the man-of-the-match award, put Army scrum-half Moss in under the posts to give the Army a six point lead. Richie Marsden scored a try for the RAF near the end, but Oz Hick missed the conversion. Major General Alan Yeoman, the director of the Army Sports Control Board, presented the trophy at the end of the game. The *League Express* report commented that "Both sides showed a level of fitness that a lot of top flight amateur sides would envy."

A year later, on 26 April 1996, the teams met again at RAF Uxbridge. By now rugby league had become a recognised sport in the RAF. The match was a thrilling 24–24 draw, but the result was largely forgotten after the RAF coach had a heart attack before the game and died on the way to hospital. He had coached the RAF team since its formation. Tim Butcher's report in *League Express* said that "He would have been proud of the efforts of his side and the dramatic way in which they snatched the draw with the very last kick of the game – a drop-goal from scrum-half Damian Clayton. It was his second of a match typical of a meeting between the two, full of pride, intensity and no small amount of skill."

The Army's tries were scored by Rob Hinton, who got two, Jason Dickinson, Wayne Braddock and Justin Thorpe. Thorpe also kicked two goals. Butcher's report concluded: "After almost a hundred years of suppression in the Armed Forces, League has now established firm roots and is set to go from strength to strength."

Army in 1996 versus the RAF at Uxbridge. .
(Photo: Courtesy Richard Naivalurua)

In 1997, the Army maintained their unbeaten record with a 25–18 win over the RAF, again at Uxbridge. The *Rugby Leaguer* interviewed Army coach Kevin Tamati about the progress the team had made. After a 46–14 win over the British Police side, Tamati felt there was still room for improvement: "They're a good amateur team," he said, "but they've got to build individual understanding and responsibility for the game and then concentrate on putting that into a team context." One of the problems found was fielding a consistent side: "Because of operational commitments, the squad can change from game to game," said Kevin "but it needs blending." However, the players' level of fitness required for their work was an advantage when facing other amateur teams: "They've got stamina and can carry through when opponents are beginning to flag." With the season played by the Army team at this time running in parallel with rugby union; most of the players were from a league background. That changed when the season moved to summer, with players able to play both codes.

By 1998 the sport had become established in the Royal Navy, and for the first time the three services competed for the NAAFI Inter-Service Rugby League Challenge Cup. Tony Hannan covered the match on 1 May against the RAF for *League Express*. He was impressed, and said that "These men are trained to fight, and it shows. A fiercely contested aggressive match, which kept impressive referee Ian McGregor on his toes throughout, was played before a sizeable and enthusiastic crowd in a hot-house local derby type atmosphere." He said that as well as 'big hits' there was 'plenty of skill' on show as well.

The Army took an early lead through tries from their hooker, Paul Roberts and prop Wayne Braddock, with the first being converted; but then the RAF pulled a try back, Banford scored with a successful conversion from Hicks. Jones then scored in the corner for the RAF to make the score 10–10. However, Army second-rower Paul Jones touched down to give his side a 14–10 half-time lead.

Soon after the break Damian Clayton scored a try for the RAF after a mistake at an Army play-the-ball. However, the Army replied with a superb individual try from Fred Oakes, and he then converted a try by Andy Sanger. By now the Army were on top, and Dean Ross sealed their win with a try four minutes from time. The Army skipper Andy Sanger commented: "This was a tremendous fixture. There's a lot of blood and bruises around, which just goes to show the commitment out there today. Forces RL is really on the up now, there's no stopping it, and both sides showed today that this game can really prosper." Tony Hannan made Sanger the 'Gamestar' in his report for *League Express*.

The Army then beat the Royal Navy 42–12 at Aldershot eight days later to win the first Inter-Services Challenge Cup. Man-of-the-match Andy Sanger led the way, and the Army were 32–0 up at half-time. The second half was more even, and Ray French in the *Rugby Leaguer* also thought that second-row Paul Jones and centre Darrell Cooper were "outstanding." Army Rugby League secretary Martin Coyd commented that: "The tournament has proved to be a huge success and has given rugby league a huge boost in the Armed Forces. All the games have been extremely competitive and there has been some excellent rugby on display. Everyone in the Army, the Navy and the RAF can be proud of what they have achieved in such a short period of time."

In 1999 the competition was played later in the year, in September. Beforehand, the Army beat the Royal Navy 36–18 in the Scottish Courage Cup semi-final, before going on to beat the Great Britain Students side in the Final. Their good form continued in the Inter-Services tournament. On 16 September they beat the Royal Navy at Portsmouth 32–16, and then faced the RAF at the Garrison Stadium in Chatham on 22 September.

In a curtain-raiser, the Army's under–21 team played the Royal Dragoon Guards. The large crowd of soldiers from the Royal School of Military Engineering then had to wait in the rain because the RAF team arrived later after being delayed in traffic on the M25 motorway. Despite their journey, it was the RAF who took the lead with a penalty from Oz Hicks.

But then their prop, Killen, was sent to the sin bin for a professional foul and Sean Fanning kicked the resulting penalty to bring the scores level. The Army withstood more pressure from the RAF, with their full-back Steve Emm preventing a try by tackling RAF centre Steve Simms. However, a move involving Darrell Cooper, Paul Jones and Baby Richards set up a try for Richie Yeomans to score under the posts. Although the RAF had been on top for much of the first half, two further converted tries for the Army gave them a half-time lead of 20–2.

The second-half was played in poor conditions, with an overcast sky and the pitch lit by six temporary mobile lights. The rain washed away some of the lines as well. Tim White and Dave Clarke scored two more tries, one of which was converted by Sean Fanning, to make the final score 30–2. The RAF beat the Royal Navy 34–18 in the tournament's other match.

The Army's unbeaten record against British forces opposition continued into the new millennium. On 29 June 2000 they beat the RAF 37–4 in the Scottish Cup semi-final at Uxbridge but lost to the British Students side 36–16 in the final at the end of July. The Inter-Services tournament was held in September, and the Army beat the Royal Navy 28–18 at Hull FC's The Boulevard on 13 September, and a week later beat the RAF 22–8 at Uxbridge. Before the match against the Navy, the two forces' under–21 sides met.

In the *Rugby Leaguer*, Ray French's report on the victory over the RAF said that "Tim White received the NAAFI Inter-Services Cup for the sixth consecutive year but he and his team mates were forced to acknowledge that the RAF had put up a bitter battle to stop them retaining the trophy." The Army were 10–0 up after 16 minutes, with tries from Darrell Cooper and Andy Kershaw. Lee Innes converted Kershaw's try. Kershaw scored again from a play-the-ball, and Innes's conversion made the score 16–0 after 32 minutes. However, the RAF came more into the game in the second half, and a converted try made the score 16–6. A penalty kicked by the RAF reduced the gap even further. However, a break by Andy Kershaw won the game for the Army. Ray French wrote that "Showing great vision he chipped over the RAF's line of defence and recovered his own kick to set up the position for the Army's match clinching try. After a quick play-the-ball, Steve Fox threw out a long defence splitting pass to the ever alert Cooper who touched down in the corner." French said that there had been "a dramatic improvement" in the standards of rugby league in all three branches of the Armed Forces.

However, all good things must come to an end, and on 7 September 2001, the RAF beat the Army 34–14 at York. Two weeks later, the Army beat the Royal Navy 13–8 at Portsmouth. The *Rugby Leaguer* reported that "the match attracted a good crowd who were treated to a close very physical match with both sides displaying a lot of rugby skills." Ratu (Rob) Kama put the Army ahead with a length of the field try which Innes converted. The Navy replied with a penalty to make the half-time score 6–2. A try by Stevie Emm and two more goals from Lee Innes clinched victory for the Army. The Navy replied with a converted try. The Army also won the development match, 29–4, to make it a successful trip to Portsmouth for the Army.

However, the RAF had beaten the Royal Navy 17–14 at Wakefield Trinity's Belle Vue to win the competition. However, it was not all defeats for the Army against the RAF in 2001. In the Scottish Courage Cup the Army beat the Royal Navy 20–8, but lost to the BARLA under–21 side and therefore did not reach the final.

In 2002, the Army beat the RAF 42–13 at Dewsbury. The Army then faced the Royal Navy at Leigh Miners ARLFC on 27 September. Graham Stone reported on the Army's 32–18 win for *League Express*. He said that "The game once again highlighted the strength and quality of Services rugby league as the Army regained the trophy from the RAF." Super League official Robert Connolly refereed the game; his appointment reflected the growing status of the series.

The Army took the lead early on with two penalties from Lee Innes, one of the Army's first BARLA Great Britain international players. Martin Walker, who was playing at his former club, replied for the Navy to make the score 4–2. However, the first try was scored by the Army; second-rower Dave Goddard touched down. However, the Navy fought back with tries from Jordan James (who went on to have a successful professional rugby league career), and 'Dutchy' Holland, to make the half-time score 12–8.

However, the Army side took control of the game in the second half. A converted try by Rees put them ahead, and further scores from Taylor, White and Hogarth put them ahead 32–12. The Navy did get a consolation try from Holland near the end, but a resolute Army defence held on for a 32–18 win that saw them regain the Inter-Services Trophy.

International events put all the service sides under pressure in 2003, and a weakened Army side lost 62–6 to the BARLA Great Britain under–21 side in March 2003 in the final of the 2002 Scottish Courage Cup tournament. The Army had qualified by winning their three group matches, and the final had originally been scheduled for November 2002, but was postponed because of the firemen's strike.

Both the Army's matches in the NAAFI Inter-Services Trophy in 2003 were played at Portsmouth. A 32–22 win over the RAF meant that victory over the Royal Navy on 10 September would see the Army retain the trophy. Before the main match, the Navy's development team won 38–6 against the Army.

The Royal Navy scored two tries to the Army's one in the first half, but good kicking by Army winger Lee Innes gave his side a 14–12 half-time lead. Neil Chapman and Fijian winger Sam Cataki scored for the Royal Navy (who having transferred from the Army is the only player to play for two Service teams in the Inter-Services Championship), while Peceli Nacamavuto ('Naca') replied for the Army. The Navy took the lead with a converted try from full-back Mark Ives, but the Army's hooker Dean Whiting touched down. The conversion made the score 18–18. A penalty from Scott Partis put the Navy two points ahead with five minutes left, but then sustained pressure from the Army saw Sean Fanning score the winning try. The RAF beat the Royal Navy 21–20 at RAF Uxbridge in the tournament's final match.

The 1998 Army team, which won the first full Inter-Services tournament, before playing the Royal Navy at Aldershot. (All photos: Courtesy Richard Naivalurua)

The 2003 Army team, after beating the Royal Navy at Portsmouth. Andy Gregory was the head coach.

The 2005 Army team against the Royal Navy at Portsmouth.

In 2004, the champions were presented with the Nick Mawston Trophy, named after Wing Commander Nick Mawston, the former chairman of RAF Rugby League, who died that year. Sadly, the Army lost both matches for the first time. *League Express* described the match on 10 September against the RAF as "the best so far" in the history of the competition. The RAF won 18–16 at Uxbridge with two tries from Will Greenwood and one from Spider LeMar. On 29 September, the Royal Navy beat the Army 19–12 at Richmond. *League Express* reported that "The Royal Navy spoilt the Army's 10th anniversary celebrations by taking the NAAFI Inter-Services Trophy from under the noses of the soldiers. In a thrilling and emotionally charged match... the Navy were crowned champions for the first time." The match was filmed by BFBS and highlights were transmitted around the world after the game. The Navy had beaten the RAF 28–14 and thus won the Trophy for the first time.

The 2005 tournament was the first to be decided on points difference, each side winning one match. In the first match, on 9 September in Portsmouth, the Royal Navy won a thrilling match against the Army 24–23. The Navy had prepared for the match by spending four days in Leeds working with the Leeds Rhinos coaches. The highest crowd so far for a match at Burnaby Road saw two teams who were at full strength.

A Lee Innes penalty put the Army ahead, but four minutes later winger Lee Heggarty scored on his debut for the Navy. Scott Partis converted to give the Navy a 6–2 lead. After a midfield battle between the packs, the Army took the lead again through a try from second-row Dave Goddard, Innes converting. The Navy lost stand-off Steve Lockton to injury, and Innes scored two more tries, converted both a kicked a drop-goal to make the half-time score 21–6 to the Army.

However, what looked like a winning lead for the visitors did not last. Partis scored a try which he converted, then Dave Roberts scored under the posts. Partis's conversion made the score 21–18. The Navy were now back at full strength, and Roberts scored another converted try to take them into the lead. The Navy had another try disallowed before Innes kicked a penalty to make the score 24–23. The Army hit the post with an attempted drop-goal, but the Navy hung on for a creditable win. Richard Naivalurua, the Army team manager, recalls "A really tough game, were all the Army bench were injured, and we had a prop at centre at the end of the match."

The Army's development side had won the curtain raiser 35–14, and the first team went on to beat the RAF 22–12 at Uxbridge. However, the RAF had previously beaten the Royal Navy 43–20, so the Army needed to win by 24 points to win the tournament. The Army's development team completed a successful campaign by beating the RAF, and the Army's Sergeant Dave Goddard was named man-of-the-tournament.

In 2006, the tournament was a very close affair. Each team won one match. The Army lost to the Royal Navy 18–13 at Richmond RFC, but then beat the RAF at Uxbridge 16–9. The RAF and the Army both ended up with a points difference of +2, but the RAF as holders kept the title. The development team lost 28–6 to the Royal Navy, but then beat the Army.

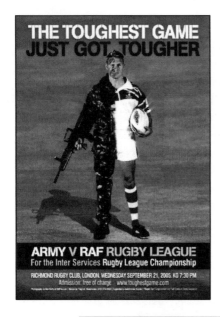

Left: A promotion poster for Army Rugby League featuring Anthony Cowburn.

Right: Ryan Swindale, who played for Army RL in the sport's early years.

Middle: The first Army ladies team in 2003.

Bottom: The Army first team 2008.

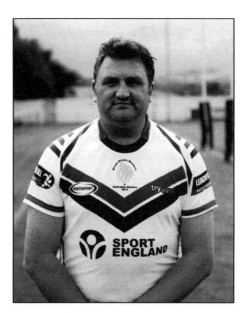

The 2007 Inter-Services

Top: The Army squad that beat the Royal Navy 18–8 at Portsmouth. Richard Naivalurua believes that this was the strongest team in his time as team manager.

Left: Steve Fox scores the winning try against the Navy.

Bottom: The Army squad that lost 15–14 to the RAF at Aldershot. In the front row are Brigadier Frank Noble, Major-General Ian Dale (who was ARL President at the time) and Lieutenant-Colonel Jeremy Bethell.

(All photos: Courtesy Richard Naivalurua)

In 2007, *League Express* reported that "The Army overcame the Royal Navy 18–8 in the opening Babcock championship match at Portsmouth. A consummate all-round performance nicely sets up the tie with the RAF ... at Aldershot." Army team manager Richard Naivalurua commented that "The Army managed to win back the Jack Harrison VC Trophy for the first time in my four year tenure as head of the first team... The defensive effort from both sides was outstanding with only the bounce of the ball separating the two sides." Steve Fox scored two tries for the Army, and Lee Innes touched down once. However, the RAF then won 15–14 at Aldershot to take the title.

In 2008, the Army started the tournament well, with a 14–10 win over the RAF at Uxbridge. In his report as Director of Army RL, Richard Naivalurua wrote that "The defensive effort from both sides was outstanding in appalling conditions." Tim Tamani, Lee Innes and Ratu Kama scored tries to see the Army home. Army skipper Stuart Silvester was chosen as man-of-the-match by Harlequins RL head coach Brian McDermott, and Naivalurua said that Silvester and "player-coach Sean Fanning both led from the front putting in some immense hits." However, the Army lost Marc Donnelly and Gerhard Wessels with injuries, and they missed the match against the Royal Navy.

Twelve days later the Royal Navy came to Aldershot and won 40–18 to take the title for the first time. The Army had both centres, Naca Nacamavuto and Mojee Matau injured in the first three minutes, and the Navy's pack dominated the game. They also won the tournament, after also beating the RAF.

In the development matches, the Army drew 22–22 with the Royal Navy, and then beat the RAF 56–6. This was the first year that there was a Ladies tournament, and the Army won it comfortably, without conceding a point.

The 2009 tournament saw each service win one match, with the RAF winning the competition on points difference. The Army's first match was against the RAF, at Aldershot on 9 September. The day started well for the Army, with a comfortable 54–4 win for the women's team, who were 38–0 up at half-time, including seven tries.

A comfortable victory for the development team followed. They ran up 100 unanswered points and scored 18 tries. Their skipper, Paul Doherty scored 34 points, Vuniani Cavailati scored five tries and Sam Speight got a hat-trick.

The main match, played in the evening, was far closer. Dave Groce reported on the Army RL website that after the Army took the lead with a try from Tim Tamani, "the match continued with aggressive running and fast play from the Army side which was met with ferocious defence from the RAF." Modjee Matau put the Army 8–0 ahead with a run over half the length of the pitch before he gathered his own kick through to touch down. The RAF then pulled back a try through Jimmy Bargett, to make the half-time score 10–6. The second half started in the same way as the first, with "both sides demonstrating some excellent lines of running and hard hitting tackles." A try from Gareth Evans for the RAF made the score 10–10. The RAF were on top at this stage, but then the Army took the lead again through a try from Bav Bavou, which was converted by Ceri Cummings. Gareth Evans scored his second try for the RAF with 20 minutes left. Despite, according to Dave Groce, both teams exhibiting "great handling, dynamic running and a desire to win" there was no more scoring, so the Army hung for a narrow victory. Ceri Cummings was named as man-of-the-match by RFL president Chris Hamilton.

Sixteen days later, the Army teams travelled to Portsmouth to face the Royal Navy. Once again, the day started well, with victories for the Veterans side, Women's team and development team. Mick Scholes's report on the Army Rugby League website said that the match started with "impenetrable defence" and "thundering tackles". The Army suffered an early blow when their skipper, Stuart Silvester, was knocked out and had to leave the field for the rest of the first half. The Army came close to scoring twice. Tim Tamani just failed to touch down a kick through, and second row Bav Bavou was held up over the line. Two successful penalties made the score 2–2 before Tamani scored in the corner, completing a set of tackles that he had started when he caught a cross-field kick near his own line. He then had a try disallowed for a forward pass so the half-time break saw the Army lead 6–2.

The Army failed to capitalise on pressure on the Navy line early in the second half, and the home team came back to score in the corner to level the match at 6–6. Four minutes later, Tamani got his second try to put the Army 10–6 ahead.

The Army then lost possession from a penalty, which allowed the Navy to equalise to make it 10–10. With passions running high, a mass brawl saw a player from each side sent to the sin-bin. The Navy took the lead for the first time with a drop-goal, 11–10. Neither side could score again, so the Army missed out on the championship by just one point. Bav Bavou was chosen as man-of-the-match by a Combined Services panel.

The development team won both their matches comfortably, as did the Ladies side. This was the first year that a Vets competition was held, and the Army beat the RAF, and then beat the Royal Navy 24–22 to take the inaugural title.

In 2010, the Army won the Championship outright. Their campaign opened with a close match against the Royal Navy at Aldershot on 2 September. An enthusiastic crowd, which included RFL President Bev Risman, saw the senior team win 16–10. Earlier in the day the Veterans, Women's and Development teams had all won their matches.

The first half of the senior match was very tense, with the only scores being a penalty by each team. The Army had taken the lead in the 10th minute through Andy Gray before Kev Botwood replied for the Navy. A try from Yabia put the Army ahead early in the second half, but the Navy struck back five minutes later to level the scores at 6–6. A mistake from the Royal Navy near their own line saw the ball come loose and Tom Howley scored near the posts. Gray's successful conversion put the Army 12–6 up. Ten minutes later Mojee Matau scored to make the score 16–6. Wagstaffe gave the Royal Navy some hope with an unconverted try near the end, but the Army held on to win 16–10, and reclaimed the Jack Harrison Trophy.

After the narrow win against the Royal Navy, the visit to the RAF turned out to be a more comfortable win. Earlier in the day the veterans and development teams had both won, and the senior side retained the championship with a 36–8 win.

The Army RL Veterans – Rats – inaugural winners inter service competition 2009 versus RAF.

The Army first team at RAF Uxbridge.

Army RL Veterans team after beating the Royal Navy at Aldershot in 2010 (Photo: Peter Lush).

Army versus Royal Navy 2010

Development match: Five Navy players stop one Army attacker.

Development match: Presentation of the man-of-the-match award to Dave Kearns.

(Photos: Peter Lush)

Veterans' match:
Left: The Army going forward.
Middle: Half-time: Sean Fanning preparing the team for the second half.

Ladies match: The Army team after beating the Royal Navy.

(Photos: Peter Lush)

The Ladies' match: The Army squeeze in for a try.

The Ladies' match: Major General Ian Dale presents the player-of-the-match award. (Photos: Peter Lush)

Left: The first team match: Army captain Stuart Silvester receives the Jack Harrison Memorial Trophy.

Middle: Army RL Chairman Brigadier Frank Noble with Bev Risman and Army RL President Major General Ian Dale.

Bottom: The man-of-the-match award presented by RFL President Bev Risman.
(Photos: Peter Lush)

The Army after beating the Royal Navy with the Jack Harrison Trophy.

Left: Army RL President Major-General Ian Dale and coach Andy Sanger with the Jack Harrison Trophy.

(Photos: Courtesy Richard Naivalurua)

RAF versus The Army at RAF Cranwell, September 2010.

Top left: Riordan Slade Jones in action in the Academy match.

Bottom right: A word after a tackle!

(Photos: sbsphotos.co.uk)

In 2011, the Army prepared for the Inter-Services tournament with a series of friendly matches in July and August. East Hull and Castleford Panthers were beaten; there were draws with GB Police and Myton Warriors, and the team lost by one point to a BARLA side.

The preparation paid off, with the senior side beating the RAF 47–14 at Aldershot. Earlier in the day, the Women's team had won 44–0 against an inexperienced RAF team, and the Army's development team won 40–8. From that Women's match was that Army players Sarah Roper and Dani Phan were invited to train with the Leeds Rhinos women's team.

For the senior side, head coach Sean Fanning fielded a strong team. The Army took an early lead through a drop-goal by Ceri Cummings. Mojee Matau set up the first try for Andy Gray. The Army's second try soon followed; Knox Veikune collected a kick from Cummings to score. The Army lost Gittens with a knee injury, but continued to apply the pressure and Qasevakatini scored. Then Veikune offloaded to Nacamavuto who scored under the posts. However, Veikune was then injured and had to come off. The RAF scored a converted try just before the break, and at half-time the Army were 23–6 ahead. The RAF started the second half well and soon pulled a try back. However, the Army replied with Qasevakatini's second try, converted by Cummings. The Army won comfortably 47–14.

The matches against the Royal Navy were played just over two weeks later on 16 September. The development team lost 14–4, but the Women's team won 36–14 to continue their domination of the tournament. Caz Roberts scored 14 points and Tatilia Bani scored a hat-trick of tries. The players were presented with caps for the first time, and Army RL sponsors SAAB presented the award for Army player-of-the-year to Tatilia Bani.

The senior side drew 12–12, and because the RAF beat the Royal Navy 20–18, the Army retained the Inter-Services title with a win and a draw from their two matches.

In 2012, the Army's campaign opened at RAF Cranwell in wet and windy conditions. The home side were on top in the first half, but the Army came back in the second half to draw 22–22. This was only the second draw between the two teams. Before the main match, the RAF's development team beat the Army 11–4, the first time they had beaten the Army.

In their first match, the RAF won 19–10 at Portsmouth against the Royal Navy. So when the Navy came to Aldershot on 28 September, if the home side won, they would take the title if they won by 10 points or more, but if the Navy won, then the RAF would take the crown with three points from their two matches. A draw would also have meant the RAF taking the title. The day started well for the Navy, with a 26–14 victory in the Development match over a young Army side. The Army Ladies team then faced the Navy, and won comfortably, 68–0. However, in the senior match, the Royal Navy won comfortably, 32–6, so Damian Clayton, for the RAF, received the trophy at the end of the match.

Al Scarborough, the Academy team manager said that: "Overall it was a good season… even though the results at the Inter-Services didn't reflect that. We see ourselves as the pathway to the first team … the overall goal is to ensure the best possible players push through to the senior side." The end of the season also saw Jack Horner finish as Academy head coach, after four years. Al Scarborough said that "The Academy and the first team have benefited hugely by his contribution to the development of rugby league players."

Army Ladies versus RAF 2011

Top: Sarah Roper passing to set up an Army move.

Left: Tatilia Bani being tackled. (Photos: sbsphotos.co.uk)

Top: Army captain Katie Garside running into two RAF tacklers.

Middle: The Army defence ready for action.

Bottom: Army Ladies team 2011.

(All photos: sbsphotos.co.uk)

The Army versus RAF, Inter-Services 2011 at Aldershot

Top: Gareth Lodge charges forward.

Middle: Gus Qasevakatini touches down by the posts.

Bottom: Andy Gray scores a try for the Army.

(All photos: sbsphotos.co.uk)

2011 Army team which beat the RAF and went on to win the Inter-Services.

Fijians have made a great contribution to Army Rugby League. Richard Naivalurua is joined by two fellow Fijians, Kuki and Tim Tamani, who in 2011 were the first brothers to play for the Army in an Inter-Services match. (Both photos Courtesy Richard Naivalurua)

Royal Navy versus the Army Inter-Services 2011

Top: A spectacular try for the Army.
Middle: The players remember the fallen before the match.
Bottom: The Army celebrating after the game.
(All photos: sbsphotos.co.uk)

RAF versus The Army 2012 Inter-Services at RAF Cranwell

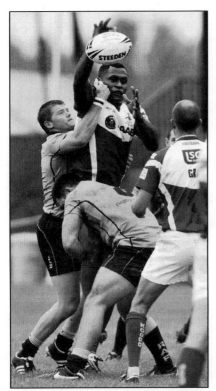

Top: The Army offload under pressure.

Middle: Two Army defenders stop an RAF winger

Bottom: Two Army defenders keeping an RAF attack under control.

(All photos: sbsphotos.co.uk)

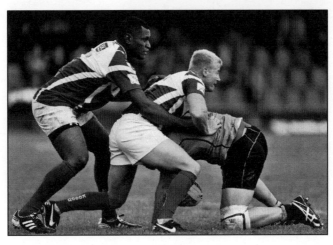

Army versus Royal Navy Inter-Services 2012 at Aldershot

The Academy team on the attack. (Photo: Peter Lush)

The Ladies team going forward. (Photo: Peter Lush)

Army Ladies team versus Royal Navy at Aldershot 2012. (Photo: Peter Lush)

The Ladies' player-of-the-match receives her award. (Photo: Peter Lush)

Army Development team before playing the RAF in 2012. (Photo: Peter Lush)

The Army first team before playing the RAF in 2012. (Photo: Peter Lush)

2013

The Army won the 2013 tournament. On 13 September, at a rainswept Aldershot Rugby Stadium, the first team beat the RAF 18–4. A week later they followed this up with an 18–6 win over the Royal Navy at Portsmouth to take the title. The RAF were runners-up after beating the Royal Navy. The Academy side also won both their matches, with a narrow 16–14 win over the RAF at Aldershot, and then a 40–30 win over the Royal Navy. The Ladies side continued their run of success, with a 64–0 win over the RAF followed by a 66–4 win over the Royal Navy. The Ladies had a notable win in one of their warm-up matches, beating a Yorkshire Select 12–10.

4.   The Challenge Cup

By 1999, rugby league was recognised and established in all three Armed Services. Reflecting the development of the sport, the question arose of entry into rugby league's most prestigious and well-known competition, the Challenge Cup. Martin Coyd recalls that initially, only one place was going to be offered to the forces, but the RFL were persuaded that all three teams should enter the competition.

Unlike the FA Cup, which started when football was largely amateur, the Challenge Cup has always been mainly a competition for the professional clubs. However, from the early years there has always been a place for amateur clubs. Until the wider development of the sport over the last 20 years, this was often restricted to a couple of teams, usually qualifying through winning an amateur competition the previous season. However, the growth of the sport geographically, and into new areas such as students and the Armed Forces, has seen a wider entry into the Challenge Cup. In the Super League era, those clubs enter the competition at quite a late stage, the last 32, and the first two rounds now are for clubs outside the sport's professional structures.

The teams from the Armed Forces have played a summer season, and with the Challenge Cup often starting in December, this has put them at a disadvantage because, as with teams from the Rugby League Conference, they are playing 'out of season', adding to their usual difficulties in fielding their strongest team with players on active service in different parts of the world.

Despite the difficulties, entry into the Challenge Cup has raised the profile of all the services teams, and allowed them to test themselves both against good standard amateur sides, and on occasions semi-professional sides.

Many of the Army's players and officials who were not from rugby league backgrounds remembered watching the Challenge Cup on television and to take part in the competition was very special. Andy Kershaw outlines: "In 1999–2000 we reached the third round of the Challenge Cup and played Rochdale Hornets. I'd watched the Challenge Cup on television as a kid, and it was special to be part of it. There was big coverage of the Army team, which was good for us and the game. We only got together a couple of days before the matches, and faced teams who played together regularly. Had we been playing together regularly and for longer, maybe we could have beaten Rochdale."

Anthony Cowburn also says it was special to play in the Challenge Cup: "It is something you can always look back on and say 'I've played in that competition'. Every year we go to Wembley to watch the Final and it's nice to know you were part of that and gave it your all. It's a part of national rugby league history. It's a privilege and an honour to have been involved."

The Army's first match was away to one of the amateur game's great names, Dewsbury Celtic. Sean Fanning recalls: "The Army entered into the Challenge Cup in 1999 and received great coverage from the BBC with a report going out on television, it was the first time the services had competed and no one knew what to expect, some people thought we would get humped but we had some great players and a great team spirit. We had been drawn against a team from Yorkshire who were the champions in their own league and this was seen as a tough draw. We trained at Aldershot and we were going to play at the newly built Aldershot rugby stadium. After being filmed training by the BBC on Queens Avenue the excitement for the game really was built up. The cameras were all there and the opposition had former Wigan star Va'aiga Tuigamala's brother playing for them and looked like a capable outfit.

The game kicked off and straight away the Army took control and it seemed like the opposition were intimidated by us. We won easily that day. It was a great game for me personally that day; I scored four tries and was interviewed after the game by Ray French after receiving the man-of-the-match award. After that game I missed the following rounds having been posted away to Colchester for a few months. I remember Mick Scholes trying to have me released from work to play, but he was unsuccessful. The team went on to play Oulton Raiders and won. Then we were through to the third round and were drawn against professional opposition in the shape of Rochdale Hornets."

The Dewsbury Celtic match was covered by Steve Tranter for *League Express*. He wrote that "The Yorkshire Cup finalists started well enough with a drop-goal from former Batley stand-off John Roadnight after only three minutes. Chris Hannan swiftly followed up with a converted try six minutes later after the Army had fumbled the ball from the kick off. The Army continued to make mistakes, squandering possession early on. After 15 minutes though, good work from scrum-half Andy Sanger put Richie Yeomans through on the left wing and the Army, having lost their early nerves, began to dominate in the pack. Man-of-the-match, former Leigh half-back Sean Fanning, kicked them closer with a penalty for holding down in the tackle.

The next score was going to be crucial and it was Darrell Cooper, after more excellent work from Sanger, who weaved his way through to give the Army the lead. Debutant Andy Kershaw followed up with a typical winger's try just before half-time to give the Army a 14–7 lead at half-time."

The Army's pack was now dominant, with Wayne Braddock and Paul Jones leading the way, and combining well with hooker Baby Richards. Sean Fanning set up a try for Sanger early in the second half. Tranter commented: "Celtic heads visibly dropped and a hat-trick from winger Dean Ross and three more from Fanning had Dewsbury fans shaking their heads in disbelief as Cooper scored again to complete the rout of a thoroughly dispirited Dewsbury side.

Army: Steve Fox, Dean Ross, Darrell Cooper, Ritchie Yeomans, Andy Kershaw, Sean Fanning, Andy Sanger, Wayne Braddock, Baby Richards, Stuart Silvester, Paul Jones, Kevin Sutcliffe, Dave Clark.
Subs: Chris Brown, Gary Windle, Ben Hughes, Dean Lewis.
Scorers: Tries: Fanning 4, Cooper 2, Ross 3, Yeomans, Kershaw. Goals: Fanning 5
Dewsbury Celtic: Jamie Graves, Phil Kain, Dave Massey, Mark Brierley, Paul Akaidare, John Roadnight, Shane Hussein, Andy Wilkinson, Sean Cummins, Mick Poutney, Chris Hannon, Carl Gibson, Lee Massey.
Subs: Dave Pepper, Peter Greensmith, Andy Tuigamala, Richard Brook.
Scorers: Try: Hannon, Goal: Hussein, Drop-goal: Roadnight.

Two weeks later, another home draw saw another Yorkshire team visit Aldershot, this time Oulton Raiders. Steve Limb covered the match for *League Express*, and said that "Even though Oulton raiders didn't underestimate the power of the Army after their 54–7 annihilation of Dewsbury Celtic two weeks ago, they still found the Forces champions too hot to handle, especially in a blistering first half that saw the Army race into a 16–0 lead as their big forwards laid the platform, and a hesitant defensive line allowed the Army left flank to cut loose."

The Army established an early 12–0 lead with two converted tries by Andy Kershaw and Richie Yeomans. Steve Fox kicked both goals. Yeomans scored again to set up a 16–0 half-time lead.

Oulton improved after the break, but then Fox extended the lead to 20–0. Oulton scored a converted try, but Fox added two penalties to take the score to 24–6. Although Oulton were on top towards the end of the game, and added a second try by Adrian Pudsey, the Army hung on to win 24–10.

The Silk Cut man-of-the-match was Kevin Sutcliffe, a former BARLA under-18 representative player. Oulton's coach John Hirst commented: "When we started to apply some pressure on them they struggled a bit, but the start they got took us a bit by surprise." The Army's coach Rick Rolt was delighted with his team's win: "We set the goal of getting to the third round and we have achieved that so we have to be happy." He said. "But we are equally happy at being able to play against top sides like Dewsbury Celtic and Oulton Rangers. It has been a tremendous experience and we would like to thank them for coming down here and playing us. We've got loads of respect for the top amateur sides. It's been a great experience."

Army: Steve Emm, Nobby Pocock, Alan Ridsdel, Steve Fox, Andy Kershaw, Richie Yeomans, Andy Sanger, Wayne Braddock, Baby Richards, Stuart Silvester, Paul Jones, Kevin Sutcliffe, Dave Clark. Subs: Gary Windle, Tim White, Dean Lewis, Chris Brown.
Scorers: Tries: Kershaw, Yeomans 2, Fox. Goals: Fox 4
Oulton Raiders: Chris Owen, Adrian Pudsey, Paul Halloran, Lee Hall, Danny Elston, Richard Mee, Rob Moules, Danny Burton, Chris Whitehead, Steve Holmes, Mark Longley, Steve Jakeman, Mick Bamford. Subs: Sasch Brook, Linton Morris, Neil Bradbrook, James Mulligan.
Scorer: Tries: Pudsey 2. Goal: Elston.

The third round, which was played on 29 January 2000, saw the semi-professional teams from the Northern Ford Premiership enter the competition. The Army were drawn away to Rochdale Hornets, one of the clubs that had helped form the Northern Union, the predecessor to the Rugby Football League, back in 1895. A crowd of 700 saw the match, which was refereed by one of the sport's top officials, Russell Smith.

Gareth Walker was *League Express's* reporter at a wet and windy Spotland, and he said that the Army "can be pleased with their efforts, despite the one-sided scoreline." They "never threw in the towel against an impressive looking Hornets outfit, and deservedly received a standing ovation from the home crowd at full-time." Rochdale were 28–6 ahead at half-time and won 66–6.

Rick Rolt said that "We did some good things going forward and I thought we caused them a few problems," said Rolt. "And when you consider that we haven't played since the last round of the Cup, I thought we competed well. For 10 or 15 minutes in the second half we really put it to them, and looked equals. A few of the lads in the changing rooms are upset that we didn't play as well as we could have done, but I think that shows just how far we've come. To be sitting in the changing rooms at Rochdale Hornets disappointed because we lost shows the standard that we have set ourselves."

However, the Army could not handle an experienced Rochdale Hornets side, who had Australian man-of-the-match Dane Dorahy calling the shots from scrum-half. Hornets' coach Steve Linnane commented: "All credit to the Army, we knew it would be tough and they never gave in."

Rochdale Hornets: Lee Maher, Marlon Miller, Scott Martin, Danny Wood, Chris Hilton, Phil Waring, Dane Dorahy, Danny Sculthorpe, Gavin Swinson, Shayne McMenemy, Chris McKinney, Darrell Delrose, Chris Newall. Subs: Darren Robinson, Gavin Price Jones, Sean Cooper, Martin Bunce.
Scorers: Tries Wood 3, Hilton 2, Miller, Dorahy, McMenemy, Martin, Maher, McKinney.
Goals: Dorahy 9.
Army: Steve Emm, Mark Pocock, Andy Kershaw, Darrell Cooper, Dean Ross, Andy Sanger, Steve Fox, Wayne Braddock (c), Richie Yeomans, Stuart Silvester, Paul Jones, Kevin Sutcliffe, Dave Clark. Subs: Oz Greenley, Richie Nelson, Graham Windle, Tim White.
Scorers: Try: Clark, Goal: Fox

The match did achieve considerable publicity for Army Rugby League, including coverage of the match in the *News of the World*, among other newspapers.

Sadly, the team's success on their debut was not repeated in the 2000–01 competition. The Army were given a tough draw, away to one of the leading Cumbrian amateur sides, Wath Brow. The match was played on 18 December 2000, after being postponed twice. The result was a 41–6 defeat, with Agnew scoring a try for the Army, which Lee Innes converted. The Army had been planning to fly players in for the original date, but couldn't do that when the match was eventually played. Anthony Cowburn recalls a tough trip to Cumbria: "I remember that freezing cold day up in Cumbria when we played Wath Brow, a very good amateur team. Having to trek through the village streets in boots to warm up on a very boggy school pitch to playing in what can only be described as a bog on the coldest day I can remember, needless to say we lost the game, no hot water and an old man saying 'Are you the best the British Army can offer?' That hurt, especially as team captain!"

However, things looked up in the 2001–02 season. The Army were drawn away from home again, this time to Saddleworth Rangers. It was an interesting match for the Army's team manager, Tim White. He couldn't lose. He regularly played at prop for Saddleworth, and would appear for them in the next round if they won, or would be organising the Army side if they won. It was his managerial role that proved to be successful, as the Army won 15–6. Colin Clare's report in *League Express* said that the victory was "much more comprehensive than the scoreline suggests."

Saddleworth were in the National Conference League's Premier division at the time, and this was the Army's best result to date against amateur clubs. Their fitness probably helped, because the game was played on a "gluepot" pitch, and the Army's strong pack was a key factor in their win.

Clare wrote that "The master tactician in the Army camp was stand-off Sean Fanning – a former professional with Leigh and Highfield – who had a marvellous rapport with half-back partner Jonathan Gregory that maximised the solid base of a pack in which Anthony Cowburn, Dean Lewis and Ross Coombes were outstanding. On top of that, they had the twin threat of the BARLA Player of the Year Daryl Cooper at centre and fellow BARLA international Lee Innes on the wing."

A try from Anthony Cowburn put the Army ahead after 15 minutes, and at half-time they were narrowly in front, 6–4. A penalty goal to each side followed, and then a try from Lee Innes put the Army clear. Another penalty conversion by Innes and a drop-goal by Sean Fanning saw the Army home 15–6.

Saddleworth Rangers: Ryan Duckworth, Nick Leeming, Brian Quinlan, Danny Carrigan, Chris Beck, Kevin Fitzpatrick, Mike Coates, Lee Fletcher, Chris Garforth, Gary Ainsworth, John Lowther, Jimmy Rogers, Emerson Jackman. Subs: Ray Garside, Mark Davenport, Jason Brassington, Paddy Slicker.
Scorers: Try: Quinlan, Goal: Coates.
Army: Rob Smart, Ben Taylor, Mark Pocock, Daryl Cooper, Lee Innes, Sean Fanning, Jonathan Gregory, Ross Coombes, Kevin Agnew, Stuart Silvester, Dean Lewis, Darren Gilmore, Anthony Cowburn. Subs: Steve Sampher, Wayne Durnard, Karl Stockley (dnp), Conrad Bispin.
Scorers: Tries: Cowburn, Innes. Goals: Innes 3. Drop-goal: Fanning

Two weeks later, the Army headed north again, this time to face Simms Cross, the North West Counties League champions. Although the final score was 34–10, it was only in the latter stages that the Army saw the game go away from them. Tries from Capewell and McGiever gave Simms Cross an early lead. John Redmond commented in *League Express*: "But the Army were never going to take such setbacks lightly and with second-row man Paul Jones absolutely outstanding and stand-off Sean Fanning, Lee Innes and Daz Gilmore always a threat, the visitors grabbed a neatly taken try from winger Mark Pocock to cut the half-time deficit to 10–4."

However, further tries from Capewell and McGiever saw the home side stretch their lead in the second half. Just before the final whistle, Innes scored a "richly deserved" second try for the Army which he converted.

Simms Cross: Paul Roberts, Darren O'Brien, Brian Capewell, Kel McGiever, Paul Walsh, Neil Percival, Paul Tobin, Peter Grady, Mark O'Connor, Peter Worthington, Andy O'Neil, Lee Swain, John Bowles. Subs: Lee Ashton, Tony Burns, Matt Carmichael, Kevin O'Neil.
Scorers: Tries: Capewell 2, McGiever 2, Percival, Ashton. Goals: Capewell 5.
Army: Rob Smart, Mark Pocock, Andy Kershaw, Steve Fox, Lee Innes, Sean Fanning, John Gregory, Ross Coombes, Kev Agnew, Stuart Silvester, Dylan Griffiths, Paul Jones, Daz Gilmore. Subs: Terry Windle, Carl Stockley, Wayne Burnard, Conrad Bispin.
Scorers: Tries: Pocock, Innes. Goal: Innes.

In 2002–03, the Army were drawn at home in the first round, but faced tough opposition in National Conference League side Hunslet Warriors. On 30 November 2002, the Leeds-based side won 22–10. A penalty from Lee Innes saw the Army take the lead after 10 minutes. However, the Warriors replied with a try from Omar Mahedi two minutes later, and by half-time were 14–2 ahead. Another penalty increased the Warriors lead before John McNairn replied for the Army. But the Warriors added another try and a penalty before a consolation try for the Army from centre John Batu made the final score 22–10 to Hunslet Warriors.

This match was notable for the appearance of Ben Cockayne, then a young soldier, for the Army team. In an interview in *Rugby League World* (May 2013), the Wakefield Wildcats winger admitted that life in the Army had not been for him, although one of his problems had been being posted to Germany, where he could only play rugby union. He was discharged from the Army, and managed to go on to have a successful rugby league career in the Super League.

The 2003–04 season saw the Army drawn away to East Hull, one of the leading amateur clubs, based in one of the sport's strongholds. The National Conference side ran up a 22–0 lead before the Army fought back to make the final result a more respectable 22–12.

In February 2005, the draw for the first round saw the Army return to Hull, this time to face West Hull. Mark Chestney's report in *League Express* said that "The Army produced a crushing victory over National Conference League giants West Hull. The Hull outfit fielded a number of under–18s and veteran former internationals Gary Lumb and David Roe, but the Army were all round too powerful in every department, with second-row man and man-of-the-match Simon Hillam proving inspirational. Add such as Fijian winger Jona Manu and his centre Jali Tomasi, and the Army are certainly a side that had flair and panache, as well as power. [For West Hull] youngsters like Mathew Williams, Christian Richardson, Carl Pettman and Simon Townend worked hard and Lumb and Roe tried to use all their considerable experience to good effect, but the Army were too well drilled."

To beat West Hull 38–8 on their own ground was a stunning achievement. A try from Paul Riley put the visitors ahead after four minutes. Jona Manu then scored again, and Innes's conversion made the score 10–0. Baird replied for the home side, but then Mosese Matau scored again for the Army. Richardson scored for West Hull, but a try from Ben Taylor just before half-time saw the Army 18–8 ahead. Taylor scored again early in the second half, and three more tries saw the Army home as comfortable winners.

West Hull: Glen Ellerby, Mark Baird, Leon Scott, Wayne Magee, Matthew Williams, Gary Lumb, Rob Shaw, Brian Newby, Michael Taylor, Andy Townend, Chris Richardson, Stuart Taylor, Paul Hatton. Subs: Glen Pettman, Glen Donkin, Dave Roe, Simon Townend.
Scorers: Tries: Baird, Richardson.
Army: Lee Innes, Ben Taylor, Jali Tomasi, Mosese Matau, Jona Manu, Paul Riley, John Kenway, Alan Robinson, Anthony Cowburn, Inoke Veikune, Simon Hillam, Gareth Lodge, Dave Goddard. Subs: Ben Hodgson, Daffyd Gould, Inla Lalakobau, Stuart Butters.
Scorers: Tries: Taylor 2, Riley, Manu, Matau, Hillam, Robinson, Lodge. Goals: Innes 3.

However, two weeks later the Army's chances of facing professional opposition in the third round came to an end in Oldham, in a narrow defeat to National Conference League Division

Two side Waterhead. David Bland wrote in *League Express* that "the Army came away with plenty of plaudits for yet another top show in which the likes of Simon Hillam from the Royal Logistics Corp, Royal Artilleryman Paul Riley and Royal Engineer Dave Goddard at loose-forward again showed up extremely well in a well-drilled side that will count themselves unlucky to lose."

It was a tight game throughout, with each side soring three tries. One conversion and a drop-goal near the end were enough to win it for Waterhead. The home side led 10–4 at the interval, with the Army's try scored by Inia Lalakobau. Riley scored in the second half to make the score 10–8. Waterhead scored again with eight minutes left, and a drop-goal made them secure with a seven-point lead. The Army's final try came from Mosese Matau; leaving Waterhead winners 15–12.

Waterhead: Keiran Greenald, Paul Joyce, Micky Fogerty, Darren Nixon, David Hewitt, Paul Bennett, Lee Charlesworth, Rory Frank, Kyle Lancashire, Daniel Parker, Matthew Barrow, Tony Pemberton, Warren Druggitt. Subs: Terence Fitzgerald, James Campbell, Martin Blanche, David Byrne.
Scorers: Tries: Fogerty, Bennett, Joyce. Goal: Lancashire. Drop-goal: Fitzgerald.
Army: Lee Innes, Ben Taylor, Mosese Matau, Jona Manu, Inla Lalakobau, Paul Riley, John Kenway, Neville Boyd, Anthony Cowburn, Inoke Veikune, Simon Hillam, Gareth Lodge, Dave Goddard.
Subs: Ben Hodgson, Stewart Butters, Al Robinson, Jali Tomasi.
Scorers: Tries: Lalakobau, Riley, Matau.

In 2006, the draw for the first round was held at the Royal Armouries Museum in Leeds. All three forces teams were drawn at home. The Army were drawn at home to West Hull, and team manager Richard Naivalurua, was pleased to face the Humbersiders again. In an interview with *League Express* he outlined: "We're delighted to play West Hull because they hosted us royally up in Hull last year and it was great to play in the heartland of rugby league. We'll bring them down to Aldershot and hopefully host them as well as they hosted us and give them a very good game of rugby. At least 10 of our first team squad are on operations at the moment, but we are confident we can put out a strong team to give them a game."

The match was at Aldershot on 4 February. The score was closer than the previous year, but the Army still won comfortably, 38–18. Trevor Hunt reported in *League Express*: "The Army dumped West Hull out of the Powergen Challenge Cup for the second successive season after a comprehensive 38–18 victory. Centre Naca Nacamavuto was the scourge of the West Hull defence, grabbing a hat-trick of tries and having a hand in three others as the Hull side struggled to stop his powerful running and telling offloads."

Nacamavuto scored after six minutes, after West Hull had taken the lead through a penalty. A Chris Smith try put West Hull try level, but Nacamavuto's second saw the Army regain the lead. West Hull hit back through a Mark Cassidy try, converted by Hewitt to take the lead. But it was short-lived and Nacamavuto put Seru in for a try that Innes goaled for a 16–12 interval lead.

Nacamavuto claimed his hat-trick try four minutes into the second half, only for Cassidy to claim his second for Hewitt to goal and close the gap to four points. But prop Peter

Cowburn crashed in for a two tries and Innes added a conversion to put the Army clear. Nacamavuto then put in Innes for a try and the conversion sealed a memorable win.

Two weeks later, Bradford-based side West Bowling came to Aldershot in the second round and won 20–14. It was an unusual match for Lee Innes, because he played for the visitors regularly in the National Conference League. He kicked three goals, but the visitors' extra experience saw them win through to the next round.

Gary Hill reported in *League Express*: "The Army battled throughout with prop Rob Southern and veteran former Leigh halfback Sean Fanning getting great support from the likes of Innes and former BARLA internationals Darrell Cooper and Dave Goddard, whilst Fijian centre Naca Nacamavuto certainly took some holding.

The Army struck first with a ninth minute try from Cooper for Innes to goal, but Bowling hit back with two tries from Sutcliffe in four minutes as he fended off a number of would-be tacklers for tries in the 18th and 22nd minutes for an 8–6 lead the visitors held to the interval."

Two further converted tries early in the second half gave the visitors a 12 point lead. Hill continued: "The Army threw everything onto attack and in the 56th minute lively loose-forward Anthony (Pud) Cowburn crashed in for an Innes-goaled try. Bowling's defence was tested to the full as the Army laid siege to their try line before the final whistle went to signal a Bowling victory."

Army: John Hogarth, Lee Innes, Darrell Cooper, Naca Nacamavuto, Ben Seru, Sean Fanning, Stuart Butters, Rob Southern, Rob Smart, Carl Stockley, Ris Risdale, Al Robinson, Anthony Cowburn. Subs: Liam Garside, Neville Boyd, Ben Kay, Dave Goddard.
Scorers: Tries: Cooper, Cowburn. Goals: Innes 3.
West Bowling: Peter Simpson, James Dewhurst, Martin Tordoff, Tim Sutcliffe, Ryan Smith, Gareth Cullington, Steve Illingworth, Gareth Shepherd, Glen Barraclough, Paul Hutchinson, Nigel Halmshaw, Ian Wormald, Daniel Ramsden. Subs: Sha Basha, Phil Chappell, Liam Martin, Martin Kites.
Scorers: Tries: Sutcliffe 2, Tordoff, Dewhurst. Goals: Simpson 2.
Referee: Chris Nielsen.

The next year, the Army faced top class amateurs again in the first round when Leigh Miners Rangers came to Aldershot, and won 28–20. Steve Farrell reported in *League Express*: "In a bruising battle at Aldershot, Leigh Miners Rangers withstood the Army's late siege of their try line to move through to the second round of the Carnegie Challenge Cup. The superbly fit Army side made up for a lack of finesse with plenty of firepower and although they never held the lead they ensured that the National Conference League leaders were always within their sights.

With prop Stuart Glister, the ageless Sean Fanning ... and Ken Dowding the pick of a resolute and determined Army side, the Miners were certainly given the stiffest of tests. But in centre John Woods, and second row Simon Warhurst the Leigh side had plenty of class and that eventually saw them through. It was Woods who got the Miners off to a flyer with a third-minute try which he then goaled. But the Army were soon on the scoresheet when the impressive Lee Innes linked to put in Liam Garside for an unconverted try.

The Miners ... created a try for winger Mark Jones which Woods again converted on 18 minutes.

Within seconds of the restart it was Chris Humphrey jinking his way through as the Miners' slick handling created an opening for the try which Woods again goaled. But Innes hit back for the Army and added the extras before a Woods penalty ensured the Leigh side were leading 20–10 at half-time.

The Army blasted at the Miners' line at the start of the second half with Glister, Beckerl Nacamavuto, Colin McKenzie and Dave Goddard's constant threat alongside former BARLA Player of the Year Darrell Cooper, but the Leigh defence held firm. Then Wood struck again on 67 minutes to claim his second try with a long-range run.

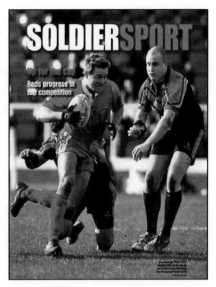

Fanning pulled back a try but Humphrey claimed his second before McKenzie completed the scoring with the Army's fourth try two minutes from time."

Army: Lee Innes, Ben Seru, Nacamavuto, Darrell Cooper, Ratu Kama, Stuart Butters, Sean Fanning, Stuart Glister, Rob Smart, Colin McKenzie, Liam Garside, Dave Goddard, Ken Dowding. Subs: Tyson El Wairinqolo, Ben Cannes, Mark Aspinall, Ken Taylor.
Scorers: Garside, Innes, Fanning. Goals: Innes 2.
Leigh Miners Rangers: Darren Pilkington, Paul Wingfield, Chris Humphrey, John Woods, Mark Jones, Gary Fitzmartin, Scorr O'Brien, Dean Balmer, Aaron Gorton, Danny Mole, Adam Higson, Simon Warhurst, Martin Lewis. Subs: Craig Wingfield, Danny Trimble, Danny Galvin, Tom Farrimond.
Scorers: T: Woods 2, Jones, Humphrey 2. Goals: Woods 4.

In 2008, Sean Fanning recalls that "Another good Challenge Cup run came to an end when we were put to the sword by a strong professional outfit, Oldham RLFC. We had home advantage but the game was over as a contest by half-time. The second half saw Army winger Ben Seru score a brace of tries and have one disallowed. This encouraged Oldham to offer him a professional contract. As a team they were too strong for us."

The Army's cup run had started at home to St Helens-based amateurs Thatto Heath Crusaders in the first round. After early pressure from Thatto Heath, the Army took the lead after 23 minutes with a converted try from Gareth Lodge. Lee Innes then broke free from a three-man tackle to score and converted his own try.

A penalty saw the Army go in at half-time 14–0 ahead. Two further penalties made the score 18–0. Thatto Heath then had a man sent to the sin-bin, and with a one man advantage the Army scored again through Paul Riley. Martin Shea came off the bench for the visitors to score their first try, converted by Stott. Lee Innes then scored his second try, which he also converted. Thatto Heath got their second try through Jimmy Hitch, Stott again converting. The final try was for the Army, with Ben Taylor touching down. Innes's kick hit the post.

However, despite the score line, and a 24–2 penalty count against them, Thatto Heath enjoyed their day in Aldershot. Their club match report said: "The disappointment of the on-field result was however equally, if not more so, balanced out with the treatment we received off the field. The facilities at Aldershot were second to none and the hospitality laid on for our travelling spectators and players were fantastic, and for that we pass on our sincere thanks to The Army and wish them well in the next round."

Soldier Sport magazine covered the cup run, and featured Anthony Cowburn on its cover, playing against Thatto Heath (see above).

Army: Eugene Viljoen, Lee Innes (c), Sean Fanning, Ben Taylor, Ben Seru, Paul Riley, Paul Greenwood, Stuart Silvester, Rob Smart, Marc Donnelly, Mark Devine, Gareth Lodge, Anthony Cowburn. Subs: Temo Alipate, Bruce Francis, Dave Bethell, Sam Cataki.

Scorers: Tries: Innes 2, Lodge, Riley, Taylor. Goals: Innes 7.

Thatto Heath Crusaders: Shaun Quinn, Matty Garner, Mike Woods(c), David Johnson, David Sutton, Andrew Stott, James Hitchmough, Neil Belshaw, Paul Gauchwin, Greg Mannion, Mark Beech, James Clarke, Lee Gannon. Subs: Adam Walsh, Graeme Johnson, Daniel Slater, Martin Shea

Scorers: Tries: Shea, Hitch. Goals: Stott 2.

Three weeks later, the Army travelled to one of the game's great strongholds, Wigan, to play Ince Rose Bridge. A hard-fought match saw the Army win 26–25, which brought Oldham to Aldershot in the third round.

Oldham scored three tries in the first 12 minutes, and although Ben Seru pulled one back for the Army, which Lee Innes converted, the half-time score was 34–6 to Oldham. The second half was closer, but Oldham won comfortably, 56–10. Seru scored a second try for the Army near the end. A crowd of 400 saw the match, the first time the Army had entertained professional opposition at Aldershot.

Army: Eugene Viljoen, Ben Seru, Paul Riley, Sean Fanning, Lee Innes, Steve Fox, Paul Greenwood, Stuart Silvester, Rob Smart, Marc Donnelly, Gareth Lodge, Ben Taylor, Anthony Cowburn. Subs: Bruce Francis, Sirino Veresa, Andy Smith, Sam Cataki.

Scorers: Tries: Seru 2. Goal: Innes.

Oldham: Marcus St Hilaire, Paul O'Connor, Mick Nanyn, Craig Littler, Danny Halliwell, Neil Roden, James Coyle, Jason Boults, Phil Joseph, Warren Stevens, Adam Robinson, Robert Roberts, Tommy Goulden. Subs: Richard Mervill, Chris Baines, Tommy Grundy, Matty Brooks.

Scorers: Tries: Coyle 3, St Hilaire, O'Connor, Joseph, Boults, Roden, Nanyn, Littler. Goals: Nanyn 8.

Fijian winger Ben Seru spent a couple of years with Oldham, but Army commitments meant that his playing opportunities were limited. He also played rugby union 7s for the Army and club rugby union for Stockport.

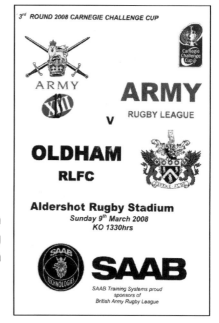

The 2009 campaign saw the Army progress again to face professional opposition beating teams in London and Castleford to end up being drawn against strong opposition in Featherstone RLFC. This again was a game too far and a heavy defeat not a fitting reward for their efforts.

The Army had entered the competition in the preliminary round, and were drawn away to West London, one of the capital's leading Rugby League Conference teams. The match was at Grasshoppers RUFC in Isleworth on 18 January, having been postponed by two weeks after the pitch had been unplayable on the original date. The Wembley Stadium arch could be seen from the pitch, could either team get there?

West London took the lead, but the Army came back to lead 12–10 at half-time with tries from Viljoen and Boyd, both converted by Stu Butters. In the second half the Army took control, and as West London tired, further tries from Andre Zwijnen and Ryan Taylor, with one more goal from Stuart Butters resulted in a 22–10 win.

Army: Lee Innes, Tim Tamani, Mosese Matau, Ryan Taylor, Ben Taylor, Eugene Viljoen (c), Stuart Butters, Enoke Levanatabua, Tim Brewer, Gary Debaughn, Neville Boyd, Dave Goddard, Darrel Winn. Subs: Marc Donnelly, Colin Mackenzie, Andre Zwijnen, Sean Fanning.
Scorers: Tries: Taylor, Viljoen, Boyd, Zwijnen. Goals: Butters 3.

The first round match followed six days later, with the Army facing student opposition. Northumbria University faced a long journey to Aldershot, but had the advantage of being in the middle of their season. However, the Army dominated from the start, and were 22–0 ahead at half-time. Fifty unanswered points came in the second half for a 72–0 win. All the backs except skipper Stu Butters scored tries, and Butters added 10 goals. It was a good workout for the team before facing more testing opposition, and keeping a clean sheet was a credit to the defence.

Army: Stuart Butters (c), Lee Innes, Ryan Taylor, Tim Tamani, Sam Cataki, Paul Riley, Gareth Slade-Jones, Marc Donnelly, Tim Brewer, Rushi Naisau, Ben Taylor, Dean Wildbore, Darrel Winn. Subs: Rob Smart, Dave Goddard, Gary Debaughn, Liam Garside.
Scorers: Tries: Riley 2, Slade-Jones 2, Innes, R. Taylor, Tamani, Cataki, B. Taylor, Winn, Goddard, Debaughn, Garside. Goals: Butters 10.

The second round draw produced a trip to Featherstone, not to play the Rovers, but their amateur neighbours Featherstone Lions. This was still a tough match, but the winners would have the chance to face professional opposition in the third round. On 14 February, the team arrived in Featherstone to find the Mill Pond pitch very heavy. A strong defence saw the Army pack take control in the first half, and at the break the Army were 16–2 ahead. The second half was more even, but in the end a 30–12 win was a good result in difficult conditions. Full-back Lee Innes was man-of-the-match.

Army: Lee Innes, Tim Tamani, Mosese Matau, Ryan Taylor, Sam Cataki, Paul Riley, Rob Smart (c), Marc Donnelly, Andy Parkinson, Rushi Naisau, Koms Komaisavai, Inoke Veikune, Darrel Winn. Subs: Andre Zwijnen, Dave Nunnerley, Gareth Lodge, Gary Debaughn.
Scorers: Tries: Riley 2, Matau, Smart, Nunnerley. Goals: Innes 5.

However, the draw for the third round produced one of the toughest matches possible – a return trip to Featherstone on Sunday 8 March to face the Rovers at Post Office Road. One of the legendary grounds of the professional game also saw awful weather again, with snow and hail. With the opposition including former Great Britain international Iestyn Harris, it was not surprising that the half-time score was 52–2, after the Army had led 2–0. The final score was 94–2, but Featherstone would have expected a similar result against any amateur opposition. Inoke Veikune was the *League Express* man-of-the-match for the Army.

One of the Army's subs, Anthony Cowburn, was there as part of the coaching team. He recalls: "I had retired and just finished a stint at Headley Court with a trapped nerve, courtesy of playing against [former Leeds and Great Britain forward] Barrie McDermott for Army veterans against Great Britain Veterans. Dave Goddard pulled up in the warm up, and our team manager, Richard Naivalurua, looked round and finding no other replacements said "Get your boots on. I could not say 'No' to Nav and still haven't said 'Thanks'."

Featherstone Rovers: Ian Hardman, Waine Pryce, Joe Hirst, Tom Saxton, Sam Smeaton, Iestyn Harris, Andy Kain, Tony Tonks, Joe McLocklan, Stuart Dickens, Matty Dale, Tim Spears, Jamie Field. Subs: Tom Haughey, Jack Lee, James Houston, Sean Hesketh.

Scorers: Tries: Kain 4, Smeaton 2, Hirst 2, Pryce 2, Lee 2, Dale 2, Tonks, Field, Saxton, Hesketh. Goals: Dickens 6, Harris 4, Kain.

Army: Tim Tamani, Sam Cataki, Siona Tunisa, Mosese Matau, Andre Zwijnen, Paul Riley, Rob Smart (c), Inoke Veikune, Tim Brewer, Bruce Francis, Dave Nunnerley, Ben Taylor, Darrel Winn. Subs: Andy Parkinson, Ryan Taylor, Gary Debaughn, Anthony Cowburn.

Scorer: Goal: Smart.

Referee: Warren Turley.

Attendance: 1,763.

The first round in 2010 saw yet another trip to Featherstone, but this time to face the less daunting Lions on 23 January. A minute's silence was observed before the game to mark soldiers lost by battalions represented in the Army team and from the local Featherstone community.

Playing conditions were good, albeit with a heavy pitch, and the home side dominated the early exchanges. They led 14–0 after 24 minutes, but then the Army came more into the game. Four back-to-back sets put pressure on the Featherstone line, and in first half injury time Paul Doherty scored a crucial try to make the score 14–4 at the break.

The second half was a different story. Playing down the slope, the Army dominated the match. Captain Gareth Lodge was man-of-the-match for a strong defensive display, and the final score was 24–14. Paul Doherty and Rob Smart, with two apiece and Sam Speight all scored tries, and Stu Butters added two goals. The Army had five players, Sam Speight, Paul Doherty, Scott Sarsons, Skelly Sauliga and Ledua Jope, making their debuts, so it was a satisfactory result all round.

Head coach Andy Sanger was delighted that for a first run out under his tenure the players figured out what went wrong in the first half, learnt from it, and pout things right in the second half. It was a good win against a strong team, with more to come from these players.

Army: Stuart Butters, Sam Speight, Noxi Levanatabu, Rob Smart, Paul Doherty, Scott Sarsons, Andy Gray, Garry Windle, Andy Kay, Gareth Lodge (c), Skelly Sauliga, Andre Zwijnen, Darrel Winn. Subs: Colin McKenzie, Ben Taylor, Andy Parkinson, Ledua Jope.
Scorers: Tries: Doherty 2, Smart 2, Speight. Goals: Butters 2.

The second round draw took the Army to another of the game's great venues, a decaying Wilderspool Stadium to play the local amateur side, Warrington Wizards. A crowd of 250 locals sat in the Bevan stand and get good value for their £3 admission fee. After missing an early penalty, a cross field kick saw Colin Marangon score the first try, which was converted by Rob Smart. The Army added to their lead when skipper Gareth Lodge scored. The conversion was missed, but the Army were 10–0 ahead after 20 minutes.

Just after the half hour, a try from Rob Martin after a tremendous run by Sam Speight saw the Army go in 14–0 up at the break; a great achievement for a team with four players making their debut. However, the second half was a different story. The break revived the Wizards. Their winger Shaun Gilmour scored after five minutes, and then had a try disallowed. A series of penalties against the Army gave Warrington possession and on 58 minutes Alan Reddecliff scored a converted try to make the score 14–10. Lee Coe scored a converted try to take the Army 10 points ahead. Sam Speight then had a try disallowed, and Army full-back Rob Martin was then sent to the sin-bin. Reddecliffe scored a converted try to make the score 20–16 to the Army. With three minutes left, Nick Braide gave Warrington the lead with a converted try, and despite further pressure from the Army, a further converted try from Tom Wilde gave the home side a 28–20 win and a home match with Swinton in the next round.

Army: Rob Martin, Tim Tamani, Mags Marangon, Masirewa Viliame, Sam Speight, Rob Smart, Andy Gray, Garry Windle, Andy Kay, Gareth Lodge (c), Darrell Winn, Andre Zwijnen, Andy Parkin. Subs: Scott Sarsons, Adam Baker, Jack Kirkmond, Lee Coe.
Scorers: Tries: Martin, Marangon, Lodge, Coe. Goal: Smart.

In 2011 the first round draw took the Army to South Wales for the first time, to Nelson RFC, to play Welsh Conference side Valley Cougars. However, for once the Army were not facing a team who were in the middle of their regular season – it was the Cougars' first match of the season as well as the Army's.

A try from Chris Holcombe gave the home side the lead on 21 minutes, but the Army came back with tries from Marangon and Kay to take the lead. A converted try from Thatcher restored the Cougars lead, and the half-time score was 12–10. Kay and Hunter put the Army ahead again in the second half, and Turaga extended their lead. However, the home side came back with a converted try from Steven Bray, and then levelled the match with a try from Liam Thomas. However, a converted try from Josh Lyons put the Army 30–24 ahead, and they defended their line as the Cougars pressed for an equaliser to go through to the next round.

Valley Cougars: James Thatcher, Liam Thomas, James Allen, Kev James, Ricky Alssop, Ceri Cummings, Paul Emmanueli, Troy Brokbank, Rhodri Morris, Isaac Duffy, John Saniger, Adrian Owen, Phil Carlton.

Subs: Steve Bray, Mark Jones, Ben Thomas, Chris Holcombe.
Scorers: Tries: Holcombe, Thatcher, Bray, Thomas. Goals: Emmanueli 4.
Army: Stu Butters, Marcus Turaga, Jonny Gregory, Josh Lyons, Max Vave, Andy Gray, Andy Kay, Lagoia Buruilakeba, Andy Parkin, Andre Zwijnen, Chris Tipton, Casey Shaw, Darrel Winn. Subs: Danny Hunter, Colin Marangon, Marc Donnelly, Gareth Lodge.
Scorers: Tries: Kay 2, Marangon, Hunter, Turaga, Lyons. Goals: Butters 5.
Referee: M. Woodhead.

The second round saw a home draw, and the visitors to Aldershot were familiar opposition, the RAF. This meant that one services team would be in the third round. Both teams included some younger players with more experienced players unavailable, and an entertaining match saw the Army win through 27–16. The Army's half-back pairing of Andy Gray and Danny Hunter were crucial in the home side's win, ably supported by Andy Kay at hooker (pictured above), and second row Andre Zwijnen.

However, the satisfaction of beating their longest-standing rivals resulted in a return to familiar territory – another trip to Featherstone in the third round to face the Rovers. Twelve points behind after just six minutes, the half-time score was 36–0, and the final score 86–0; showing the huge gap between a top-class semi-professional side, and an amateur team who did not play together regularly in the early part of the year. Army coach Sean Fanning's frustration showed when he told *League Express's* Chris Westwood: "I don't like being nilled, and I'm disappointed by one or two things; our errors and the way we gave Rovers back-to-back sets. The game was fatiguing enough without that. But let's face it; we played a team at the top of their game and who are going to finish at or near the top of their league this year so I can't be too critical. I thought we gave of our best."

The Army hooker Andy Kay was a former Featherstone player, and Westwood wrote that "large numbers of Rovers fans were by now cheering them [the Army] on" during the first half, reflecting the mutual respect the two teams had. Westwood said that the 'gamestar' was "The entire Army team for fronting up to Rovers".

Featherstone Rovers: Tom Saxton, Bryn Powell, Ian Hardman, Liam Welham, Tom Carr, Greg Worthington, Liam Finn, Tony Tonks, Ben Kaye, Jon Grayshon, Andy Bostock, Tim Spears, Sam Smeaton. Subs: Mufaro Mvududu, Dominic Dee, Cayci Pearson, Matty Johnson.
Scorers: Tries: Welham 4, Hardman 3, Carr 2, Johnson 2, Worthington, Finn, Powell, Bostock, Mvududu. Goals: Finn 11.

Army: Stu Butters, Ben Seru, Jonny Gregory, Josh Lyons, David Kearns, Andy Gray, Michael Brown, Marc Donnelly, Andy Kay, Sanivalati Ligani, Jamie Laing, Andre Zwijnen, Colin Marangon. Subs: Rob Smart, Darrell Wynn, Vuniani Cavailati, Casey Shaw.

In 2012 the Army were given a bye to the second round, but in some ways this did them no favours, because it meant that their first match of the year was away to BARLA National Conference side Oulton Raiders, who were in the middle of their season. The Army team had held a training camp during the week before the game to have the best possible preparation. A minute's silence was observed before the game to mark the deaths of six soldiers in Afghanistan. The Army had chances early on, but Oulton took the lead with a try in the corner, and then scored a converted try from the kick-off to take a 10–0 lead. Ceri Cummings kicked a drop-goal to get the Army on the scoreboard, but the raiders scored again before half-time to make the score at the break 14–1. The Raiders scored the first try in the second half to go 18–1 ahead, but good play by Marc Donnelly and Colin Marangon put pressure on the home side. Andy Parkin touched down for the Army, but the raiders then responded with a drop-goal to make the final score 19–5. Army head coach Stewart Ridsdel commented: "I was disappointed with the result but as it was our first game of the season. I saw lots of promise in key positions, all I have to do now is make sure I keep the group together for the remainder of the year."

Army: Ceri Cummings, Eppy Naulumatua, Viliame Masirewa, Colin Marangon, Leo Tuliva, Danny Hunter, Andy Hullock, Gareth Lodge, Andy Parkin, Ryan Taylor, Ben Cartmel, Casey Shaw, Tim Timani. Subs: Marc Donnelly, Ben Taylor, Ben Niayaga, Andy Gray.

Scorers: Try: Parkin. Drop-goal: Cummings.

The 2013 season saw the Army drawn away to Leigh East. The restructuring of the amateur game meant that both teams were at the start of their season. This looked to be a good draw for the Army; Leigh East were in National Conference 2, and were rebuilding after a large group of players had left the club. However, on a cold and wet day it was not to be. Leigh East scored early on, but the Army came back with a try from Milburn, converted by Danny Hunter. A further try from Hunter, which he converted, put the Army 12–10 ahead at the break. However, the second half was dominated by the home side, despite having a player sent off. The Army scored two tries near the end to make the score 28–24, but missed out on a trip to play Sheffield Eagles, who beat Leigh East 112–6!

Leigh East against The Army

Action from a tough match in Lancashire.
(Photos: Peter Lush)

5. Internationals and tours

On 27 August 1994, an Army team faced international opposition for the first time since the mid-1950s, when a couple of matches had been organised by the RFL.

The British Forces Germany side faced a French Army team from the Batallion de Joinville. The French side won comfortably, 67–3. The chief guest was Major General S.C. Grant.

In 1999, an Army under-18 team based on the Army Foundation College at Harrogate toured the south of France. Although there were some heavy defeats, the tour was seen as a success, providing a great experience for the players and showing the development of rugby league within the Army. The same year the Royal Engineers toured Australia, playing three matches, including the Australian Army Engineers team.

Many rugby league followers do not have good memories of the 2000 World Cup. It was not well organised, the weather was dreadful, and Great Britain did not reach the final. But for Army Rugby League there were two important aspects of the tournament.

The Army team played the full Tonga team at Harrogate in a warm-up match for the tournament, and hosted their opponents at a dinner after the match. And in the 'Emerging Nations' tournament, Lee Innes and Darryl Cooper played for the Great Britain BARLA side who won the tournament.

Army RL versus French Army in the Grant Cup, played in Bruggen in Germany.
(Photo: Courtesy Martin Coyd)

Just seven years after recognition, and that first historic victory over the RAF in 1994, at the end of April 2001, Army Rugby League embarked on its first international tour, to play three matches in New Zealand, finishing with a test match against the New Zealand Army side.

Duane Fyfe was in the New Zealand Army for 22 years, and played a major role in New Zealand Army Rugby League. He is now based in Dubai, where he is involved in the developing the game. Rugby Union is the main winter sport in the New Zealand Army, but he says that " are three main Army Camps that have well-established clubs that play in the local club competitions within their province on a week-to-week basis from March to late August. Two other smaller camps have had teams on a 'on again, off again' basis due to military restructuring and operational commitments. The oldest Army club is the Burnham Chevaliers that have been established and competing in the Canterbury competition for the last 30 years in the South Island. Linton Camp (the most populous camp in the North Island) is the next strongest club.

Annually the NZ Army conducts an inter-regional competition between Southern, Central and Northern Regions for Army honours from this tournament players are selected to represent Army at the annual Inter-Services tournament versus Navy and Air Force.

There were regular trans-Tasman matches between Australia and New Zealand as curtain raiser for the Annual ANZAC international test between NZ Kiwis and Australian Kangaroos, but this feature match stopped a few years back for reasons unknown to me. Whenever a NZ Defence team is scheduled for a match Army fixtures take a back seat as the strength of NZ Defence team come from Army. International matches are rare due to the distance, internal support and operational commitments especially over the last 10 years. So the reciprocal tours of 2001 and 2002 were very special for NZ Army Rugby League."

On the pitch, the tour was a great success. Two out of three matches were won, including the test match against New Zealand. In the tour report in *League Express* by Paul Wright, one of the tour management team, Army coach Rick Rolt commented: "The tour received big coverage in the press in New Zealand and the New Zealanders are already planning a revenge mission to the UK next year. The amount of interest the games attracted surprised the Kiwis and it has done the game a lot of good over there, which is really gaining ground at the moment. Obviously it was a very productive tour for us as the Kiwis were a very good side. It was just a wonderful tour from start to finish, although the NZ Army's arrangements for transport for us were thrown into a bit of chaos because of their commitments in East Timor. But we couldn't be critical in any aspect. The results show just how far rugby league has come in Britain – remember that it was only in 1994 that anyone was allowed to play rugby league in the Armed Services. And those who represented Britain deserve a lot of credit for their commitment and dedication."

Apart from Paul Wright and Rick Rolt, the tour management team included Jimmy Aspinall as tour manager, who replaced Mick Scholes who had to pull out, and Rick Nolen as assistant coach.

Sean Fanning recalls that the "rugby turned out to be the best part of the tour", but feels that "it was a learning curve for a lot of the people involved" and that future tours were organised differently. He believes that a code of conduct would have been advisable, as it is "essential with young guys on tour." He also remembers the huge distances travelled in an old bus that could not go faster than 30 miles an hour, but "the lads made of the best of it and we had some good nights out, and the rugby was great."

The team's arrival in New Zealand was difficult. After a long journey via Los Angeles, the outbreak of Foot and Mouth in Great Britain meant that the players' footwear was inspected, and in some cases muddy boots were not allowed to enter the country. One player was rigorously searched, delaying things further. However, when the players arrived in Palmerston North, where the first match was played, Sean recalls that "Accommodation at the camp was great, and we all had our own rooms. The food was great as well; the New Zealand lads liked their scoff. We got settled in and went out to socialise. The town was quiet, but as with any squaddies we made the most of it."

The first game was against the New Zealand North Army side. The Army fielded their strongest side with the aim of getting off to a good start. Sean remembers: "Like any tour we were not quite sure what we were going up against and the team we faced didn't disappoint – any ideas of an easy tour were squashed when we saw the size of the Kiwis."

The match was played in a tropical storm, and the Home team took the lead after three minutes from a penalty. Sean Fanning kicked a penalty to bring the Army level, but the Kiwis scored the game's first try and went into the break 8–2 ahead. In the second half Lee Innes scored, and Fanning's conversion levelled the match. A well worked move saw Innes score the winning try. BARLA under-21 international Kevin Agnew played well at hooker, but the man-of-the-match was the Army's second row Paul Jones.

Sean Fanning remembers a tough encounter: "They were very physical with some monster hits going in on our boys. After the initial onslaught we settled into our game and got some completions under our belt. The New Zealanders were trying to offload at every opportunity. At first this caused us loads of problems, but later in the first half we started to gain the upper hand as a lot of their offloads didn't work. Towards the end of the second half we seemed to get well on top, and definitely finished the stronger."

The team now headed off in the bus to the South Island, after a night out to celebrate their win. Sean was struck by the scenery on the ferry trip: "We saw some of the most fantastic scenery I'd ever seen, I could see why the film Lord of the Rings had been made in New Zealand." He also remembers one of the forwards falling asleep, and "anything and everything" being put on him, with photos taken. He was not happy when he woke up...

The second match was played at Coronation Park at Burnham Military Camp near Christchurch on ANZAC Day. Some of the British party were invited to attend the ANZAC Day ceremony at daybreak, a very moving experience. Sean recalls that "Accommodation and facilities were again good and we got on with training for the second game. We had made a decision to try and give everyone a game in this match, as we wanted to play our strongest team against the New Zealand Army team in the last match. We were confident because we had a good squad and we needed to rest some of the boys from the first game. However, things didn't go to plan and we were under the cosh from the start." The half-time score was 28–4 to the New Zealand side, with the Army's points coming from a try by Nick Pool. Richie Yeomans and Alex Wright came on for the second half, and in what League Express described as "a no holds barred game... that had the large crowd on tenterhooks" the Kiwis hung on to win 32–30. Paul jones scored two tries, and Andy Kershaw, Richie Yeomans and Lee Innes also touched down.

Army tour to New Zealand 2001

On the team coach.

The team at Uxbridge before departure.

(All 2001 tour photos Courtesy Jimmy Aspinall)

The players – ready for action.

The team with the British High Commissioner.

The British and New Zealand team management groups.

The players travelled to Wellington for the final match. The British High Commissioner and New Zealand Chief of the General Staff were present at Davis Field in Trentham Military Camp to see a famous British win.

Sean explains that "After our defeat we weren't quiet as confident, which may have been a blessing, the final game would be against the best players from the first two games. By this time we had our share of bumps and bruises but the guys were up for it. A lot of talk was of how physical the NZ players were and we wanted to match them up front, we had Alex Wright and Sly Silvester playing in the front-row and in my time as an Army player they probably are our biggest hitters, and we would need them to muscle up if we were going to win this. The New Zealand players had obviously taken a lot from their win and as far as they were concerned it was one all, with their strongest team to play us.

Game on and straight away both packs got stuck into each other with Alex and Sly more than matching the opposition front row. Tim White was in the pack that day and, even though he was coming to the end of his playing days, he too was getting into their faces. Anthony Cowburn was everywhere and half-back Richy Yeoman was one of the players of the tour. The New Zealanders team were again trying to play expansive rugby and it just wasn't coming off for them. We were just concentrating on set completion and our coach Rick Rolt had us sticking to a simple structure in those days; three drives one way and then get it wide hitting a centre or second row. This was quite effective when guys run good lines, and if that failed we had Lee Innes at full-back scooting away. Not many guys could pick up and go as well as Lee and he was very hard man to put down, as I had found out on many occasions when playing against the Royal Engineers.

At half time we had our noses in front, but we were feeling the pace, it was the end of the tour. But the New Zealand lads didn't seem happy and we got on top in the second half and won by two scores. I thought that the Kiwis that day just didn't seem to gel together, maybe trying to make two teams into one, who knows? Anyway we had won and to the victors goes the spoils and we were in the mood to party. The New Zealand players all wanted to swap shirts after the game, because our Army shirts were great, better than theirs. But we did anyway just to make the effort and be gentlemen about it. Well, some of us did, but the other lads ran off so they didn't have to."

The Army had gone behind to an early try, but then tries from Alex Wright, Andy Kershaw, Rob Smart and Alec Wright secured a 22–10 victory for the Army team. Rick Rolt commented in *League Express*: "We knew they would come out of the blocks at 100 miles per hour. Hanging on in there early in the game was the key. Once we'd handled that we fancied our chances of pulling away late in the game – and that was pretty much how it panned out."

Duane Fyfe recalls: "I remember the team management attending our Dawn service for ANZAC Day with us and the players making the most of the hospitality in the places they visited, but that goes without saying really. The management of both teams got on very well and lasting relationships were forged which the best thing I took away from the visit.

The loss in the Test match was unexpected from our point of view as were confident going into the match and we had purposely staged the venue for Wellington as most of NZ Army HQ is stationed there so were wanting to raise the reputation and profile of rugby league as a viable sport to our own 'Brass' first and foremost."

The British Army players had a good celebration with the New Zealand players after the game, and then had a couple of days relaxation before getting back on the bus to the airport to fly home.

Eighteen months later, towards the end of October 2002, the New Zealanders came on tour to Great Britain. The party arrived at Heathrow, and initially stayed at Aldershot. They played their first match in Aldershot, and beat the British Army (Germany) team 46–32 before moving to Nestcliff Barracks in Shrewsbury. The first test match was played at the Donnington base, near Telford, Army Rugby League vs New Zealand Army Rugby League. The New Zealanders on comfortably 54–14.

The second game was at Catterick, and the new Zealanders stayed at Maine Barracks. This time it was closer, but the Kiwis won the match 52–22 to take the series. (Some reports say the result was 36–20).

They then faced the Great Britain Students side, and lost 20–18. They were winning 18–10 four minutes from the end, but two tries for the Students gave them a notable victory.

The third game against the Army was at Leigh Miners ARLFC, and the tourists stayed at Nestcliff. Sean Fanning recalls that "We lost the tour 2–1, but all our Royal Engineers players were away for the first two matches. Then when they returned we won the last game." The Army side beat the Kiwis 22–21 in the tour's final fixture.

Duane Fyfe was the tour manager for the New Zealand ARL side. He has many good memories of the tour; as with the British team's visit to New Zealand, the team bus "became like a second home" and did 6,000 miles during the trip.

Duane recalls: "The huge effort put in by Jimmy Aspinall to host us amidst the struggles of a nationwide fire fighters' strike which refocused resources and priorities for many of the arrangements made for us. From a team point of view the players were very good about the changes that needed to be made and were just happy to be there.

Jimmy put a sign in the front window of the bus 'NZ Army Rugby League Tour'. The Kiwi rugby league team were touring the UK at the same time as us, many fans saw the sign on our bus and mistook us for our national side, waving and asking for autographs. In particular when we went to watch the Kiwis play St Helens at Knowsley Road, the ground security also thought we were the Kiwi team, opened the gates and let the bus in. By the time they realised the mistake our lads were off the bus and into the stand. It didn't actually matter that much as we always had free entry to the match as we were part of the half time entertainment with our team versus local fire-fighters in a Tug of War competition.

The first game of our tour was staged in Aldershot and arranged there so we could be shown around the sites of London afterwards. Playing the first test at Donnington Barracks meant we got to meander into Wales and the second test in Catterick facilitated a weekend in Edinburgh.

Attending the 2002 Super League Grand Final at Old Trafford was a definite highlight. The singing, chanting crowds is something you do not experience in the southern hemisphere and having to 'book a space' in a pub close to the ground for a pre-match beer all made for the occasion.

When visiting St Helens they had the Challenge Cup trophy and the Super League trophy and gladly allowed the players to take photos with them both. Visits to Widnes and Bradford were also fantastic, but Wigan was extra special because Kiwi legend Dean Bell took us around and walking around the township of Wigan and seeing the rugby league folk who were so willingly to stop and talk about rugby league with you was just great.

The third test played in Wigan [Leigh Miners] was a cracking match and played in atrocious conditions which soon turned the pitch into an absolute mud bath. In normal circumstances the game probably would have been postponed due to the conditions but this was not possible due to time constraints and arrangements being made.

We lost our best player to injury in the warm-up game in Aldershot and not having a physio-therapist on tour with us meant he was not able to take part in any of the matches for the remainder of the tour. Jesse Royal went on to play in the NRL for the Newcastle Knights and NZ Warriors. His on-field impact would have definitely made a difference.

The manager of the English Students team, John Kain, went on to become the manager of the England Academy 18-year-old side that played the Junior Kiwis that I managed two years later. We drew that series 1–1 which meant he had a 2–1 count over me of which he so graciously reminded me and everyone else of in the after-match speech of the final game, all in good humour but a reminder of the relationships established on tour."

Also in 2002, the Royal Engineers broke new ground for Army teams, when they played two matches in Philadelphia, including beating a team that contained several American internationals.

Sean Fanning recalls organising a successful visit to Sydney; the Army Medical Services (AMS) tour in 2002: "The AMS rugby league team started life as an Aldershot medical services team formed by Nigel Rigby who was based in Aldershot and was from Warrington. This team then became the Army Medical Services team. The pinnacle for this team was its tour to Sydney in Australia in 2002. This was put together by a group of us including Gower Haywood, Nigel Rigby, Chris Jenkins and me. The only officer on tour was a great rugby player, Doctor Dillon Griffiths. Money for the tour was raised from various sources included the Army Sports Lottery and some mess funds; but we did receive some funds from the lads' watering hole, Emma's Night Club. This allowed us to obtain a fair amount of sports gear for the guys to wear on tour.

The tour was very relaxed and we had a wide range of player abilities because some players had dropped out or been take off at the last minute for work issues. This is always the case and I remember trying to persuade some footballers to come at the last minute. In fact if someone had the £200 personal contribution in the last week they were in.

The first game was at a stadium just outside Sydney were Bondi United play. The curtain- raiser game to us was a game involving the New Zealand under-16s who looked awesome and a massive professional looking outfit. I began to think we might have pitched at the wrong level. Some of the last minute recruited footballers were asking me if they really needed to play. The opposition turned up and they were massive. We thought we were going to be mauled. When the game kicked off we were up against it and lost some of our best players injured. Pat Hoyte broke his hand and Dillon had a bad hamstring, we still rib him about it now. But we held our own and only lost by a couple of scores. That wasn't bad considering how big the team we were up against was and that it was our first game.

A highlight of the tour was the meal we went for in the revolving tower overlooking Sydney. The food was great and you could eat any meat from the continent. So as we were all tucking into kangaroo and crocodile steaks we had one of our tour photos taken, which I am sure the lads will keep as a great memory of the tour.

Left: The 2002 Army Medical Service tour to Australia.

Below: A night out on the tour.

The next rugby was to be played in a service competition in Randwick barracks, which was our accommodation at the time. I always remember the heat and conditions on one of the training sessions we did. I was attempting to coach after the guys had been out on the booze. There were flies all over one of my mates; he just couldn't move for them. He must have had just the right scent because they wouldn't leave him alone. The lads were in stitches. Not the best training session.

The next game was a round robin tournament and was meant to be an Army trial for the Australian Defence team. We got beaten, but all the games were close and the guys enjoyed it. The weather was scorching hot and some of the guys had not even played rugby before so it was great experience for them. Then it was out on the town and the lads really made the most of it. Some of the stories still told today."

In February 2003, a team from the Army Foundation College in Harrogate toured Australia, and played two established junior clubs from the Penrith area. The Army players were all under-17, had joined the Army in September 2002, and one a third of the squad had played rugby league before joining the Army. The team had been coached for four months before the trip by RFL coaches Andy Harland and Steve Fairhurst. The team manager for the trip was Captain James Fisher.

Rugby League World reported that in the first match the Army team lost 24–12 to Windsor, after being eight points down after only two minutes. They then faced St Mary's in 40 degree heat, and won 13–12 after the home team hit the post with a conversion in the last minute. Jamie McIlroy was player-of-the-tour, while man-of-the-tour was second-rower Paul Garner. The players also visited Sydney Harbour, the Blue Mountains and Bondi Beach in their two week trip. Huddersfield Giants development manager Stuart Sheard, who was in Sydney during the trip, commented that "The boys who toured behaved in an exemplary fashion and were a credit to the British Army." The Army Foundation College repeated the trip in 2004, and narrowly lost both matches.

Also in 2003, the Royal Dragoon Guards Regiment team toured in Australia for three weeks, and were based in South Sydney. Jason Grant recalls that they "had a great time". One of the highlights for him was meeting Australian rugby league legend Brad Fittler.

The Army's next major tour was to Australia, in 2004. This marked the 10th anniversary of Army Rugby League. It showed how much the sport had developed from the early days. The tour was sponsored by Skanska, Blanchard Wells and RWL Employment Law consultants.

Sean Fanning was the Army's coach for this tour, which comprised three matches. Sean remembers: "As with a lot of the tours some of our best players were unable to tour. Some of the places were taken by guys who had finished their playing careers, but were drafted in. Army Rugby League needed to take part in something special for their anniversary and what better than a tour to where the game is at its best. Australia is not only the best place to tour for intensity and competition, but it is a great country to visit as a tourist. The tour set out to reward some of the guys that had given so much to Army Rugby League in the past,

Also on the tour was a mate of mine, Mark Wells, who I was coached by in my time at Gosport and he coached the side with me. Mark was also one of the team's sponsors. Also assisting in the coaching was Darrel Cooper, who was recovering from a knee reconstruction similar to me, but his was more recent and he was only just out of early rehab. We planned to use the tour to rehab him and get him involved in the backs coaching; trying to develop the older players into future coaches was always something we encouraged. Even though we were slightly under-strength this didn't dampen the enthusiasm and the lads were buzzing. Uxbridge was again the departure point and pre-tour training camp and kit issue was all done before we left. We did some physical preparation at an early hour before breakfast, then onto principles of play and the way we were going to play the game over there. This was done throughout the tour; a bit of physical work in the morning and then some game related training after breakfast.

Some of the old guard were on the tour as part of the management, but later ended up playing because of injuries. Steve Emm, who was assistant manager, played in the final game and even Nav, who was the tour manager played in that game as well. Nav had put a massive amount of effort into the logistical organising of the tour. He is very thorough, and with the help of his backroom staff the trip was not just about winning a few games. Over the time he was in charge as team manager he had built up a very strong squad and it could be never be said that the Army fielded a weak side on his watch.

We had the usual social in Uxbridge before we left. The tour itinerary was tight and we had to cram in three games in eight days. There was no room for lads suffering from too much alcohol on the plane, added to the usual jet lag. Everyone had their warnings and we were all advised on the ways to combat the fatigue of such a long flight. The flight passed without incident and the lads made the most of it.

In Australia we were initially based on the outskirts of Sydney and for the final game flew north to Townsville which is where the majority of the Armed Forces were based. The games scheduled were against New South Wales (NSW) University Students, then NSW Combined Australian Services and the last game was against the Australian Army, which would be a very tough fixture especially with an under-strength British Army side. A lot would depend on how many injuries we incurred and how well we bonded together.

The first game was against the Students. It was in the evening and was really quite cold. We had selected our strongest side to get the tour off to good start; the plan was to use the second game to give some of the development players and old guard a game if we went well and rest certain players for the last game which we expected to be the toughest.

We got off to a flyer and within 20 minutes were in front by a couple of scores. The lads were on fire and playing really well, sticking to our sets and retaining possession. We were beating the Australians at their own game, a little bit safe, but nevertheless effective rugby. Anthony Cowburn was the skipper and did a great job of not letting the lads get carried away as sometimes happens when a team goes in front early on. Some of the first choice front-row players such as Sly and Dave Goddard were not available, but we had some young players on tour who really stepped up to the plate. Gareth Lodge, a young Parachute

Regiment soldier, really got stuck into the Australians and has been a first choice player ever since. Another player to step up was Liam Garside who really played well on that tour and also became a first choice player after the tour.

The second half was much like the first. We started well and totally dominated the game. I thought this was an opportunity to get some of the players rested because of our tight schedule. With 20 minutes to go I rang the changes. I felt confident and the only downside was a couple of injuries, one serious, and meant the end of playing on tour for John Hogarth, who had a dislocated shoulder.

No sooner had I made the changes then the game turned on its head. A few knock-ons and a few debatable penalties and we were under the cosh. We had all spoken about the refereeing and were not expecting any favours, but I felt that the referee had used the substitutions as an excuse to bring the Australians back into it, coupled with a few more injuries, including Ben Taylor. We were really suffering. I had brought Gareth Lodge and Nacka off and it seemed like the team had fallen apart, before I knew it they were within a score and with a few minutes to go I was sweating. We just couldn't get a decision our way. We have all felt frustration with referees, but the coach has to take the full responsibility and in the last minute of this game, after another two penalties against us, the Australians scored and snatched the game from us.

Losing 22–20 was frustrating for the players, but I remember taking it badly. I felt to blame because we were in total control until my substitutions had changed the game, or so I thought. However, on reflection there were many reasons and even though I will always blame myself, I just had to get on with it. A tour can feel like it is going to be ruined when a team gets defeated and I needed to get it back on track because we were playing in a few days.

The second game was against the NSW Combined Services at the St Mary's Club in Penrith, and was a game we had to win. We had our strongest side out, but had already lost John Hogarth and were unsure what sort of opposition we were going to face. Morale and confidence was dented, but we had trained well and were ready for the next test. We had to go with a strong line up again which I didn't really want to, but losing the first game had forced my hand and with a couple of injuries already we were under pressure to get a win. I had blooded a few of the fringe players in the first game, so I wasn't sure if these lads would get a game again because we had our toughest game next. We didn't want to go into that game with two defeats under our belts.

However, the Army played well and in particular Nacka, who was playing in the centre had a great game. Gareth Lodge and Liam Garside were also strong for us in the pack and we won the game convincingly.

The coin was tossed by former international player and Royal Australian Navy veteran Ferris Ashton who served in the Second World War, played for Easts and went on to win eight caps against Great Britain and New Zealand, including being a member of the 1952–53 Kangaroos.

The 2004 Army squad that toured Australia.

The tourists with Great Britain and England international Adrian Morley, who was playing in Australia at this time.

The Army and New South Wales Combined Services sides after the match. (Courtesy Richard Naivalurua)

The game started ferociously and there wasn't anything between the teams with big hits everywhere. An interception by Stewart Ridsdel relieved some of the pressure on the Army, but the game was going from end-to-end and neither team could get on top. After 20 minutes we were 4–2 down and I introduced my first substitute which was our manager, Nav, who we hadn't planned on playing. However, injuries had forced us in considering different options and we had Steve Emm and Nav in to bolster the squad; this had a good effect. Nav was brought on for his no nonsense defence and safe hands, but ended up scoring a great try in the left hand corner after selling a cracking dummy with a left foot step, one Paul Newlove would have been proud of it. This seemed to give the Army team the kick up the backside it needed and it was great for Nav after all his efforts

and a first game loss, to score a try that was part of getting the tour back on track. The rest of the team responded, we went on to dominate the match, and ran out clear winners 34–14. The tour was back on track and everyone seemed to play well; the old guard stepped up and Nobby Pocock and Stewart Ridsel had great games. One of the candidates for player of the tour, Liam Garside, had another great game. The man-of-the-match for me was close between Patty, whose work rate was immense, and Nacka, who seemed to cause the opposition problems every time he had the ball with his footwork and elusive skills. But it was a game where everyone seemed to play well, the lads really stuck to the sets and we needed to do that. One worry was that we seemed to make too many errors as a team, and we were heading towards our final and toughest game.

Photo: Team manager Richard Naivalurua ('Nav') came out of retirement and is shown scoring a great try for the Army side. (Photo: Courtesy Richard Naivalurua)

The final game was against the Australian Army. We trained well, but had selection problems with injuries and Nav and Steve Emm donned their boots. They had come on tour as part of the management team. The game was ferocious and as with any Australian side there were big hits all over the place. The game was played in very hot conditions and this obviously suited the Australians because we had not really had time to acclimatise. Nonetheless at half-time I was quite confident when we went in 10–10. The one worrying thing for me was the possession stats and I knew we hadn't had as much possession as they had. This would prove decisive later because we faded in the second half. This was compounded by our error count in the second half, coach-killing mistakes like running into touch on the first tackle and not making touch from penalties. The final result was a 28–14 loss, which meant that our tour record was one win and two defeats. This put a dampener on the tour, especially for Nav and me. Nav had done all the hard work organising, and as coach, I was absolutely gutted.

The tour finished with some 'R and R' and we were ideally positioned to visit one of the natural wonders of the world, the Great Barrier Reef, which I had always wanted to see. So Wellsy, Steve Emm and I took full advantage of the opportunity. We sailed over it in a Catamaran, got the diving gear on and scuba-dived on it and then took a helicopter flight over it, it doesn't get any better.

Looking back, the weather proved to be a real hindrance for that final match. However, it gave the team a chance to visit a different part of the country, normally these tours are based around Sydney for obvious reasons, but most of the Australian Army is based in the North." One additional treat for the tourists was meeting Australian Rugby League legend Laurie Daley, and having a team photo taken with him.

In November 2004, the Army faced the touring Australian Combined Services side, and lost 22–10 at Dewsbury's Ram Stadium. *League Express* reported that: "The Aussies looked to be cruising when they led 10–0 after just 11 minutes through tries from Peter Ibbott and Nick Matthews, and increased the lead just before half-time by a further six points when Adam Wallace crashed over adjacent to the posts.

The Army, coached by former Great Britain international Andy Gregory, scored twice in eight minutes through John Hogarth and Dean Lewis to get a sniff of victory. But it was left to Australia to make sure of success when centre Grant Killen finished off a back-line movement with 12 minutes remaining.

Army: Brad McFaul, Rob Matheson, Jon Vatu, Tony Karavaki, John Hogarth, Rob Smart (c), Dan Tuibucaa, El Wainoqola, Dean Whiting, Pete Alipate, Liam Garside, Dean Lewis, Skip Signor. Subs: Ginge Windle, Ben Hodges, Paul Brolone, Ray Baselala, Web Webster, Tim White, Steve Emm.
Tries: Hogarth, Lewis. Goalkicker not known.
CAS: Michael Green, Scott Taylor, Brad Saunders, Grant Killen, Brad Woodward, Brain Jones (c), Cameron Earea, Rick Kelly, Adam Robinson, Nicholas Matthews, Kurt Bryant, Peter Ibbott, Adam Darby. Subs: Kevin Grinham, Anthony Piggott, Chris Woodhouse, Aaron Power, Chris Wright, Adam Wallace, Josh Hansen.
Tries: Ibbott, Matthews, Wallace, Killen. Goals: Earea 2, Piggott.

In 2006, the Royal Armoured Corps team toured Australia. They stayed at a hotel in Darling Harbour and trained at an Army Camp near Sydney, and played three games against civilian sides. One was the Paramatta Eels third team, at Cabramatta Stadium. The RAC lost 32–10. They then played a Portuguese RL side, which was composed of Australians of Portuguese origin, at the New South Wales Academy side, which they won, and then beat another civilian side in the final match. It was a great achievement to win two out of three games.

Two other international matches were played in 2006. A Lebanon team, made up of domestic-based players, went to Cyprus where they played two sides from British military bases on the island. In the first match, they beat the Western Sovereign Base Area Combined Services side 38–4; but then narrowly lost to the Eastern Sovereign base team. But with the political upheaval at home, it was an achievement that the games were played at all, and they gave the Lebanese team a morale boost.

In 2009, the Army headed off to South Africa. This tour was organised to mark the 15th anniversary of rugby league being played in the Army. It was the first time that an Army team faced a full national side.

The idea for the tour came from a tour by the South Africans to Great Britain in 2008, when they played three BARLA County sides, and then the BARLA Great Britain team. Some of the Army squad watched their match at Dewsbury and from meeting the tour management then the Army Rugby League tour was planned.

As well as playing three matches, Army rugby league ran a two-day coaching course and referees clinic to support the development of the game.

South Africa has produced some great rugby league players who have played professionally at the top level in Great Britain and Australia. However, the sport has always struggled to establish a firm presence in the country. In modern times, the sport was relaunched in 1988 by Dave Southern and Tony Barker, two British exiles. Following the major changes in the country's political structure which started in 1990, South Africa was able to participate in international sport, and competed in the 1995 and 2000 World Cups. However, the current team is built on home-based amateur players, playing in the rugby union off-season. They lost all four matches on their 2008 British tour heavily. However, playing at home in their own conditions, the matches would clearly be a major test for the Army.

The Army tourists arrived in South Africa on 21 June. Chairman of Army Rugby League, Colonel Frank Noble, commented: "This is a fantastic opportunity for British Army Rugby League and South African Rugby League to work together in developing and promoting the sport. When so many of our Army players and support staff are away on operations around the world, it is a privilege to be able to represent the British Army and tour such a respected rugby playing nation as South Africa. For our players, the opportunity is second to none as a chance to represent their country whilst developing their teamwork, leadership and playing skills.

We have some very experienced players alongside some new members of the Army squad. I am delighted that we carved out a hard fought and deserved win in our first game. We are now looking forward to the match against the full South African Test side ... I am certain that we are going to have a great tour playing the top rugby league teams in South Africa." Lance Corporal Don Donnelly from 39 Engineer Regiment was due to be deployed to Afghanistan later in the year. He said: "I love the game and to have the opportunity to represent the Army on a tour like this is just brilliant."

The tour party included three physiotherapists. One of them, Captain Caroline Zelaya outlined: "We are carrying a number of injuries in the squad. However, all of the soldiers are naturally very fit and robust. They have trained hard, come through the first game with great spirit and I hope we can keep all of them on the pitch for the whole tour."

The opening game of the tour was played at the South African Defence Force Sports Ground, Thaba Tswane, just outside Pretoria against the South African Rugby League (SARL) national 'A' side.

The South African team lived up to their national rugby reputation – physical, strong, determined and passionate. After only three days in the country, and at an altitude of 1400 metres, the Army faced a tough and determined Rhinos team. The crowd was vocal and passionate. However, the Army had picked up a couple of Welsh Lions supporters who were staying at the same apartments and thus had their own travelling fans.

Dave Groce reported on the Army RL website: "The Army made a strong and disciplined start. Over the first half, the Rhinos stayed in the game with some clever and accurate kicking, leading to tries from the open play that followed. By half time, the Army had played the better rugby but the Rhinos were still in close contention at 16–10.

Following the break, the Rhinos came out strong with repeated assaults on the Army line. The Rhinos began to pull ahead and a number of injuries disrupted the Army cohesion. However, the Army's fitness levels, playing discipline and spirit began to tell. The Rhinos' discipline began to break in the face of a steadfast Army defence and a determined attack. Over the last quarter of the match, the Army pulled away with some outstanding driving runs and open play. By the final whistle, the Army had carved out a well-deserved 40–22 win. For his outstanding running and all round contribution to the team effort, the Army winger Ratu Kama was awarded man-of-the-match."

The Army: Lee Innes, Stuart Harries, Ryan Taylor, Darrell Cooper, Ratu Kama, Rhydian Slade-Jones, Luke Simmonds, Col MacKenzie, Stuart Silvester (c), Garry Windle, Darrell Winn, Dean Wildbore, Tom Howley.

Subs: Jamie Frazer, Frenchie Debaughn, Nobby Pocock, Leigh Coe.

With only a day to recover from that match, the Army then faced the full South Africa team at the same venue. A dozen of the travelling British Lions fans were present to support the team.

2009 tour to South Africa

Enjoying an ice bath.

Relaxing by the pool.

The team and support staff. (All photos: Julie Hulatt)

The playing squad.

Supporters at the first game trying to keep warm. Julie Hulatt is on the left.

The two teams at the end of one of the matches. (All photos: Julie Hulatt)

Dave Groce outlined: "Before the kick-off, a minute of silence was observed in memory of a Major who was killed in Helmand Province, Afghanistan, on the day the South Africa tour began (19 June 2009) and was repatriated to the United Kingdom on the day of the Test (26 June 2009). May they all rest in peace.

The Army faced everything that they had expected from the South African national side: passion, direct running, brutal aggression and big hearts. The first half was comfortably the Army's. The Rhinos were comprehensively out played by an Army team that was on fire. The Army discipline, game plan and structure held firm in the face of a brutal South African defence. A number of high tackles eventually led to a South African sin bin. The Army held a half time lead of 24–6.

True to their rugby tradition and heritage, the Rhinos came out after half-time energized and determined to get back into the game. They put aside the in-your-face rugby to play the game and before long they were putting the Army under pressure. A combination of strong direct running with effective width produced a series of Rhinos tries. The Army continued to score, but the Rhinos were closing the gap. In the face of such pressure, the Army produced one of their most resolute, disciplined and stalwart displays to hold out for a 38–34 victory. Rarely has victory tasted so sweet. Truly an awesome test. After the game, the South Africans declared the spectacle to have been the most amazing display of rugby league in South Africa for many years.

The Army: Lee Innes, Stuart Harries, Ryan Taylor, Darryl Cooper, Ratu Kama, Rhydian Slade-Jones, Luke Simmonds, Col MacKenzie, Stuart Silvester (c), Garry Windle, Don Donnelly, Dean Wildbore, Tom Howley. Subs: Anthony Cowburn, Sean Fanning, Darrell Winn, Leigh Coe, Rob Martin.

The final match of the tour was against the Northern Bulls club team. The official report on the tour says that this was "a game too far". The tour manager, Dave Williams, and tour guide, former Royal Engineers player Bokka Viljoen, were on the bench. The Army were 12–10 down at half-time, and lost 32–24. The tour report concluded: "The Army had learnt a valuable lesson, perhaps underestimating the intensity of a test series and the ability to recover for another game so soon. The warmth and generosity of the Northern Bulls in the club house after the game brought the tour to a very satisfactory conclusion."

The Army: Lee Innes, Rob Martin, Ryan Taylor, Sean Fanning, Ratu Kama, Rhydian Slade-Jones, Luke Simmonds, Col Mackenzie, Stuart Silvester (c), Garry Windle, Frenchie Dabaughn, Anthony Cowburn, Darrell Winn. Subs: Nobby Pocock, Leigh Coe, Matt Startin, Dave Williams, Jamie Frazer, Eugene 'Bokka' Viljoen.

Sean Fanning has good memories of the tour: "I had been to South Africa with the rugby union team and stayed in five star hotels in Cape Town. The rugby league team played in Pretoria, and we were in apartments. Bokka Viljoen organised things for us, and Dave Williams and his wife helped out with the food shopping.

The South Africans are natural rugby players, very physical, but there is no emphasis on rugby league there. They could be a top rugby league nation. The rugby was really tough, it was a good tour. We ran refereeing and coaching courses for them to help with their rugby league development."

In 2011, the Royal Engineers had a short tour to the south of France. On 10 July they beat Gratentour 58–22, and three days later beat a Salses XIII 22–6.

In July 2013, the 1 MERCIAN Regiment team toured Malta. After a warm-up match against a Gozo Invitation XII, which they won 50–4 after being 16–4 ahead at half-time, they faced the a Malta XIII side. The home side gave a debut to 16-year-old Maltese-Australian Brad Littlefair, but did not have any of their players who play in Super League or the NRL.

The Maltese led 6–0 early on, but a converted try by Jese Kauleta brought the score back to 6–6. A penalty put the Maltese side ahead 8–6, but Si Luvawaqa beat two defenders, and a successful conversion gave the Mercians a half-time 12–8 lead.

In the second half, a converted try by Steven Naylor put I MERCIAN 18–8 ahead, but then two tries from the home side saw them ahead 20–18. A further converted try by the home side's captain-coach Chris parker made the score 26–18. Luvaqwaqa then scored his second try, but the final score was 26–24, a narrow win for the home side.

Colour Sergeant Alan Boyle said that his team were a credit to the British Army and showed great determination to match the Maltese side: "It was a great effort from the boys tonight. It's still very early for us in terms of development and these guys really showed great pride, passion and determination to get as close as they did."

Since 2009, the full Army side has not played any international opposition. However, it is important to recognise various players who have played for amateur international teams. Apart from Lee Innes and Darryl Cooper, in 2004 Dave Goddard played for BARLA Great Britain, in 2008 Rob Smart played for Scotland and Ben Taylor for the Great Britain Community Lions. Tom Howley, Marc Donnelly and Colin Marangon have also played for the Great Britain or England Community Lions, and from the ladies team, Sarah Roper was capped by England.

6.   Combined Services

The development of a Combined Services side was very important for rugby league in the Armed Forces. It gave the players a new level to aspire to play at, and the opportunity to play Combined Services sides from other countries.

The Combined Services side could only come into being when the game was established in the Royal Navy, so that all three services could be represented. However, before this, in July 1994, a Joint Service team played in Morocco, in a tournament. They beat the Moroccan national team 38–10, and the Moroccan students 72–6, but lost 39–20 to the British students side. This was the first time that a joint services team played.

After the first full Inter-Services tournament finished in Aldershot in May 1998, with the Army crowned champions, the selection for the first Combined Service squad was decided in a meeting with all three services represented. Martin Coyd became the first secretary of Combined Services Rugby League. Damian Clayton (RAF), Wayne Okell (Royal Navy), Sean Fanning and Richard Naivalurua were all involved from the beginning. They all started as players, and later became coaches or part of the management teams. Dave Mortimer has also been involved with the Combined Services team from the beginning, as the logistics manager for matches and tours.

A date was set for the first game and a coach was nominated. It was decided that this was going to be Ray Unsworth, who had a great deal of experience in the professional game, including with Wigan. The opposition for the first game had to be pitched at the correct level, and when the French Army pulled out, it was decided to play Redhill, who were the 1998 BARLA National Cup winners first. The game was played at RAF Uxbridge and the squad met up a few days before for training.

Sean Fanning recalls: "Combined Services were successful that day and won. It must have been difficult in the first selection meetings because the Army had the majority of players in the early years." However, all the services have been well represented in the Combined Services matches.

Damian Clayton has been involved with Combined Services from the beginning, along with Sean, Richard Naivalurua, Wayne Okell and Dave Mortimer. Damian recalls: "The first time we got together, we played Redhill at Uxbridge, who were one of the best amateur teams at the time and beat them. That gave us the confidence to compete, raised our profile in the sport, and showed that we could compete at an amateur level. Later on, we played the full BARLA team at Hunslet and got beaten 22–21, but should have won. They were the top echelon of amateur players. Early on the French Army had beaten us easily, but then we beat them, and we haven't played them since."

Dave Mortimer, who is universally known as 'Shippers' brings a unique perspective to Combined Services, because he has actually served in all three: "I originally got involved through Damian Clayton in Germany. I played until I was 38, and then did some coaching. I

The joint services (Army and RAF) team on tour in Morocco, June 1994. The tournament was to celebrate the King's birthday. (Photo: Courtesy Martin Coyd)

Combined Services versus Australian Police, 1998 at Farnborough. Lieutenant Colonel Keith Hitchcock, Secretary Army Sport Control Board in the front row. Head Coach, Ray Unsworth. (Photo: Courtesy Martin Coyd)

became the kitman for the RAF in 1997, and when Combined Services started in 1998 I was their kitman, and have been doing that ever since. I went on both tours to Australia, in 2006 when we won all three games, and when we won the World Cup in 2008.

I am a players' person, I bond with them, Army, Navy and Air Force, they respect me, I've always had that. I think I'm someone to talk to, maybe a 'father figure'. I've just retired. In 1976 I joined the Royal Marines for six years, then I was out of the services for a short time. Then I was in the Territorial Army, then in 1987, I joined the RAF. I retired after completing 26 years' service.

I think my nickname, 'Shippers' comes from my time in the senior service, because I tell a few stories that relate to my time at sea. I'm good friends with Wayne Okell, who is one of the 'originals' who were there at the start of Combined Services, along with Nav, Sean, Damian and me."

In 1998, Combined Services played the Australian Police, who were touring Great Britain. The match was played at Farnborough.

It wasn't long before there was a need to set up the under-23 academy side for the Combined Services and there were plenty of players of the right quality. Many players from those early under-23 sides went on to be capped and tour with the GB Armed Forces team. A ladies team was formed in 2009, and a veterans team in 2010.

Some players won honours in both codes for Combined Services, including 'Nelly' Nelson, Andy Sanger, Ben Hughes, Eugene Viljoen, Gareth Slade Jones and Bruno Green.

Having worked hard to set up the Combined Services team, the team only played occasionally until 2006. 1999 was their most active season, and started with a 42–12 victory over the French Combined Services at RAF Uxbridge on 30 April. This was the highlight of the season. A Rugby League Conference side was beaten 20-2 on 5 September at Coventry RUFC. On 23 October, there was a one point defeat, 17–16, against the Great Britain (BARLA) under-23 team at York RLFC.

It is a pity that the match against the French Combined Services did not become an annual fixture. It could have provided a climax to the season following the Inter-

COMBINED SERVICES
V
BARLA GREAT BRITAIN
UNDER-23s

SOUTH LEEDS STADIUM

FRIDAY 12TH OCTOBER 2001

NAAFI *Sponsoring Services Sport*

Services matches. In fact, up to 2012, the fixture has not been repeated.

In 2000, the Great Britain under-23 side beat Combined Services 34–0 in October at Warrington. The Great Britain side represented the best up-and-coming amateur players in the country. As with all forces representative sides, the Combined Services side probably had little chance to train together, and operational demands always influenced the selection of these sides.

On 12 October 2001, the BARLA Great Britain Under-23 side beat Combined Services 26–22. Eight Army players were in the team, which was captained by Sean Fanning: Mark Pocock, Richie Yeomans, Lee Innes, Tim White, Kevin Agnew, Gary Windle, Anthony Cowburn. Lee Innes scored a try and three goals.

Combined Services next played in 2003, going down 42–16 to the Great Britain under-23 side, in a match played at HMS Caledonia in October 2003. A week earlier, they had beaten a Four Nations Select at Leigh, 24-16. The match was part of a Great Britain Amateurs selection festival.

Combined Services next match against Forces opposition was in 2004, against the Combined Australian Services side. This was the final match of the Australians' first tour of Great Britain, and resulted in a 7–6 win for the home side at Hull KR's Craven Park. A drop-goal from the Royal Navy's Scott Partis clinched victory after Lee Innes had successfully converted three penalties. From the Army, Johnny Hogarth, Riz Ridsdel, Sean Fanning, Anthony Cowburn, Stuart Silvester, Dave Goddard, and Ben Hughes were in the Combined Services side.

The Australians were on top early on, and Blewiit, Goddard and Hughes from the Combined Services pack did great work to hold them at bay. They took the lead on 21 minutes when a kick beat Lee Innes, and Jones scored. A penalty from Wallace made the score 6–0 to the visitors. Combined Services opened their account with a penalty from Lee Innes to make the half-time score 6–2 to the visitors.

Strong words from coach Andy Smales and Combined Services captain Sean Fanning saw the home side put more pressure on the Australians. Two penalties early in the second half were both converted by Lee Innes to make the score 6–6. The Australians had opportunities from penalties to restore their lead, but preferred to run the ball. Combined Services established a position in the Australians' half, which created the opening for Partis to kick the winning drop-goal.

Combined Services: Kieron Kavanagh (RAF), Johnny Hogarth (Army), Riz Ridsdale (Army), Sean Fanning (Capt - Army), Lee Innes (Army), Damian Clayton (RAF), Scott Partis (RN), Al Blewitt (RAF), Anthony Cowburn (Army), Stuart Silvester (Army), Dave Goddard (Army), Ben Hughes (Army), Tom McKenna (Royal Navy). Subs: Steve Lockton (Royal Navy), Sam Laskey (RAF), Heppy Hepworth (Royal Navy), Scott Andrews (RAF).

In October 2004, the Wales under-21 side beat Combined Services at Aberavon RUFC. The match was played as a curtain-raiser to the Wales versus Ireland international. In 2005, Combined Services only played once, a 24–14 win over the Great Britain under-23 side at Portsmouth on 29 October. In 2006, Combined Services made their first tour, a trip to Australia. Permission was given by the RFL for the team to be called Great Britain Armed

Forces. This meant that the team could wear the Great Britain kit and use the British Lions logo. The official report of the tour, by the Navy's Nick Stenhouse, then chairman of Combined Services RL, said: "The Great Britain Armed Forces Rugby League's inaugural tour to Australia was an outstanding success on and off the field. Three games were played and all were victories for the tourists, with 126 points scored and only 46 conceded." It outlined the aims of the tour as: "to provide the following benefits to the Armed Forces Rugby League and most importantly to its many young players:

a) Maintain the momentum and development of Armed Forces rugby league.

b) Promote the Great Britain Armed Forces in Australia and foster good relations with the Australian Defence Force and the Australian Rugby League authorities.

c) Develop the skills and collective ability of the British players.

d) Reward the players and coaching staff for their commitment and efforts to date. It would also send a strong and unequivocal message to potential rugby league players that the sport is now in the main stream of Army, Navy and Air Force sports."

The players met at RAF Uxbridge, and after a two-day training camp the party left for Sydney. They arrived in Sydney on 18 April, having flown via Hong Kong, and were accommodated at Randwick Barracks. After training on the first day, there was a tour of the Sydney Cricket Ground, and a formal welcome in the evening at the NSW Leagues club in Sydney. The welcoming speech from Warrant Officer Graham Cavenough, on behalf of the Australian Army, "suggested that we may need some tissues for our journey back to 'Pommie land'." He was made to eat his words!

Adrian Morley and Mark Lennon, who were both playing in Australia at the time, both came to meet the tourists. Their support, which continued throughout the tour, was very welcome. The first match was on 21 April, against the Australian-based Portuguese team. This was a good run-out for the Combined Services side, who were 16 points up in the opening 6 minutes. A 40 point half-time lead eventually resulted in a 66–6 victory. The scoring was opened by Sean Fanning. Danny Johnson got a hat-trick of tries, and Partis kicked eight goals.

The next day some players and staff went to watch an NRL game at Cronulla. On 24 April there was a training session before the big game the next day, and a meal in the evening at the revolving Centre Point restaurant which overlooks the whole of Sydney.

The match against the Australian Defence Force side was played at Aussie Stadium on Anzac Day, as a curtain-raiser to the St George Illawarra Dragons against Sydney Roosters match. *League Express* reported that: "The Great Britain Armed Forces were worthy winners against a determined Australian Armed Forces side, running out 22–18 victors in front of a 31,000 Anzac Day crowd in Aussie Stadium last Tuesday.

The match, refereed by ex-Super League whistle blower Russell Smith, was a tribute to rugby league at this level, with strong, athletic and skilful play from both teams.

The Lions started the game like a house on fire, with the Navy's Andy Vance scoring wide in the corner after a quick play the ball. Two more tries by prop Stuart Silvester (Army) before half-time, both converted by playmaker Scott Partis (Royal Navy) sent the Brits in at the break 16 points to the good. Another try after the restart by Chris Gordon (RAF) seemed to put the game beyond the Aussies. But roared on by the large partisan crowd the green and golds fought their way back into the match, scoring three converted tries. A Partis penalty from 40 yards out maintained the Brits' four-point buffer up to the final hooter and an historic victory for the British Armed Forces on Aussie soil. The Royal Navy's Steve Lockton was the deserved man-of-the-match for his incisive decision making." Adrian Morley joined the team's celebrations in the evening.

The team's final fixture, against a New South Wales Combined Services team, had been cancelled because the Australians had players away for operational reasons. An alternative fixture was arranged with Bondi United, a feeder team for the Sydney Roosters.

The tour report outlined: "The hosts, augmented by a few Sydney Roosters reserve grade players, started brightly taking an 8–0 lead after about 10 minutes. But the tourists began to get up a head of steam and pulled back the score to 8–8 through tries from centre Wagstaff and full-back Innes. The play was end-to-end stuff with both teams scoring again before the end of the half, the visitors going in 16–12 up.

Although the second stanza started well for Bondi with a converted try, the British players showed tremendous composure and began to put together exciting power plays to stamp their authority on the game, scoring four unanswered tries, the last coming after a brilliant piece of footwork and handling by scrum half Partis who deftly fed the ball to prop Jamie Goss to score under the posts. The final score was 38–18. Man-of-the-match went to the Great Britain skipper Sean Fanning for his inspirational leadership."

After a couple of days sightseeing, the tourists arrived back at Heathrow on 3 May. The official tour report said it was "a great achievement and a great experience for all."

The players were: S. Butters, L. Garside, A. Cowburn, D. Goddard, S. Fanning, R. Smart, L. Innes, S. Silvester, A. Robinson, S. Ridsdel (all Army), R. Hepworth, J. Goss, K. Cagney, S. Partis, G. Sharp, J. Wagstaff, J. Barnes, D. Johnson, D. Fallon, S. Lockton, A. Vance, (all Royal Navy), D. Aven, M. Lodge, C. Gordon (all RAF). Commander Nick Stenhouse was in overall charge of the tour, and the coach, Wayne Okell, also came from the Royal Navy.

Combined Services played one more match in 2006, a 30–8 defeat against BARLA at Parkside Golbourne ARLFC in Warrington on 14 October. In 2007, only one match was played. In July, Combined Services played the Australian Universities side at RAF Uxbridge, and lost 48–20. However, arguably the greatest achievement of services rugby league was on the horizon. In 2008, the team travelled to Australia to play in the Armed Forces World Cup. (See chapter 7)

In 2009, Combined Services only played one match, against the Great Britain Police team. The match was played before the England versus France match at Doncaster. The Combined Services Ladies team also played on the same afternoon (See CS Ladies section below).

The Police team was coached by former Bradford Bulls forward Jon Hamer, and were the current holders of the Skanska Cup. However, the Combined Services team, which included only three players from the Army – Tim Tamani, Darrell Win and Andy Kay – won comfortably 34–18. The Police took an early lead through an unconverted try. Combined Services equalised, and were 16–8 ahead just before half-time when a converted try from the Police made the half-time score 16–14. The Police were ahead again with an unconverted try early in the second half, but once Combined Services regained the lead at 22–18; two more converted tries produced a hard-fought 34–18 win.

Combined Services: Si Wray (RAF), Tim Tamani (Army), Gareth Evans (RAF), Wilson Tulakepa (Royal Navy), Silivenusi Bunamasi (Royal Navy), Danny Johnson (Royal Navy),Chris Lodge (RAF), Jamie Goss (Royal Navy), Johnny Ledger (RAF), Richard Sharp (Royal Navy), Dale Jinks (RAF), Chris Gordon (Capt, RAF), Darrell Winn (Army).

Subs: Andy Kay (Army), Johnny Platt (Royal Navy), Atu Vuniwaqa (Royal Navy), Matt Watkins (RAF).

In 2010 Combined Services played two matches, and lost both. A 38–12 defeat against Great Britain Students on 21 November at Cheltenham was followed 10 days later by a 50–0 defeat against the Australian Universities side at Portsmouth on 1 December. For the match against the Students, the team had just three days preparation at HMS Temeraire, which was reflected in a half-time deficit of 32–4. At the beginning of the second half, the Students went further ahead with a converted try. However, the Combined Services side improved, and the rest of the match was more even. Army prop Gareth Lodge set up Gary Dunn for his second try. Steve Cooper added a third try for the Services side.

The Combined Services side that faced the Australian Universities side showed seven changes from the previous match. Within 20 minutes, the Australians were 18–0 ahead, and they added a further converted try to make the half-time score 24–0. The second half was more of the same, and the final score was 50–0. The Australian side completed their tour unbeaten. For Combined Services, the Army's Gareth Lodge and Marc Donnelly worked hard in the forwards.

The senior team did not play any matches in 2011. However, reflecting the development of the sport in the three services that make up the Combined Services, in men's rugby league Academy and Veterans matches have been played, and the Combined Services Ladies has played regularly since its debut in 2008.

Ladies

The Ladies team made its debut in 2008 against a North West Counties Ladies side. In 2009 the team played the Great Britain Students for the Pankhurst Cup, which has become an annual fixture. The match was played at Doncaster on the same day as the Great Britain versus France full men's match. The players were introduced to the 11,000 crowd.

The Combined Services team won comfortably 48–4, after leading 20–4 at half-time. The team was: Joulandi Joubert (Army), Alvi Beanie (Army), Lou Redmond (RAF), Kelly Douglas (Army), Sam Alderson (Royal Navy), Sarah Roper (Army), Sarah Hudson (Army), Lisa Joseph (Army), Zoe Waring (Royal Navy), Vicky Dillon-Davies (RAF), Rosie Haigh (Army), Jane Leonard (Army), Kim Field (RAF). Subs: Sarah Simms (Royal Navy), Lou Clarke (Royal Navy), Emma Gilbert (Army), Titillia Bani (Army).

In 2010 the Ladies team had their most active season to date. They played four matches, and lost the first three to strong opposition before beating the England Students 52–20. The first match was against an England Development side, who beat the Services side 28–0 in Bradford. In July they faced the France Ladies team at Wakefield Trinity's ground, and lost 20–14. The Services side took the lead early on with a try from Carice Allen, which was converted by Kim Field. The French scored two tries to take the lead at half-time. Tries from Field and Sarah Mitchelson were not enough to stop the French side winning in the end. 13 Army players were in the Combined Services squad of 17.

The England Ladies side proved to be too strong for the Combined Services side, and won 66–0 at Leigh. However, the Ladies won their final match of the season, and retained the Pankhurst Trophy with a 52–20 victory over England Students at RAF Cranwell.

In 2011, the Ladies only played one match, a 28–18 victory over the England Students side on a hot October day in St Helens. The match was played at Thatto Heath Crusaders ARLFC. The referee allowed extra water breaks on 20 and 60 minutes due to the heat.

In the first half the Students side took a 12–0 lead. They had recently played two matches, while the Combined Services side only had a few days training before the game. Sarah Roper pulled a try back for the Combined Services side, with Carrie Roberts converting. However, at half-time the score was 12–6 to the Students. Early in the second half Tara-Jane Stanley scored for the Students and converted her own try, and the Students must have felt they were going to win the Pankhurst Trophy for the first time. However, the Services side's superior fitness started to tell. The Army's Rosie Haigh touched down, with Roberts converting. Then Sarah Hudson scored, and Roberts's conversion made the scores level. A great move from the Services side saw the Army's Joulandi Joubert touch down. Combined Services were now on top, and Fiesha Greene scored near the posts. Roberts converted to give the Services team a 10-point margin of victory.

CSRL Ladies: Rosie Randfield (Army), Lou Clarke (Royal Navy), Marianne Classen (Army), Carice Roberts (Army), Joulandi Joubert (Army), Sarah Hudson (Army), Zoe Wareing (Royal Navy), Sarah Roper (Army), Emma Swinton (Royal Navy), Rosie Haigh (Army), Francesca Morton (Royal Navy), Fiesha Greene (Royal Navy), Katie Garside (capt, Army). Subs: Sophie Hinds (Royal Navy), Kareena Brooks (Army), Mahayla Attis (RAF), Louise Redmond (RAF).

In 2012, Combined Services retained the Pankhurst Trophy against the England Students in October at RAF Cranwell. The Services were ahead 8–4, and two further tries in the second half saw the Services side win 18–8. Combined Services' half-back and captain, the Army's Katie Garside, was the player-of-the-match.

Academy and Veterans

In 2008, a Combined Services Academy side faced a BARLA under-21 side at Featherstone, and lost 54–4. Their next match was in November 2012 against Hemel Hempstead. In 2010, a Combined Services Veterans side played for the first time. This reflected the development of Veterans' rugby league in all the services. They faced a Yorkshire side at Featherstone, for the Stow Trophy, and lost 46–38.

114

The first Combined Services Veterans team, who played a Yorkshire Veterans side for the Stow Trophy in 2010. The trophy was named after Brian Stow, who started the Army RL Veterans team. The team had stayed at the Headingley Lodge, and used the ground to take the photograph. In the front row, fifth from left is Damian Clayton (RAF), Richard Naivalurua (CSRL Secretary), Sean Fanning, and Wayne Okell. They had all been involved in the Combined Services side from its foundation. (Photo: Courtesy Ray Calvert)

An Army Veterans (RATS) side at Colchester in 2009. (Photo: Courtesy Ray Calvert)

Left: A bloodied Ceri Cummings the only player in all three services who played in the inaugural RL and RU Defence Forces World Cups. (Photo: Courtesy Richard Naivalurua)

Top right: Damian Clayton, Great Britain assistant coach for the 2013 Armed Forces World Cup, and one of the original stalwarts of the Combined Services side (Photo: Peter Lush)

Left: The Combined Services RL Originals: Richard Naivalurua, Wayne Okell, Sean Fanning, Ray Unsworth and Dave Mortimer ('Shippers') at Aussie Stadium in 2008.
(Photo: Courtesy Richard Naivalurua)

7.   The Armed Forces World Cup

The 2008 World Cup in Australia was the sport's first for eight years. The senior tournament was won by New Zealand, with a memorable (and generally internationally welcomed) victory over the hosts. For the past two tournaments the sport had staged an Emerging Nations tournament with the senior tournament. This time, various sections of the sport staged competitions, including women, students, the Police and the Armed Forces.

The original plan for the tournament was for six teams to play in two groups, with the winners meeting in the final. However, the withdrawal of Russia meant that the remaining five teams played each other, with the top two battling out the final. This meant that the Great Britain side played five games in 12 days, also having to overcome jet-lag and 35 degree heat.

The management team for the tournament from Combined Services was:
President: Air Marshal S.W. Peach CBE (RAF) (Ex Officio)
Chairman: Major Michael (Mick) Scholes (Army)
Secretary: Chief Petty Officer Clive (Perry) Mason (Royal Navy)
Team manager: Captain Richard (Nav) Naivalurua (Army)
Tour manager: Flight Sergeant Colin (Col) Davies (RAF)
Head coach: Mr Ray Unsworth (RFL)
Coach: Warrant Officer Class 1 Wayne (Wayno) Okell (Royal Navy)
Captain / Players' representative: Sergeant Sean Fanning (Army)
Physiotherapist: Captain Nicola Rush (Army)
Support Manager: Flight Sergeant Dave ('Shippers') Mortimer (RAF)

There was a pre-tour camp in London, and then when the tourists arrived in Australia; it was made clear at the opening ceremony and dinner that they were expected to lose. This proved to be good motivation for the team.

Three days after arriving Great Britain played the New Zealand Defence Force in the tournaments' opening match. Dale Jinks (RAF) scored to put Great Britain ahead after three minutes. He scored a second try, and further tries from Rob Kama, Tim Tamani and Sean Fanning, all from the Army, and the RAF's Gary Dunn, and six conversions from Dane Smallbone (Royal Navy) resulted in a comfortable 36–26 win.

The next match was a curtain raiser to England's defeat by New Zealand in the main tournament. Great Britain swept Papua New Guinea aside 86–4, with 14 tries and ten goals. The Army's Mosese Matua scored two tries, and Ceri Cummings kicked seven goals. Cummings and Matua were both among the scorers in a 36–16 victory over the hosts, and Great Britain's place in the final was ensured with a 40–20 victory over the Cook Islands. Once again Cummings was successful with the boot, with six goals, and Kama scored a hat-trick of tries.

The 2008 Armed Forces World Cup winners.

The Australians had won their other three games, narrowly beating the Kiwis 18–13, so Great Britain faced the hosts again in the final. The match was at the Sydney Football Stadium, before the Australia versus Fiji semi-final on 16 November.

Former Great Britain coach Brian Noble spoke to the players before the game, and the British team was never behind, although the match was in the balance until the final stages. A try and three goals from Martin Wood (RAF) gave Great Britain a 10–4 half-time lead. The Army's Kama and Tamani scored tries to put the British side further ahead, 20–4, but then two converted tries from the Australians reduced the lead to four points. However, the Navy's Jamie Goss crashed over for the try that clinched the World Cup, and the conversion from Wood made the final score 26–16.

Coach Wayne Okell commended the players: "We've played five games in 12 days and during all that time our players have never been behind on the scoreboard for one second. They are a credit to themselves, the British Armed Forces and their country." Head coach Ray Unsworth commented: "I was involved with the Combined Services at the outset in 1998 and I was proud to again coach them, this time in the very first Defence World Cup. Services Rugby League has gone from strength-to-strength during the past 10 years as result of the attention to detail both in the playing calendar and their preparation for this event. The players are of an excellent standard; they are very professional and focused and their achievement was a result of the processes they have put in place. It is a satisfying experience for me to coach the World Cup winners and a privilege to be involved with everyone who has helped make that happen ...these guys are a pleasure to be around. We all know how professional they are in their day-to-day attitude to the work they do and it's no different in sport ... they have just won the World Cup".

An awards ceremony took place at the end of the tournament in the Penrith Panthers lounge. Sean Fanning, as the British captain was presented with the World Cup, and the World 17 (see below) was named from the tournament's best players. The British players featured heavily in the squad.

The RAF's Dale Jinks was awarded the Player of the Tournament, and was presented with the award by Lieutenant General J Hurley AO, DSC, Vice Chief of the Australian Defence Force. The team were subsequently voted Combined Services Sports Team of the Year. Prince Edward, Earl of Wessex, presented Sean Fanning and Wayne Okell with their team award at a ceremony in London held at the RAF club.

The team for the final was: Ceri Cummings (Army), Ratu Kama (Army), Mosese Matau (Army), Jim Barnes (Royal Navy), Silivenusi Bunamasi (Royal Navy), Martin Wood (RAF), Gary Dunn (RAF), James Goss (Royal Navy), James Bardgett (RAF), Lewis Taylor (Royal Navy), Dale Jinks (RAF), Dave Goddard (Army), Sean Fanning (Capt, Army). Subs: Tim Tamani (Army), Lee Rossiter (Royal Navy), Ben Taylor (Army), Kev Botwood (Royal Navy).

2008 Armed Forces World Cup results
Great Britain 36 New Zealand 26
Australia 38 Papua New Guinea 0
Australia 38 Cook Islands 14
Great Britain 84 Papua New Guinea 6
Australia 18 New Zealand 13
Cook Islands 50 Papua New Guinea 12
Great Britain 36 Australia 16
New Zealand 38 Cook Islands 22
Great Britain 40 Cook Islands 20
New Zealand 76 Papua New Guinea 4

	P	W	L	F	A
Great Britain	4	4	0	196	68
Australia	4	3	1	110	63
New Zealand	4	2	2	153	80
Cook Islands	4	1	3	106	128
Papua New Guinea	4	0	4	22	248

Third and fourth place game:
New Zealand 32 Cook Islands 10

A World team was selected from the players in the tournament: Henare Te Kaute (NZ), **Tim Tamani (GB), Silivenusi Bunamasi (GB), James Barnes (GB), Ratu Kama (GB), Martin Wood (GB)**, Michael Green (Aus), **Lewis Taylor (GB), James Bardgett (GB)**, Kyle Arnold (Aus), Nick Mathews (Aus), **Dale Jinks (GB).** Subs: Chris Hiette (Aus), Teina Tapurau (Cook Is), Ben Tape (PNG), Beaufa Brown (NZ).

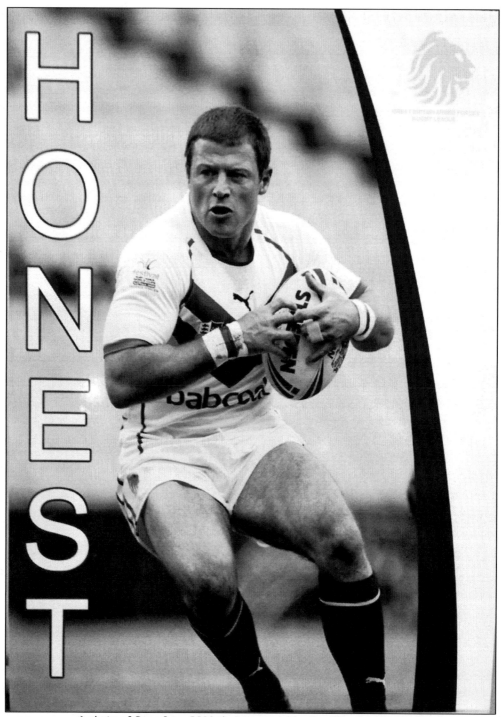

A photo of Sean from 2008 that was used by the GB squad in 2013.

The 2013 Great Britain squad at Colchester Garrison. They are in front of a Dakota aircraft, which is the World War 2 plane which Para trained personnel jumped from – it is at the gate guard at Merville Barracks in Colchester, home of 16 Air Assault Brigade.
(Photo: Julie Hulatt)

The Army representatives in the squad.
(Photo: Julie Hulatt)

2013

In 2008 in Australia, the World Cup tournaments below the national competition were played at the same time as the main competition, and in some cases were 'curtain raisers' – giving the players the chance to play at some of the sport's major venues.

The organisers in 2013, faced with holding five competitions – Armed Forces, Police, Students, Women and Wheelchair – adopted a different approach and held a Festival or World Cups in the first two weeks of July. The Police, Students and Women's competitions were held in Yorkshire, with a finals day at Headingley. The Wheelchair competition was held in Gillingham, linking with the work of the Medway Dragons in that area, and former Army RL secretary Martin Coyd. At least the weather was good, avoiding the monsoon conditions that plagued the 2000 World Cup in Britain.

The Armed Forces competition was held at Colchester Garrison. Originally, six teams entered, but Jamaica and Russia withdrew, leaving Great Britain, Australia, New Zealand and Serbia. The latter had only been playing the sport for four years, and while it was a sign of the sport's development that they took part, they were clearly at a very different stage of development from the other three teams. It is a pity that France, who have not played an international for some years, and Papua New Guinea – where rugby league is the national sport – and the Cook Islands, were not represented. The latter two played in the 2008 tournament, and would have contributed much this time.

The competition was run on a league basis, with three sets of double headers, and then the top team facing the bottom team in one semi-final, and the second and third teams meeting in the other.

While the tournament was well organised, and there was some local interest, the sport does not have a strong base in Colchester, and although there were probably good logistical reasons for holding it there, it meant the visiting players, in particular the Serbians, did not experience rugby league in its stronger areas.

However, it was eagerly anticipated. Air Commodore Dean Andrew, Chairman of Armed Forces Rugby League commented before the competition: "Rugby League has become the team sport of choice in the UK military. It embodies all the attributes that we look for in our own Servicemen; physical fitness, pride, dedication and respect for officials and opponents alike. Matches between the Royal Navy, Army and Royal Air Force have become some of the most fiercely contested and passionate events in the annual sporting calendar and are eagerly awaited. The World Cup promises the same but at an international level."

Of the Great Britain squad of 24 players, nine were from the Army: Scott Sarsons, Ryan Taylor, Marc Donnelly, Colin Marangon, Tim Timani, Tom Howley, Gareth Lodge, Jamie Milburn and Dominic Maloney. The latter was a new recruit to the Army, having only recently signed up after a career in professional rugby league with Dewsbury Rams, Featherstone Rovers, Barrow Raiders and Halifax. He commented: "I've just completed basic training and it was very hard," said Maloney. "It's different to anything I've ever experienced before and really pushed me above and beyond my limits both physically and mentally. But the sense of achievement you feel when you get through that, push yourself and come out the other side is immense – you know you come out of it a stronger person and there's a lot of pride in that. That type of test can only be beneficial on the pitch as well because it's made me physically fitter and stronger and mentally tougher as well and that's all important on the pitch. The set up in Great Britain camp is excellent and as good as anything I ever experienced in the professional game. The standard of the game is very high and I was slightly surprised at just how high it is and I definitely think there are a few players in the competition who could go all the way."

The squad also included two brothers, Lewis and Ryan Taylor. They are both former members of the Leeds Rhinos Academy. Lewis is in the Royal Navy, and Ryan in the Army, so it was a change for them to be on the same side, rather than playing against each other in the Inter-Services matches.

The tournament opened on Sunday 30 June. In the first match, New Zealand shocked Great Britain by taking an early lead with a penalty, but a try from Marc Donnelly, converted by Martin Wood, made the score 6–2 to the hosts. The Kiwis replied with a converted try on 26 minutes, but then Chris Gordon touched down just before the break to make the half-time score 10–8 to Great Britain. Army winger Tim Timani scored a great solo try at the start of the second half; and further tries from Darren Bamford, James Hutchinson and Lewis Taylor, with conversions from Wood, Garry Dunn and Dave Hankinson made the final score a comfortable 32–8 to Great Britain.

The second match saw the Australians score 19 tries against a young Serbian side who were clearly out of their depth. The Australians won 112–0, but the Serbians were unfortunate in the first half when both touch judges signalled that a penalty had been successful, only for the referee to disallow it. How often does that happen? The Serbians kept going to the end, but it was a tough challenge for them.

The competition resumed on Wednesday 3 July. The opening match saw Great Britain take on Serbia. The British coach took the opportunity to give players who had not played in the match against the Kiwis a run out, and Great Britain won comfortably 98–0, with 19 tries and 11 goals. Mike Haldenby scored four tries, Jordan Andrade got a hat-trick and Dave Hankinson scored 30 points from two tries and 11 conversions. The Serbians had received some coaching support from the other teams, looked more organised in this match, and never gave up.

The second match, Australia versus New Zealand, was much anticipated. And the hard-fought match that ensued lived up to expectations. Australia took the lead, and then scored again to lead 12–0. The Kiwis pulled a try back, but two further Australian tries, one of which was converted, to make the half-time score 28–6.

The Kiwis came back strongly in the second half. Two converted tries made the score 28–18, and a further converted try would have put the Australians under pressure. As it was, a fight between the two scrum-halves saw a general melee break out. Andrensek was sent off for running into the brawl, and both scrum halves were sin binned. The Kiwis made their extra man advantage count to touch down in the corner, making the score 28–22, but the Australians hung on, and scored near the end to seal victory 32–22.

This result set up the Great Britain versus Australia match on Saturday 6 July to decide which team would head the group and face Serbia in the semi-final.

These matches were played at the main Colchester Garrison stadium, and coincided with the Colchester Garrison Show, which attracts thousands of people to watch fly-pasts and military displays.

The first match saw New Zealand play Serbia. The Kiwis won comfortably, 62–6, but the Serbians were noticeably better than in their first two matches. Their defence improved, and they scored their first try – and points through Stefan Jovanovic. Velibor Sreckovic converted, and the Serbians came close to adding a second try near the end. The Kiwis won 62–6, having led 36–0 at half-time.

Several hundred people came to watch the Australia versus Great Britain match. It was reminiscent of some clashes in the professional game – Great Britain came close, but the Australians hung on to win 20–16.

The Australians went ahead early on with a try from Sean Colville. His fellow winger, Ross Hunter, then scored from a kick through, and Colville added a third try to make the score 14–0 to the Australians after 18 minutes. Tim Timani pulled a try back for Great Britain, but then Great Britain winger Kami Kamikamica was injured trying to gather a kick, and Hunter scored his second try. A successful conversion made the halftime score Australia 20 Great Britain 4.

For the first 20 minutes Great Britain could not break through the Australian defence. But then on 61 minutes Tommy Wilkinson scored, and Martin Wood converted to make the score 20–10. With 10 minutes left Chris Gordon scored for Great Britain, and Wood's conversion made the gap just four points. Great Britain had a couple of good scoring chances near the end, but the Australians held on to make the final score Australia 20 Great Britain 16, and set up semi-finals of Australia versus Serbia and Great Britain versus New Zealand.

In the first semi-final, the Australians again comfortably beat the Serbians, 110–0; and the stage was set for what all the home supporters anticipated would be a Great Britain victory over the Kiwis to set up a repeat of the 2008 final. However, the young Kiwi side clearly hadn't read the script in a thrilling contest that was settled in the last five minutes.

There was never more than one score between the two evenly-matched outfits but the home side were made to pay for a couple of defensive lapses. They had fought back to lead 16-14 with nine minutes remaining but a late, converted James Faleofa try dashed their hopes of a place in the final.

Great Britain began in positive fashion and took the lead after five minutes when a mazy run from wing Tim Timani gave them a good attacking platform. A fine pass from Martin Wood put full-back James Hutchinson over in the corner.

Both sides created more scoring opportunities over the next 15 minutes and a 60 metre sprint out of defence by Timani following another superb pass by Wood saw Great Britain cross again, but the try was ruled out due to a forward pass.

Both sides were guilty of losing the ball before the Kiwis levelled when a well-worked blind side move from a scrum saw full-back Leon Walker touchdown. It remained 4-4 at the interval but the home side put the Kiwis under pressure early in the second half and after some stern defending, they eventually cracked.

Ryan Taylor took a short pass from dummy half to blast his way over and Wood's conversion gave his side a 10-4 lead. However, two tries in four minutes put New Zealand firmly in control going into the final quarter. Adam Wilson grabbed the first after the ball was moved smartly along the back line and the wingman converted his own try from the touchline. Walker claimed the second after more smart handling to give them a 14-10 lead.

Great Britain worked hard to get back on terms but a rash of handling errors thwarted them until Dom Maloney took a short pass and crashed over by the posts. Garry Dunn's conversion edged them ahead with nine minutes remaining, but they immediately put themselves under pressure by spilling the re-start. The Kiwis took full advantage with Faleofa threading his way through a gap to touch down and Wilson's conversion took them through to the final. The final result was Great Britain 16 New Zealand 20.

The final was played on Saturday 13 July. Australia duly won the Cup, as they did in the Student, Women's and Police tournaments that had been run in the north of England. France won the Wheelchair tournament.

Australia 32 New Zealand 22
By David Ballheimer

Australia deservedly became 2013 Armed Forces World Cup winners at a baking hot Garrison Ground in Colchester on 13 July, eventually winning by 10 points. Around 500 people enjoyed the match.

The Aussies, as they had in round-robin matches against England and the Kiwis, used a strong first-half display to take control of the game and then did just enough after the break to hold on. In the third minute, Jack Blaine ran onto a short pass from Mitchell Knowles, but knocked on as he burst through what was effectively the last line of defence 15 metres out.

Four minutes later, Australia went ahead when the New Zealand defence held off as Keith Eshman ran at them. He spotted the line was uneven and angled his to run the corner. By the time covering defenders realised the danger, it was too late and Eshman touched down under little pressure. Mahn Darley's conversion missed narrowly. Two New Zealand errors led to Australia's second try, after 15 minutes. A penalty and charge down resulted in three straight sets for the Aussies and Dan Capilli burst over from five metres out.

Two tries in two minutes before the half-hour took the game away from the Kiwis. First, after New Zealand lost the ball on their first play at midfield, Australia marched downfield and Eshman replicated his first scoring run. Darley, who had added a superb conversion to Eshman's try, went on a 70-metre run on the second tackle following the restart, and no defender did more than lay a peremptory hand on him.

125

New Zealand did hit back before the break when a good move across the line sucked in Australia's cover and Adam Wilson touched down in the corner. He added an excellent goal-kick to give the men in black hope in the second half. The score at the break was 20–6. And those aspirations grew in the first 15 minutes as they added two more tries to cut the deficit to just four points. A high tackle on Wilson, in front of the Australian posts 20 metres out, gave New Zealand position and Itaefale Tolefoa crashed over from first receiver. Wilson then finished off another excellent move with his second score in the corner, but he couldn't improve it.

The turning point came in the 56th minute when Wilson was ruled to have tackled Sean Colville in the air as he contested a diagonal bomb from Mitchell Knowles. From the penalty, the ball was moved inside and Kerrod Andrensek sniped over from dummy-half. Almost immediately, Matthew Cole should have reduced the arrears but, under pressure, he lost the ball over the line. And when Eshman finished off a powerful break by Hunter to complete his hat-trick, the mountain for New Zealand was too steep to climb.

Henning Peterson did score the Kiwis' fourth try with seven minutes to go, squeezing between two tacklers from close range, but it was, in truth, little more than a consolation.

The Man-of-the-Match award went to the powerful running second-rower Capilli, though hat-trick-scoring stand-off Eshman must have pushed him close. The World Cup was presented to the Australians by Air Chief Marshal Sir Stuart Peach, Vice Chief of Defence Staff and President of Armed Forces Rugby League, who is a great supporter of the game.

Australia: Mahn Darley, Ross Hunter, Samuel Peters, Jason Brand, Sean Colville, Keith Eshman, Mitchell Knowles, Anthony Hopkin, Mitch Morton, Dany Tavita, Damien Rex, Dan Capilli, Jack Blaine. Subs: Kerrod Andrensek, Daniel Holt, Jarred Bassett, Venasia Turuva.
Scorers: Tries: Eshman (3), Capilli, Darley, Andrensek. Goals: Darley 4.

New Zealand: Leon Walker, Richard O'Flaherty, Leaongo Tanganui, Matthew Cole, Adam Wilson, Matthew Holtom, Darren Pullen, Rikki Simmonds, Kyran David, Alanson Smith, Itaefale Tolefoa, Matthew Phillips, Wade Sharland. Subs: James Faleofa, Timothy McKenzie, Leon Griffith, Henning Peterson.
Scorers: Tries: Wilson (2), Tolefoa, Peterson. Goals: Wilson 3.

Overall, the tournament was rightly seen as a success. The Serbs clearly enjoyed the experience, had a trip to Parliament and on their return home, were given an official reception at the Military Academy in Belgrade.

The head of the Academy, Major-General Mladen Vuruna said that the historic participation stressed the importance of sport in the Serbian Army and said that rugby league was a fine example of what could be achieved. Vuruna also pointed out that without support of the British Embassy in Belgrade and the British Ministry of Defence, the trip would not have gone ahead and thanked them for their help and guidance.

Jovan Vujosevic, Rugby League European Federation Regional Director commented: "This is a great example of the cooperation between a rugby league governing body and the military. As a result, we hope that we will have more Serbian Army international activities in

2014. Also, on behalf of the Serbian Rugby League Federation, I would especially like to pay tribute to British military attaché, Colonel William English. His support was essential in getting Serbia to the World Cup"

For the record:

Great Britain versus New Zealand

Great Britain: D Bamford, K Kamikika, T Wilkinson, J Hutchinson, T Timani, M Wood, G Dunn, M Donnelly, S Lockton, L Taylor, C Gordon, L Queeley, D Jinks. Subs: D Hankinson, D Maloney, S Sarsons, J Milburn.
Scorers: Tries: Donnelly, Gordon, Timani, Bamford, Hutchinson, Taylor. Goals: Wood (2), Dunn, Hankinson
New Zealand: A Wilson; R O'Flaherty, C Salmon, L Tanginoa, A Dougal; M Cole, M Holtom; R Simmonds, K David, L Griffith, I Tololeapoa, M Phillips, H Peterson. Subs: L Walker, F Ikahihifo, A Smith, D Mau'ufu
Scorers: Try: David. Goals; Wilson (2).

Great Britain versus Serbia

Great Britain: J Hutchinson, M Haldenby, C Marangon, M Watkins, K Kamikamica, D Hankinson, S Sarsons, J Andrade, N Parkin, R Taylor, J Milburn, C Gordon, T Howley. Subs: G Dunn, D Maloney, T Wilkinson, D Jinks
Scorers: Tries: Haldenby (4), Andrade (3),Hankinson (2), Howley (2), Gordon (2),Watkins, Hutchinson, Sarsons, Wilkinson, Marangon, Jinks. Goals: Hankinson (11)
Serbia: Sreten Drazovic; Srecko Drazovic, R Tajsic, M Cuk, D Samardzic; N Perovic, V Sreckovic; M Radisavlevic, M Stasin, A Mladenovic, M Ilic, S Jovanovic, N Cojic. Subs: S Stupar, D Ristic, V Popadic, U Pancic.

Great Britain versus Australia

Great Britain: D Bamford, K Kamikamica, T Wilkinson, J Hutchinson, T Timani, M Wood, S Sarsons, D Maloney, S Lockton, J Andrade, D Jinks, L Queeley, T Howley. Subs: C Gordon, L Taylor, M Watkins, D Hankinson
Scorers: Tries: Timani, Wilkinson, Gordon. *Goals:* Wood 2.
Australia: M Darley, R Hunter, S Peters, V Turuva, S Colville, K Eshman, M Knowles, A Hopkin, M Morton, D Tavita, D Rex, D Capilli, J Blaine. Subs: J Brand, D Holt, J Bassett, D Halliday.
Scorers: Tries: Colville 2, Hunter 2. *Goals:* Darley 2.

Great Britain versus New Zealand (semi-final)

Great Britain: J Hutchinson; M Haldenby, T Wilkinson , C Maragon, T Timani ; M Wood, G Dunn; G Lodge, S Lockton, R Taylor, L Queeley, C Gordon, T Howley Subs: D Hankinson, D Maloney, D Jinks , S Sarsons
Scorers: Tries: Hankinson, Taylor, Maloney. *Goals:* Wood, Dunn
New Zealand: L Walker; R O'Flaherty, D Pullen, L Tanginoa, M Cole; M Holtom, D Pullen; R Simmonds, K David, A Smith, M Phillips, I Toleafoa, W Sharland Interchange: J Faleofa,, T Mackenzie, H Petersen. L Griffiths
Scorers: Tries: Walker (2), Wilson, Faleofa. *Goals:* Wilson (2)

Group matches:

Australia 112 Serbia 0   Great Britain 32 New Zealand 8
Great Britain 98 Serbia 0   Australia 32 New Zealand 22
New Zealand 62 Serbia 6   Australia 20 Great Britain 16

	P	W	D	L	F	A	Pts
Australia	3	3	0	0	164	38	6
Great Britain	3	2	0	1	146	28	4
New Zealand	3	1	0	2	92	70	2
Serbia	3	0	0	3	6	272	0

Semi-finals:

Australia 110 Serbia 0   Great Britain 16 New Zealand 20

Final:

Australia 32 New Zealand 22

Great Britain appearances and scorers

		Start	Sub	Try	Goal
Jordan	Andrade	2	0	3	0
Darren	Bamford	2	0	1	0
Marc	Donnelly	1	0	1	0
Gary	Dunn	2	1	0	2
Chris	Gordon	3	1	4	0
Mike	Haldenby	2	0	4	0
Dave	Hankinson	1	3	3	12
Tom	Howley	3	0	2	0
James	Hutchinson	4	0	2	0
Dale	Jinks	2	2	1	0
Kitione	Kamikamica	3	0	0	0
Steve	Lockton	3	0	0	0
Gareth	Lodge	1	0	0	0
Dominic	Maloney	1	3	1	0
Colin	Maragon	2	0	1	0
Jamie	Milburn	1	1	0	0
Nathan	Parkin	1	0	0	0
Lee	Queeley	3	0	0	0
Scott	Sarsons	2	2	1	0
Lewis	Taylor	1	1	1	0
Ryan	Taylor	2	0	1	0
Tim	Timani	3	0	2	0
Matt	Watkins	1	1	1	0
Tommy	Wilkinson	3	1	2	0
Martin	Wood	3	0	0	5

Great Britain management and support staff

Officer in Charge	Major Richard Naivalurua (Army)
Second in command	WO1 Clive Mason (RN)
Team Manager	Lt Jason Steele (RN)
Head Coach	W01 Wayne Okell (RN)
Assistant Coach	WO Damian Clayton (RAF)
Trainer	POPT Danny Johnson {RN)
Trainer	SSGT Andy Hunter (Army)
Physio	Capt Nicola Rush (Army) POPT
Assistant Physio	Mr John Hulatt
Rehabilitation Manager	James Barnes (RN)
Conditioner	Mr Samuel Dovey
Conditioner	Mr John Buckland
Kit Manager	FSGT Dave Mortimer (RAF)
Statistician	Mr Stephen Smallbone

The 2013 Armed Forces World Cup

Great Britain versus New Zealand: Britain on the attack.

Great Britain versus Serbia: The home team dominated the game against inexperienced opposition.

Great Britain versus Australia:

Left: A big crowd watched this battle to finish top of the group.

Below: Great Britain stop an Australian attack.

The New Zealand and Serbia teams after their group match. The Serbians lost 62–6, but showed considerable improvement on their first performance.

Above and below: Great Britain on the attack in the semi-final against New Zealand.

Great Britain look to set up a scoring chance in the semi-final.

Dave Hankinson scores against the Kiwis.

Australia charging forward in the Final.

Left: Fighting for the ball.

Below: The two teams after the Final.

Sir Stuart Peach and Australian captain Dan Capilli.

All photos of the 2013 World Cup by Peter Lush (London League Publications Ltd).

Part 2: People

8.   Players, coaches, referees and officials

A huge number of people have been involved in different ways in Army rugby league since 1994. The people included here are a selection of players, coaches, referees, officials and volunteers. Some people who played an important role we were not able to contact; either because they had left the Army and we did not have contact details for them, or were on operational duties.

Various people commented that rank did not matter on the pitch, everyone was a team member. Therefore, the people here are included in alphabetical order, without regard to rank or length of service.

Ian Allison
Jimmy Aspinall
Mark Bairstow MBE
Jeremy Bethell
Emma Bowes-Crick
Wayne Braddock
Christopher Brown
Darrell Cooper
Anthony Cowburn
Martin Coyd
Jamie Doig
Katie Garside
Dave Goddard
Jason Grant MBE
Dave Groce
Rob Hinton
Ben Hughes
John and Julie Hulatt
Lee Innes MBE
Andy Kershaw
Richard Naivalurua
Andy Sanger MBE
Mick Scholes
Stuart Silvester
Kevin Tamati
Eugene Viljoen

Ian Allison

As a new sport in the Army, one of the key areas that needed to be developed was match officials. Without referees, no matches could happen. While the RFL has supplied referees for the Inter-Service and Combined Services matches, for the Lawson Cup and Yeoman Cup to function, it was important for the Army to develop a group of referees.

The current director of rugby league referees for the Army and Combined Services referees development officer is Ian Allison. He has been the Army's director since 2009. From 2009 until 2012, he was director of the Combined Services Society; he states "I handed over to Micky Brighton due to my move to Warminster. Workload got the better of me and something had to give, the Army has to come first".

Each post is very demanding. Ian explained the duties for each one as follows: "The Director of Army Referees means being part of the Executive Committee for Army Rugby League and decide on the structure of the competitions which are run. This includes encouraging players to take to the field at the lowest level. Specifically, we would develop through training courses new referees to take up the whistle and would mentor and develop through training and assessment those referees already in the Society. I also lead on ensuring that every game in the Army has a qualified Referee of a standard required for the individual game being played.

The Director of Combined Services RL is part of the Executive Committee for CS Rugby League. The executive decides on appointments of coaches and support staff for Combined Services teams – first team, Academy, Ladies and Vets. I also decided on how officials are managed at CS and Inter-service levels, and worked closely with the RFL to ensure close working links.

As Development Officer for Combined Services, I help through training, mentoring and assessing new members of the Referees Society to improve their skills to get more personnel to take up the whistle. I also ensured in the last two years that every coach that qualifies in the Services Rugby League community at either level 1 or 2 also qualifies as a referee. This has seen a huge improvement in touchline behaviour because coaches have become more aware of the role of the Referees." Maybe this is a model the RFL could use in other areas of the game.

Ian recalls how he became involved in sport: "I was heavily involved in sport at my secondary school, Branksome in Darlington. I represented the school at football, cricket and rugby union, and also for three years did Judo at weekends. I played union at open side flanker for Mowden Park RUFC in Darlington at under-14, -15 and -16. I was not given the opportunity to play rugby league until I joined the Army, and immediately loved the game."

Ian had joined the Army – the Royal Engineers - in 1986, as a junior leader. After rugby league became a recognised sport in 1994, he represented the Royal Engineers, Adjutant General Corps and British Army of the Rhine at right centre and hooker; however, "a knee injury ruled me out of playing and I qualified as a coach and match official in 1998. I was head coach of 36 Engineer Regiment (Maidstone) from 1998 until 2002, and coach of the Adjutant General Corps from 2002 until 2004."

Ian then concentrated on refereeing, and has become one of the Army's leading officials. He was the referee for the Lawson Cup Final (Corps) 2005, 2008, 2010, and for the Yeoman Cup Final (Unit) 2006, 2009, 2011 and 2013. He has also refereed Inter-Service matches at Vets, Ladies and Academy level since 2005. He was a touch judge for the ladies Combined Services match against the French National Side in 2011, and in three Army versus Navy matches, in 2009, 2010 and 2012. In 2009, he travelled to Cyprus to referee in a 2 Lancs 9s tournament and incorporated coaching sessions with the unit prior to the tournament.

He has also refereed in civilian rugby league: "On behalf of the RFL I have refereed in Student matches, Ladies matches, the Regional League Conference and the London Merit League."

Ian says "I enjoy working at grass roots level, developing the skills and knowledge of people who take up the great sport of rugby league. It is a sport suited to the challenging military environment; it reinforces core principles of teamwork, controlled aggression and extreme physical fitness. Almost all of the Army values and standards are transferrable: selfless commitment, courage, discipline, integrity, loyalty and respect for others are all rules which Soldiers live and breathe. They are all seen, both on the field of play and in Soldiers' daily lives, either in camp or operations."

Inevitably, there are times when refereeing is not pleasurable: "I do not enjoy turning up for games when due to poor discipline, poor self-control, teams are more interested in causing injury rather than playing the game. This has been the case in both civilian and military circles especially in the south where the sport has developed hugely in the last 10 years, but I am pleased that this trend is reducing substantially."

Ian finds that "The one thing that stands out as the main difference between civilian and military rugby league is the physicality of the military games. The contact in the challenge/tackle area is brutal, but not illegal. The sheer brutality in this area makes games played at Army versus Navy, Lawson Cup Finals or Navy East versus Navy West excellent for spectators. In the latter; which was played at Headingley two years ago, around 5,000 spectators saw a brutal game with huge hits from both sides. The Navy play this game ahead of a Super League clash at Headingley. They use the game to select the squad for the Inter-Service games so the lads know it is all to play for. Four guys went to hospital with concussion in what was the fairest game I have been involved in. Selfless commitment, courage and integrity were all evident. By the end of the game 10,000 supporters were in the ground and gave the teams a standing ovation. The great thing about rugby league is that the game is made up of great hits and fair doses of skill. Spectators enjoy both sides and this is evident in these games."

Ian has also done some coaching in the RL Conference: "In 2011 I became the head coach of Oxford Cavaliers in the Regional League Conference West. However, due to a move to Warminster I resigned from this post at the end of the 2012 season."

He says that "Both refereeing and coaching bring their own challenges. The knowledge of coaching and developing players in the amateur game is very rewarding. When I was head coach of Oxford Cavaliers I developed two players into the Irish Wolfhounds and one player into the English Lionhearts side. Since this time, three of these players have made a jump from amateur rugby league into the Oxford semi-professional team (Jack Briggs, John Connaughton and Ruari Lynch). All could go further. The frustration in the amateur game, especially in the south, is getting players onto the field of play. I remember confirming a squad of 18 to travel to Bristol Sonics for a game. I spoke to every player on the Thursday and Friday before the game and all confirmed they would travel. We then travelled with six. It can be soul destroying.

Refereeing, on the other hand, can be very rewarding; especially when you are having a good game. Like players and coaches, officials make mistakes and when this happens it can be a very lonely road. I do self-assessments after every game, but wait 24 hours before completing them and focus on what three things I did well and what three things I could do better. Due to my position in the military, I think I have taken on more referee appointments than I would have done otherwise, but I have now grown into this role; so I would say I now prefer officiating to coaching.

What can be very annoying though is when I see match officials put their interests above that of the game. Some match officials I have had contact with think the game is played for them. Without a coach, without players and without a referee the game could not go ahead. Match officials must be integrated into the whole game and must help develop and coach new young starter teams and assist them get off the ground. This has been my main focus over the last few years."

Ian has also had some contact with the Super League officials: "Ian Smith took my referee course in the late 1990s and I worked with Stuart Cummings on a regular basis when I was Director of Referees for CS. My contact in the RFL since handing over the appointment of Director has been George Taylor (Development Officer CS) and Danny McNeice (Development Officer Midlands). Unfortunately, both have suffered from the RFL down scaling due to the reduction of the Sport England bid, but both are with us on a consultant basis for the Armed Forces World Cup."

Ian's work has been recognised both at Combined Services level and within the Army. He was awarded the Chairman's award for outstanding contribution to Combined Service Sport in 2010 (this award that has only been issued twice); and was awarded the Adjutant General Corps Sporting Colours for outstanding contribution to rugby league in 2011.

Ian was also in charge of organising the match officials for the Armed Forces World Cup at Colchester in July 2013.

Ian has now been in the Army for over 27 years, and has had a wide-ranging military career. He recalls: "My first few tours were spent in the United Kingdom, Northern Ireland, Falkland Islands and Germany in a variety of combat engineer, clerical and instructional posts including posts with 3 Royal School of Military Engineering, 14 Independent Topographical Squadron RE and 26 Engineer Regiment.

On 1 April 1992, while serving with 26 Engineer Regiment I was transferred to the newly formed Adjutant General Corps (Staff Personnel Support) under Options for Change."

He then did a tour of the Falkland Islands before joining 1st Princess of Wales Royal Regiment in 1994 while they completed a tour as the resident battalion in Omagh, Northern Island. Then "In 1996 I moved with the unit to Canterbury and carried out various operational deployments back to Northern Ireland, Albania and the Congo. In 1997 I moved to 5 Airborne Brigade to work in the Headquarters before being promoted later that year to Sergeant and posted to 36 Engineer Regiment in Maidstone. During this time I completed an operational tour to Bosnia. In 2001 I was promoted to Staff Sergeant and appointed Regimental Accountant."

In 2004 Ian moved to Worthy Down as an Instructor at trade training and in 2005 took the lead on all UNICOM Training and the migration of this information onto the new Joint Personnel Administration System. In May 2006 he was assigned to Media & Communication, Headquarters Land Forces as the Chief Clerk. He was heavily involved in moving the Branch of from Plans Directorate into the new, much larger, Media & Communication Directorate.

In September 2008, Ian returned to finance work as Financial Systems Administrator at 4 Logistic Support Regiment RLC at Abingdon. In 2009, he deployed to Iraq and Kuwait on Operation Brockdale (the mission to withdraw British troops from Iraq) as Force Cashier Middle East. In October 2011, he moved to his current post as Chief Clerk Directorate Land Warfare.

Ian believes that sport is "An integral part of life within the services. Sport and fitness work hand in hand with the wellbeing of all our people. Rugby league is a sport that requires dedication and controlled aggression. Working within a team is also very important; all together the skills are easily transferable into an operational environment."

He has played a major role in developing the sport in the Army and the Combined Services, and hopefully will continue to do so in the future.

Jimmy Aspinall

Having been born and bred in Wigan, it is maybe not surprising that Jimmy Aspinall has had a lifetime's involvement in rugby league. He played for local teams as a schoolboy, and has been involved with Ince Rose Bridge ARLFC for many years as a committee member including a spell of six years as club secretary.

As well as his involvement with Ince Rose Bridge, Jimmy has played an important role in amateur rugby league as manager of the English Community Lions (formerly Great Britain Community Lions). He has also been involved in various roles in rugby league in the Army, but the highlight for him was the first Army Rugby League international overseas tour to New Zealand in 2001, and the Kiwis' return trip to our shores in October 2002.

Jimmy recalls: "Mick Scholes was the team manager of the Army RL side. We were preparing for our first international tour, and Mick unfortunately had to pull out. Colonel Mike Bowman, the then chairman, and Paul Wright, the secretary, asked if I would become team manager. For me it was a tremendous honour, a very successful tour and one I will cherish for the rest of my life. Overall, every player enjoyed the tour as we won two of the three matches against the New Zealand Army team.

Prior to flying out we assembled at RAF Uxbridge to put the final touches which included kit issues and photographs. After an overnight stay we travelled the short distance to Heathrow Airport and boarded our flight for Auckland via a six hour transfer at Los Angeles. Overall the flight was particularly arduous; however the short stop-over in Los Angeles airport gave us enough time to relax in a beach bar just a short taxi drive from the airport!

When we arrived in New Zealand, we had a 13 hour journey by coach, to Linton Army Camp in Palmerston North. It was a very old coach, with a maximum speed of around 30 mph." Transport arrangements had been affected by the New Zealand's Army's commitments in East Timor.

"I remember that when we arrived in NZ the foot and mouth outbreak in the UK was on-going, and the customs officers checked our luggage very carefully, especially the players boots. If any of the players had dirty boots they could not bring them into the country. I had a friend in the New Zealand Defence Force, Captain Michelle Chadwick, who had transferred from the British Army; she served in the Queen Alexandra's Royal Army Nursing Corps and was based at Linton Camp Palmerston North. She proved very helpful with local knowledge and the lie of the land. This was very helpful in my role as team manager. The accommodation was superior to that available to the majority of UK soldiers, single rooms, good food and very good training facilities."

However, it was clear that it was going to be a tough test for the Army team: "The New Zealand Army play Rugby Union as their main sport, and we were under no illusions that it would be a very tough test. Everyone knew we would be up against it and the games would be very close and tough. The Kiwis don't take a backward step, they hit you with everything they can muster. Off the field they were generous and their hospitality was second to none.

The day we arrived we were expected to attend a reception at local Services Legion club – similar to our British Legion here, however on a larger scale. The whole party were very tired, but everyone did their duty impeccably and spent a couple of hours there talking to the locals." We won our first game on North Island and after a huge celebration we headed to Christchurch on the South Island. We got the ferry from Wellington to Picton, a town named after Sir Thomas Picton, the Welsh military associate of the Duke of Wellington, who was killed at the Battle of Waterloo. The scenery was incredible as we approached Picton through the Marlborough Sounds. When we disembarked we had a four hour coach journey to Burnham Military Camp which is situated near Christchurch. As before we were looked after very well by our hosts. Apart from playing an international game we were fortunate to be there for ANZAC Day. We accepted an official invite to be part of the ceremonies, however it meant being up at 4am to take part in the ceremony, which was held at daybreak. It was a very cold morning with frost on the ground and as we stood there in our Army Rugby League blazers and ties absolutely freezing what evolved was a truly remarkable experience. Our contingent was Captain Paul Wright, Warrant Officer 2 Tim

White, Sergeant Paul Jones and myself. To be involved in that service and to see how they performed it was a tremendous honour. We all felt the hairs rise on the backs of our necks and I will forever always remember it.

As well as the rugby, we enjoyed a visit to Christchurch centre which was beautiful; there was a particular street that was like New Orleans which was very attractive. The Avon river runs through the city and one of the popular attractions is punting on it. A number of us sat in the flat-bottomed boats with no keel, with a chap dressed in striped blazer, braces, and wearing the straw hat pushing us along using a long pole. A number of players went whale watching from the air, which for them was a very memorable trip."

On ANZAC Day the Army faced the New Zealand Army South Island team, and lost narrowly 32–30. Jimmy recalls: "Having had a great time in Christchurch we moved back on to Wellington to Trentham Army Camp which was located in a suburb called Little Hut, which is about 15 minutes outside the city. The final game was played there, against the full New Zealand Army team. The British Ambassador and other members of the consulate came and watched the game. It was good of him to take the time out of his busy schedule to come and support us." We won the game 22–10 to wrap up the series 2–1.

During our stay at Trentham camp a number of our party toured the West Pac Rugby Stadium and the TE Papa Museum in Wellington where we took in a little bit of New Zealand culture. After travelling back up north to Auckland we stayed at Devonport Naval base from which a number of the party visited the Ericsson Stadium (now called Mt Smart), where the New Zealand Warriors play their NRL games. We also went up the Sky tower in the centre of Auckland. We left New Zealand contented that we had experienced a wonderful country whose inhabitants were warm, friendly and very accommodating." As well as being a great experience, Jimmy found being a tour manager demanding: "Managing a team is very different from playing. The players play and train, and have no worries. Managing means working all the time, and sorting out problems."

However, international rugby league also involves making friendships that last a lifetime: "I am still in contact with Duane Fife and Barrie Law who I met on that trip. Duane is involved now in developing rugby league in the United Arab Emirates. Duane brought the New Zealand Defence Forces team to Great Britain on tour."

Jimmy played a leading role in the Army hosting the Kiwis when they toured in 2002: "There had been no cost to us when we had toured New Zealand other than the return flights. In New Zealand transport, food and accommodation was provided by our hosts. I felt that we had to reciprocate in the same way so I managed to secure use of a coach, a 'white rhino' from Catterick."

Major Stuart Eaton who had been involved with Army RL in the early years was very instrumental in arranging the loan of the coach. He had also been the secretary of British Forces Germany Rugby League. Jimmy drove the coach and picked up the NZ team at Heathrow. He had arranged accommodation with units around the country who had facilities for 40 players and management staff and recalls: "This was quite difficult at times; however he gained tremendous support in this area from unit Quarter Masters who were very understanding."

The Army were due to play the NZ Army in three test matches; however the locations of the test matches would be dictated by the location of the accommodation. After leaving Heathrow they travelled the short distance to Aldershot where they stayed for the first couple of days to allow the NZ party some time to get acclimatised before setting off to Nesscliffe training camp just north of Shrewsbury. The first test match was played a short distance down the road at Parsons barracks, Donnington Telford. The second test match was played at Catterick, the team stayed at Marne Barracks home of 5 Regt RA and the now disbanded 8 Transport Regt RLC. The third game took place at Leigh Miners ARLFC, which is in Wigan. "We lost to the NZ Army at Donnington and Catterick, which meant they had won the series before the final match at Leigh Miners ARLFC."

Jimmy ensured that the Kiwis had the opportunity to see some of the British culture whilst they were over here: "I arranged a day out to Edinburgh Castle and a tour of London which included the Imperial War Museum. I also took them to some of the Super League clubs. We visited Wigan Warriors at what was then called the JJB Stadium. We dropped lucky in that former New Zealand professional rugby league player Dean Bell was at the Stadium and he gave his fellow countrymen a personal tour of the stadium, along with a small bag of mementos for them to remember their time there. We also visited Knowsley Road home of the then current Super League champions St Helens and managed to take some photos with the Super League Trophy.

I was allowed the time off from my normal duties to look after the tourists while they were here which ensured everything ran smoothly. At the end of the tour we returned back to Aldershot for a final night before I returned them to Heathrow for their flight back to New Zealand."

However, Jimmy did allow his club loyalties influence the tourists: "As a Wiganer, I obviously wanted to promote Wigan to them. My mother helped me by scouring secondhand shops in Wigan for secondhand Warriors RL jerseys to give to the players. As previously stated we had visited other Super League clubs, however I wanted them to support Wigan rather than someone else." In 2004, Jimmy managed the Ireland team that toured Russia and played in the Victory Cup. The New Zealand Defence Forces team was also involved, and he once again he met some of the people from New Zealand on that trip.

Jimmy first got involved with Army Rugby League through the Royal Logistics Corps (RLC) team. From 1995 to 1996, he was posted to 8 Transport regiment at Catterick. He recalls: "Major Neil Songhurst was the team secretary, but he was posted for a short tour of duty to the Falkland Islands. "I pulled a team together to represent 8 Regiment RLC, and then became secretary of the Royal Logistics Corps Rugby League in the absence of Neil."

In 1997, the RLC played REME at The Stoop in a curtain raiser to the London Broncos versus Canberra professional game. The Director General of the RLC, Major General Martin White, and the Director General of Equipment Support attended the game, before the match they was introduced to the players. Martin Coyd refereed the game which was eventually won by the REME, however after the game the head of the Buck, the Broncos' mascot, ended up in Padre Paul Wright's car on its way to Aldershot! Paul had to hastily return it with a slight sense of embarrassment; however it was all taken in good spirits!

A posting to Germany followed for Jimmy. Army Rugby League had a base in Germany, and Jimmy soon got involved in helping develop the game over there: "As well as the Army playing the game, Damian Clayton was working tirelessly hard with the RAF developing rugby league. I was based in Herford with HQ 1 (UK) Armoured Division as the Staff Master Driver. Although rugby had and was being played Germany it needed a strategy and sponsorship support. In the three years I was there which included a tour of Yugoslavia I managed to form an inter-corps league competition, an Inter-unit 9s and a 13-a-side knock out tournament. One of the highlights was securing the main arena at the Rhine Army summer show to hold a competition. Many thousands of people watched the teams play rugby league over the weekend and probably for the first time. We also held referees seminars to get people qualified, because if you don't have referees, you can't have organised games. I also managed to secure sponsorship from Scottish and Newcastle and Rover Deutschland. There were a lot of troops based there then, with their families. People wanted things to do at the weekend, and events we organised were well supported." It was a great three years, however to maintain the momentum it required someone with a similar amount of passion and sacrifice to their own personal life to continue the job, however unfortunately it did not happen.

Jimmy also used his Wigan connections to get some famous players to come and help: "Graeme West, a former New Zealand international player and captain, Wigan player, captain and head coach came to Germany to support the development which included presenting winners and runners up medals at the competitions. On another occasion, Mick Cassidy, having just played in the Super League Grand Final at Old Trafford for Wigan flew out to Paderborn again to make presentations and attend a Sportsman's dinner on behalf of Germany rugby league. Andy Gregory, who is arguably one of the best scrum halves rugby league has ever seen, assisted by visiting the RDGs in York Barracks Munster to attend their end of season dinner and present the player awards.

It was all about developing rugby league on a more structured basis. When I left, Brian Stow continued the work for a short period of time before he was posted and, as I said earlier, things took a downward turn when there wasn't anyone there to keep the momentum going. Another contributing factor was unit withdrawals, especially the RAF pulling out of Germany, which all added to the game of rugby league falling foul to the circumstances."

During the time Jimmy was there he organised a BA (G) representative side made up of players from different units. They played the RAF before he was then posted back to the UK to take up the position of Staff Master Driver HQ 5 Division in Shrewsbury: "On arrival back in UK in 2001 I got back involved in rugby league through Paul Wright who was the secretary at the time, I became competitions secretary and ran the Lawson and Yeoman Cup competitions. I was coming towards the end of my military career as a soldier when I was in

Shrewsbury having been in the Army for 22 years initially with the RCT and then the RLC after the amalgamation in 2003."

When Jimmy left school in 1978 he became an apprentice bricklayer. However, he found there was little work at the time – "They were demolishing old houses, not building them" he recalls – and ended up joining the Army. "A friend of mine had joined up", he remembers, "and he had all this flash gear and seemed to be doing well. I didn't realise that he had been doing his basic training, had been stuck in a base camp and had saved all his pay." Jimmy joined up in 1980, and was initially in the Royal Corps of Transport, which in 1993 was amalgamated with other Corps to form the Royal Logistics Corps often known as the 'Really Large Corps'.

"My first posting was to Germany, with 8 Regiment RCT in Munster. I remember a match in Germany where we played rugby league under the hospices of rugby union which no one to this day ever found out about."

In 2002 he was looking to move on: "I was looking for a commission, but the window of opportunity was very small. There were a lot of quality guys around who were Warrant Officer Class 1. I was not successful in getting a commission in the regular army, however an ex commanding officer who was Commander RLC TA at Grantham Colonel Chris Murray heard that I was about to leave, and suggested that I consider a commission in the Territorial Army (TA).

I got an interview with the Commanding Officer of 156 Transport Regiment and he was willing to have me. I finished in the regular Army on a Friday, then as a commissioned officer joined the TA. While serving in 156 Transport Regiment a full-time job opportunity arose in his home town of Wigan as the Permanent Staff Administration Officer (PSAO) of a TA unit which he applied for and was successful in securing. It was a 'non deployable' post with the Royal Mercian and Lancastrian Yeomanry, which is part of the Royal Armoured Corps.

Over the years I have kept in touch with many of the people involved in running Army RL, such as Mick Scholes and Richard Naivalurua. I see Martin Coyd from time to time at various events around the country and it is always great to catch up with him. I have great admiration for him, he showed great commitment to get Army Rugby League going, and people like him, from top to bottom have helped develop Army Rugby League to what it is today. He put in a hell of a lot of work at the initial stages, and we wouldn't be where we are today without that."

During his tenure as Great Britain (now England) Community Lions manager, Jimmy arranged practice games for the Great Britain team against the Army RL side. The Army team played the Great Britain community Lions at Hindley before going to South Africa. He says: "We have always tried to give the forces players an opportunity to play for the Great Britain and England teams. Matches like that gave us a chance to look at the Army RL players. Marc Donnelly, who also players for Myton Warriors, is a member of the 2012 England Community Lions team which won the Four Nations tournament and he was selected to tour Canada with the England team in November 2012". Jimmy has now handed over the duties of managing the English Lions international team for the past seven years and has returned once again back to his amateur club Ince Rose Bridge to help them in their quest to gain National Conference League honours.

Mark Bairstow MBE

An ongoing priority for Army Rugby League is to develop coaches. The current Director of coach education and development is Major Mark Bairstow. Mark has now been in the Army for over 30 years. He was originally in the Royal Electrical and Mechanical Engineers (REME), and is now in the Educational and Training Services Branch (ETS) of the Adjutant General's Corps (AGC), which he was commissioned into in 2001. So his role in the Army provides valuable experience for his work in rugby league.

He says that the main focus of his post is "To generate sufficient qualified, competent, current and motivated Army Rugby League UKCC Level 2 coaches in order to support and develop rugby league within the Army." He believes that "Coaches are an essential requirement both to ensure that the sport is played effectively and safely and to encourage participation and promote the game of rugby league across the Army. As such, they are the 'lifeblood' for enabling the sport to be played. Coaches must be qualified, competent and current and approved by the RFL as the national governing body for the sport. My job is to make sure a system is in place to deliver these coaches."

The most recent Army coaches' course was in May 2013 at Aldershot. Mark's role was to outline to the candidates on the future Army RL/RFL Continual Personal Development (CPD) opportunities and the Army RL Coach Pathway.

From a personal point of view, he says that "Coaching offers you the chance to give something back to the sport! In terms of developing players, staying involved with a game that you are passionate about and in contributing to the wider growth of the game within the Army." His best memory as a coach is "Coaching the AGC to win the Lawson Cup. We were the first Corps outside of RE and REME to win it." His worst memory is "losing the Yeoman Cup Final".

Mark comes from Bradford, and played rugby league at school, as well as football and doing athletics. He joined the Army in 1982, before league was recognised, and played Union from 1984 to 1994. But then "I started to play rugby league in 1995, while at the School of Electrical and Mechanical Engineering (SEME)." He played full-back, and captained the SEME team in the Yeoman Cup, "where we finished as runners-up. I also captained the REME team to the final of the Lawson Cup in 1999, where we were also runners-up." After switching to the AGC, Mark captained and coached their team to a Lawson Cup win in 2002, and still coaches the AGC team.

Another highlight as a player was playing for the Army in the 1998 Inter-Services tournament, in which the Army was successful."

In 2004 he switched to the Army Veterans team, which he played for until 2009. He says that "In the early years of the Vets we had a number of former pros turn out against us. For me, the most memorable would be Paul Newlove, including tackling him. But my most poignant memory was playing at Rochdale Hornets ground; and after the game in the club house the overwhelming feeling of pride that the club members made us feel about ourselves and the Army. It is really hard to describe, but just the atmosphere and welcome that we received. It was probably epitomised by one spectator bidding £50 for a coat hanger in the charity auction!"

Mark was Army RL secretary from 2003 to 2004, and one particular highlight from that period was the 10th anniversary tour to Australia: "This was an epic tour over three weeks, in which the Australian Defence Force won the series 2-1. It involved getting a touring side of 32 players and support staff to Sydney and then Townsville. Particularly memorable was the fantastic hosting by the Penrith Panthers."

Mark joined the Army in 1982. It "was an aspiration that I had grown up with as a child. My father had been in the Army. I joined as an apprentice Aircraft Technician in REME. I have served in the UK, Northern Ireland, Germany and Cyprus; and deployed three times to Iraq." Mark received the MBE in the Queen's birthday honours list in 2009. He will retire from the Army in 2013 due to redundancy.

He believes that "Sport is an integral part of Army life. It provides the platform for the cohesive team building that is required by all soldiers and is at the very fabric of what we do. It epitomises the Army core values of courage, discipline, respect for others, integrity, loyalty and selfless commitment."

Mark was involved for a short period with the Bristol Sonics RL Conference team in 2003, both as a player and assistant coach. And, maybe not surprisingly, he supports the Bradford Bulls.

Jeremy Bethell

In establishing rugby league in the Army, the role of the senior officers has been very important. Rugby league has been fortunate to be well-served by the men who have had this responsibility, and they have played an important part in developing the sport.

Lieutenant-Colonel Jeremy Bethell was chairman of Army Rugby League from March 2002 to September 2007. He had previously been vice-chairman, and had become involved through helping set up a team in the School of Electrical and Mechanical Engineering (SEME) Regiment and as a referee. He recalls that "As I was the only commissioned officer refereeing, Colonel Mike Bowman, the ARL chairman at the time asked me to form the Army RL Referees Society in 1999. As we had been to school together and were great friends, it would have been churlish to refuse. Not long after that, he also asked me to become the Vice Chairman of Army Rugby League as well. Two years later, he moved jobs and was unable to fulfil his commitments as ARL chairman, so I was asked to succeed him."

Jeremy came to rugby league from a union background: "As a soldier, fitness is always a pre-requisite. I have always enjoyed team sports and my main sport was rugby union, I played at school and club level before joining the Army, then University, Unit, and Corps level when a serving soldier. I never had the opportunity to play rugby league, although I was brought up on a diet of Eddie Waring as a boy and was no stranger to the televised game." He had planned to become a rugby union referee, but the recognition of rugby league in the Army saw him become involved in a new sport for him: "I had reached the end of my rugby union playing career when I needed a back operation and I intended to qualify as a Rugby Union referee as part of my rehabilitation. This coincided with the time that rugby league was being recognised as an Army sport. Rugby union had become an open game and David Hinchliffe MP and others had succeeded in getting rugby league acknowledged within the Services. I was approached by members of the unit I commanded, who wanted to start a rugby league team. As I was already chairman of the unit rugby union club, and the Commanding Officer, this was a very simple decision to make and we converted it overnight to a single club that played both codes. As the sport was embryonic in the Army, and had little infrastructure, I applied to attend a rugby league referees course instead of a rugby union course. Geoff Berry assessed me as competent in the second ever military referees course, which was held at RAF Honnington."

By 2002 the sport was established in the Army, although Jeremy recalls that "Some players were still pressured to play rugby union, although Mike Bowman's initiative to change rugby league in the Army to a summer sport avoided most of the clashes." He saw the main role of the chairman was to ensure that there was a strong committee, "who would, in turn ensure that: strong Army sides were able to win the Inter-Services competition; that the Corps competition was well managed, to maximise the numbers playing and help identify potential Army players; and that the Unit competition was well managed, to maximise the numbers playing and help identify potential Corps players." The chairman also chaired the committee meetings, "made the difficult decisions", represented the Army at Combined Services level meetings, including taking the chairmanship in rotation, and "to be the main interface with the president, sponsors and potential sponsors and my opposite number when playing civilian clubs." Jeremy became the first chairman of the Combined Services Rugby League Referees Society in 2004.

One event that got wide press coverage during Jeremy's time as chairman was the establishment of rugby league at Sandhurst. He recalls: "Although I lobbied the senior officers at Sandhurst when the initial resistance was manifest, it was support for the infrastructure that was my prime concern, the case being led by senior officers, particularly the chairman of the Army Sports Control Board, Major General Simon Lytle, who was our strongest advocate at that time."

The Inter-Services matches are the highlight of the Army's season. One initiative that Jeremy took was to try to get Sky Sports interested in covering the matches: "I thought Inter-Service fixtures were a much better spectacle than the Varsity rugby league game that they screened. We linked up with Neal Coupland, who became a producer of the *Super League Show*, to improve our marketing. For two years, like the Varsity game, we played our 'home' games at Richmond RFC. Like them we had pre-match dinners, which were tremendous occasions, Ray French spoke at the first, and Stevo at the second, but Sky did not bite.

The most memorable achievement during my time, although I can claim little of the credit, was the inclusion of the female Inter-Services games, to be on the same day and at the same venue. They became truly an integral part of the occasion and the celebrations afterwards.

Another fond memory is the occasional provision of Super-League referees. Ashley Klein refereed a number of Inter-Services games and we have been also been lucky enough to secure the likes of Thierry Alibert and Ben Thaler. In other competitions, such as the Public Servants Cup, we were appointed up-and coming-referees, the most memorable being Robert Hicks at an age when he couldn't drive, but was driven to the game by his mother. All these experienced referees helped the development of our home-grown officials, who really appreciated the time and trouble taken.

I particularly enjoyed being the Army representative on the Combined Services committee, and was honoured when I became Chairman for a while. I was working with some tremendously dedicated people from all three services, collectively putting the administrative structures in place for the management and discipline of the Inter-Services competition and also raising the profile of services rugby league within the Rugby Football League headquarters at Red Hall and throughout the community game. We were very appreciative of the way that the services, as new boys, were enthusiastically welcomed into the administrative structure of the game by our opposite numbers in the more mature sections, such as BARLA, Student Rugby League, etc."

Playing in the Challenge Cup has been another important development for the Army team: "The first time we played a professional club in the Challenge Cup was against Rochdale Hornets in January 2000, who made us so welcome. Although we were well beaten, we were able to give a good account of ourselves, and showed that Services Rugby League had arrived and cemented the relationship between the fledgling services sport and the rest of the game. In later years we met Featherstone Rovers twice, and have receiving the most warm and positive reception each time. However, for many years we were at a disadvantage because the games were out of our main season, unlike our early round opponents. That should change now with the main amateur teams moving to a summer season."

Jeremy left the Army in 2007, after nearly 37 years' service. He joined the Army in 1971, and was commissioned into REME in 1973. He saw service in Germany, UK, Northern Ireland and the Falkland Islands (post conflict). While in the Army he did an in-service degree in Mechanical Engineering and also gained an MBA. With the Field Army, he headed units responsible for the repair of heavy armoured vehicles. He also spent time in staff appointments, and provided the strategic direction for the support for new armoured vehicles, or sub systems, entering service. He also commanded the School of Electrical & Mechanical Engineering Regiment, where newly recruited tradesmen are taught the necessary operational trade skills. He now works for Thales, a multinational defence and aerospace company: "I ensure that the products they supply for the British Army have the correct support in place: spares, technical publications, special tools, training, etc. My work is predominantly on urgent operational requirements, supporting the rapid development of vehicle-bourn systems, which counter improvised explosive devices in Afghanistan."

However, Jeremy has maintained his links with Army Rugby League. Since 2007 he has been a vice-president of the organisation, and is the founding president of Soldiers League, which he considers to be a great honour: "The emphasis of the society has changed over time. Initially the three aims of supporting the Army Rugby League, supporting soldiers who were to play representative games and raising money for three chosen service charities, had equal prominence. The service experiences in Afghanistan have thrust the charitable element to the forefront and this is now the major purpose.

There is a very strong link, naturally, between Soldiers League and the Army Veterans XIII, who unlike Masters RL, play full contact, even though some are well over 35 years of age minimum. Brian Stowe christened them as the RATS – Race Against Time and Senility. RATS games are also used to promote Soldiers League and to raise money for service charities. I hope to see this developing further in the future."

Jeremy's interest in rugby league has also developed into becoming a season ticket holder at the London Broncos. Despite living in Dorset, he attends most home matches: "I have been a season ticket holder for the Broncos since my visit to the Stoop to support the REME versus the Royal Logistic Corps as the curtain raiser for Broncos versus Canberra Raiders match on 21 July 1997. That was the day I became hooked. I do recall that Martin Coyd was the referee for the curtain raiser. Since the inclusion of the Catalan Dragons in Super-League, our annual summer holidays are now in the Perpignan area, on dates that are dictated by the fixture list.

As a referee, I have been nominated to officiate at many service establishments around the country. I was also able to contribute to the London Referees Society, unfortunately for only one season, as my military duties took me just that too far away. However, I usually had my kit in the car, and had the opportunity to fill short notice commitments. Twice, Simon Mathews, the chairman of the London Referees Society, needed urgent replacement Super League inter-change officials, because the booked touch judges were stuck in traffic on the M1 and the inter-change officials had to step up. He got hold of me as I was driving to watch the Broncos, and stepping into the breach was something I was thrilled to do.

Looking back, Jeremy thinks that the development of rugby league fits in very well with Army life: "Competitive sport is a key element of military life, it has tremendous training value. Rugby League epitomises the soldierly skills required. It requires physical fitness and the robustness required of a contact sport, team work is essential but the requirement to stand up and be counted by putting your body on the line (again and again) to make that tackle, for the rest of the team is why I think it is the perfect soldier's sport."

Emma Bowes-Crick

The development of the Army Ladies' rugby league team was an important step forward for the development of the sport, giving it a new base. The team's first captain was Emma Bowes-Crick. Before joining the Army in 1999, she had never played rugby before: "I played a lot of sport at school, but when I joined the Army I played netball, rugby union and did equitation (horsemanship). I used to provide medical cover for Army men's under-21s for many years, so I knew a lot of the Army rugby union players. At Sandhurst we got a team together and I played for the first time then. I got completely hooked and then formed an Army Medical Services (AMS) side.

I played for the Army rugby union team and was vice-captain for a time. During this time I ran the AMS women's side and won the inter-Corps 7s one year. Through AMS rugby I met Sean Fanning who persuaded me to help him start the first Womens Army rugby league side. I had a lot of contacts through AMS and Army rugby union so I used those contacts to form the rugby league side. Sean taught us all the rules and trained us. At that time I don't think any of us had played league before. We were all union players. Sean sorted out some sponsorship, including the well-known George pub in Gosport. From there, we had a few games which culminated in the first inter-services match at Gosport against the RAF. The Navy couldn't muster a team that year, so it was just the one game which we duly won.."

Emma has many good memories of her time playing Army rugby league: "It was a great time for us because it was all completely new, but we all loved it. I do remember literally begging people to play and putting some real beginners on the pitch to start with, but everyone loved it so people stayed with us. However, I do remember our second Inter-Services at Dewsbury when I had begged a young physio to play for us. She was new to the game and was not really that keen as she was about to get married and go on some trekking adventure for a year. We told her it would all be alright, but sure enough about 10 minutes in there was an almighty crack and she had fractured her femur in half. It was pretty nasty. Needless to say she didn't go on the trek and she never played for us again!

I think some scouts from BARLA were at the second match. We played in quite a few Army League tournaments at Corps level and I think the AMS pretty much won every tournament we played in."

The team immediately got coverage in the rugby league press: "After our first inter-services there was an article written about us in a national rugby league magazine so that was pretty special. My main memory would be Sean Fanning. Without him none of it would have happened. He had such drive and determination and was adamant it was going to succeed. He put in so much work for us and is an inspiration. It is a privilege now to see that it has become so successful and the quality of players is so high. What's interesting is to see some of the girls at various events and they don't even know who we are and how it all began. But I am proud of what we achieved and glad that all the hard work meant that it is going so strong today."

Playing against the other services was important: "It means a great deal because that's how you achieve an Army cap in the Services. Although in my day we didn't have such a thing, but just last year [2012] I was awarded mine at an ARL dinner which was a special moment." Emma never went on tour with the Army rugby league team: "We did not go on tour because it was so new back then. It was difficult enough just to get a side together, but we had some great nights out. And because most of us played Army rugby union we went on tour with them to the Akrotiri-10s in Cyprus which was brilliant and which we won."

Emma believes that sport plays an important role in Army life: "It's so important because it teaches you about teamwork. It brings together people from all over the Army that you wouldn't normally meet and puts you all on a level playing field. It's a time when a bunch of people can get together regardless of rank and all have one common goal. Obviously, it's great fitness as well and is a different kind of fitness from what you would normally do in the Army. Personally, I am not a big fan of running or going to the gym as you are on your own, but I could play hours of team sports and love every minute of it. I have found that some of my greatest friends I have met through sport, and they are friends I still have today. Before I joined the Army in 1999 I helped out a lot with the men's under-21s from about 1991. I am still great friends with a lot of them now and when I was in Afghanistan last year I bumped into a whole host of rugby players from that era."

Emma had always wanted to join the Army because "I am from an Army background. My dad was in the Royal Regiment of Fusiliers and my sister was in the Royal Logistics Corps. I spent my career as a nursing officer. I was deployed to Bosnia in 2001, Kosovo in 2002 and Iraq in 2003." Emma left the Army in 2004, but "joined the Territorial Army in 2009. I was deployed to Kenya in 2011 and on Operation Herrick 16 in Afghanistan in 2012. I mostly spent my nursing career as a trauma theatre sister. I now work in primary health, but when I was deployed to Afghanistan I was based in a forward operating base dealing with trauma and anything else that came through the door." In the TA she is the second in command of a medical squadron based in Kent.

Emma is now on the Soldiers League committee. She says that "I am so glad I am still a part of it and I go to the Annual dinner every year. I hope to always stay a part of it. Even though at the time I played more union than league, it is Army rugby league that I have continued to be involved in."

Wayne Braddock

Despite being from Wigan, Wayne (Stephen) Braddock's main sport when he was young was football: "At school I played all sports, but excelled in football and rugby. I chose football as my main sport and went on to represent Wigan Town and then signed schoolboy forms at the age of 14 for Wigan Athletic." Not being offered an apprenticeship by Wigan Athletic was one of the reasons he joined the Army on 1 September 1987.

Wayne never played football in the Army – "I wanted a break from it" – but did play rugby union at unit level, but was never invited to play for the Corps team. He did win the

Minor Units RU Cup with 216 (Parachute) Signal Squadron, although the match is also memorable because he got sent off: "...came up fighting after someone 'danced' on my back."

Rugby league was only recognised halfway through his Army career, but he particularly remembers the Inter-Services and Combined Services matches: "My highlights playing for the Army were captaining both the Army and the Combined Services for several years. I was also one of the few who were never beaten in an Inter-services game. A great highlight that springs to mind immediately was winning the man-of-the-match award against BARLA U23s at York, after narrowly losing to them. There are too many to speak of. I played every position in the pack for the Army, but was a specialist prop.

The Inter-services were the highlight of every season, even when we played in the Challenge Cup. The feeling you get when you wear the Army badge and play against either of the other services is immense, probably indescribable!"

Wayne was involved in the sport's early tours: "I went on two tours. One was with a joint services side to France. We played Battalion Joinville in a curtain-raiser to Australia versus French Presidents XIII. It was a tough game, the referee gave us nothing, the French were biting, nipping and just generally being dirty, a massive brawl ensued and the crowd went wild. The Aussie team patted all us guys on the back as we walked down the tunnel by them at the end of the game. I was also lucky enough to go on the joint services tour to Morocco. We played against a Moroccan Presidents XIII and Great Britain Students. My memories of this tour are vague. I remember playing in scorching sun, training on the beach, early morning and getting a huge crowd to watch the games."

Another international honour was playing in Germany in 1996: "I also recall playing in a tournament in Germany, British Forces Germany (BFG), France and Army. BFG thought they were going to prove a point and beat the Army, it didn't work. The French team had players like Freddy Banquet (who I played against when he was at Sheffield - I think), Fabian Devvechi and a few other internationals. They were serving their conscription. This was in October 1996; I got the man-of-the-match award against BFG, a decanter which I now have my port in. This match was for the Grant Cup."

Wayne believes that playing in the Challenge Cup was important for the development of the sport: "The Challenge Cup was a chance to show people outside of forces rugby league what we were about and what we could do. I remember the first year we played in it well, getting to the 3rd round on our first attempt; I think the world of rugby league then sat up and took the forces seriously."

His service to Army Rugby League is shown through winning the Army player-of-the-year in 1994–95 and 1996 – silver goblets – and the Combined Services player-of-the-year in 1999 – "a beautiful glass elongated pyramid". However, one of the awards he values most is the Players' player-of-the-year 1994–95 for 1 PARA, "not being Parachute Regiment this made me feel accepted..."

Wayne joined the Army as an apprentice in the Royal Signals, "because I didn't get any good qualifications from school and my future prospects in my hometown of Wigan where bleak, I'd also recently been told I wasn't being offered an apprenticeship as a footballer at Wigan Athletic." After two years at the Apprentices College in Harrogate, Wayne was at Catterick, then with the 28 (BR) Signal Regiment in St Tonis in Krefeld in Germany until 1992, then four years with the (Parachute) Signal Squadron in Aldershot, and finally five years at the Royal School of Signals in Blandford until he left the Army in 2001. He now runs his own tree surgeon business, GB Tree Services, and lives in East Yorkshire.

He believes that "sport is crucial in Army life. It gives the guys a different focus and a release. The physicality of rugby league and the discipline required to play it a decent level goes hand-in-hand with the military ethos."

Not surprisingly, he supports Wigan Warriors: "I'm a Wiganer born-and-bred and have followed them all my life. I played for London Broncos for a couple of seasons while I was posted to Aldershot. I only ever played in the reserve grade and never got the opportunity to play first team." He does remember Scotty Rosolen, Peter Gill and Tiger Carroll from his time with the Broncos and "I played under Glenn Workman and Tony Rea, and had a great time. But the training moved to Crystal Palace, and I struggled to get there, travelling from Aldershot, and also had to do career courses, so just faded away..."

Wayne is not involved in rugby now, he would like to be, but finds it difficult to make the time. But he did play a major part in the early years of rugby league in the Armed Forces.

Christopher Brown

Chris was raised on rugby league, but has spent time in both codes over the years. He recalls: "I played for Dewsbury and Batley Schools, and was chosen for the under-11 side to play at Wembley. But the Council couldn't afford the uniforms for us, so we didn't go. I played with Francis Maloney and Francis Cummins, and for Batley Boys played with Roy Powell. I might have got a contract with Dewsbury, but I decided to join the Army in 1986." Chris comes from a family steeped in rugby league. His second cousin is Deryck Fox, who played for Great Britain, Bradford Northern and Featherstone.

Chris went to the Apprentices College: "I asked about playing rugby and found myself playing rugby union. I didn't really know the difference at the time, but I started to get into union, and of course there was no rugby league in the Army at that time. I played union at Corps level for the Royal Engineers, but I think I was better at rugby league."

He was involved in rugby league for his regiment before the sport was recognised: "As a regiment we entered a tournament in St Helens. Then this tournament at Chepstow was organised, and we took a mini-bus of players down to play in it. It was a really hot day, and there were quite a few teams. Afterwards there was a meeting of 20 to 30 people to discuss starting rugby league in the Army, and people put their hands up to take positions. It was run by the junior ranks, and we didn't really know what we were doing at first. Martin Coyd led it, and there was a group of us who kept it going. Martin was originally in the Royal Engineers, and I took over from him in running the Corps team. I was player-coach in the Royal Engineers team."

Then came the first Inter-Services match at Leigh: "I came off the bench. It was a tough encounter, I didn't know what to expect. We hadn't played much and were facing a strong side. I remember that Phil Clarke presented the trophies. And it all went on from there. When I was based at Chatham, we used to play in the London League. I remember playing against the London Skolars and other London teams. We had rugby union guys, we developed their skills, taught them how to play and they loved it."

Another special memory for Chris was playing in the Challenge Cup: "I'll never forget, we drew Dewsbury Celtic, who were one of my old clubs. The local paper phoned me up, and there it was in the paper – 'Local lad plays against Dewsbury Celtic'. I was on the bench for that match, and played against Oulton in the next round. But then I was dropped against Rochdale Hornets! I was coming to the end of my career, but I was really disappointed. When I was younger I had played for the county side at places like Warrington and Keighley, so the Challenge Cup was special for me."

Chris also played in the Inter-Services matches: "I remember a big win against the Royal Navy at Aldershot. Over the years, I played in all the positions except prop or second row. I was really a half-back, but then broke my arm playing at loose-forward. I got the ball, and got smashed. I drove the ball in and took the punishment." Another interesting experience was to play for Combined Services against a strong London Broncos side in a pre-season match.

Although he is from a rugby league background, his coaching career developed in both codes. He has worked for the RFU as a defensive coach, and has done work for them in Yorkshire at county level. One particularly exciting experience was going with the Royal Engineers league team to Australia in 1999. He recalls: "It was a fantastic trip. I am a climbing instructor, and we decided that the team would abseil off the Sydney Harbour Bridge at 7am. We had no security clearance, and found out afterwards that there were sharks in the water! Beating the Aussie teams was always great."

After his time at the Apprentices College, Chris was based in Germany, and trained as a blacksmith. He then became an instructor for two training regiments, and was in the Royal Engineers for 14 years. He then transferred to the Intelligence Corps. He recalls: "There was no rugby team in the Intelligence Corps, so I set up a union side there. I see a lot of them at Twickenham each year. Three years ago I moved to the Adjutant General's Corps, so I've got three cap badges and more mess kit than anyone else!" Chris was a Sergeant in the Royal Engineers, Warrant Officer 2 in the Intelligence Corps, and was commissioned from WO2 to Captain in 2010.

Chris has recently left the Army: "I'm setting up a logistics business. I live in Lincoln, and am doing some training for Lincoln Rugby Club. There's no rugby league near me at the moment, but I hope to get back involved with the game in the future."

One of Chris's more unusual memories of the game involves the television programme *The Gladiators*: "There was a big event in Dewsbury, hosted by one of the Gladiators, wearing a Dewsbury shirt. One of the female presenters from the programme came to present the prizes. My son was the mascot."

Darrell Cooper

Over the years, a small number of Army players have won international honours in the Great Britain amateur set up; originally run by BARLA, and now the RFL Community Lions. The first players to be honoured were Darrell Cooper and Lee Innes. However, Lee was known to the BARLA set up because he was playing for West Bowling in the National Conference. Darrell was selected purely on the basis of his performances for the Army team.

And the honour was further enhanced because the two players were selected for the BARLA Great Britain & Ireland squad for the 2000 Emerging Nations World Cup. Run in parallel with the full World Cup, as well as BARLA, teams from Morocco, the USA, Canada, Japan and Italy also played.

Darrell had been approached before to attend trials, and had said he was not interested due to it being a closed shop for the three northern counties. But this time, Martin Coyd, "who could be very persuasive" got him to fly back from holiday to attend the BARLA trial.

On being successfully selected for the 30 man squad Darrell returned for a training camp in Warrington. He recalls: "It was surreal. I was 28 years old, and had been in the Army for 12 years. There were 30 selected players there, and Lee was the only one I knew. Lee was accepted by the others because he was from Bradford and played with or against them before, but I was seen as a 'southern softie' and effectively ostracised. They all had broad northern accents and seemed to be big, hard, horrible men from Cumbria. 'Who's this?' they were thinking. It was quite a thing, and I didn't feel comfortable. It was like being at school, where I was the new boy that no one wanted to play with! I decided that I would have to prove myself to them. It was not a good introduction.

The manager and coach staff were excellent. The coach had already seen me play previously as he coached the GB Students side, which I had played against them in the Public Services (Courage Cup) Cup Final at Knowsley Road, in 1999 season." This was a very difficult year for Darrell as it was only a few months after his father Steve Cooper (who was an avid support of Army Rugby League) passed away.

Darrell thinks that the Knowsley Road match "had a massive part to play in me being selected as I won man-of-the-match in the victory against the coach's team. For our first game we went to France to play the full French international team, who were preparing for the Senior World Cup. I was selected at centre, and the other centre was our captain. We defended well against the full French team, matching them all over the park. I was surprised to be voted man-of-the-match by the manager and the team, it was a great way to be finally excepted as an equal in the team. The French referee didn't give us anything in the game because he didn't speak any English, although funnily he did during the World Cup!"

The squad trained in Warrington over eight consecutive weekends. This was fine for most of the players, but Darrell who was based in Mons in Belgium at the time. He managed to swap shifts so he could attend, but had to finance 95 per cent of the ferry and fuel costs for the 1,000 mile round trip himself. Interviewed by the *RFL Bulletin* before the World Cup, he said that the travelling "...can be quite tiresome, but the Army have shown good support and let me take some time off – although I do have to make the time up later!"

He recalls: "After a gruelling 10 weeks and being accepted on merit I went on to play in all the Emerging World Cup matches. We had a phenomenal squad, and played well to get to the final. However we knew the final would be tough test against an Italian side which boasted several professionals who played in the NRL in Australian. Every player dug deep to complete 96 per cent of our sets, it was a great game and end-to-end stuff. It was one of the best line-ups I've ever been in." BARLA Great Britain & Ireland won 20–14 at Dewsbury in front of a 1,601 crowd.

Army RL Secretary Martin Coyd said that it was "a fantastic achievement" for Darrell and Lee to have been selected for the squad. He added that "Darrell is a fantastic player, a naturally gifted player and it is good to see that his talent has been recognised. It has not come easy to him, but his hard work and determination has shown through and now he has his rewards."

After the World Cup, Darrell was about to be posted to Oman when Martin Coyd told him he had to attend an event in Huddersfield, "But wouldn't tell me why. It was difficult for me to go, but then he told me I was the BARLA Player-of-the-Year for 2000. Of course I went; it was a massive privilege for someone of my background to win that award."

Darrell had overcome a serious knee injury to play in the World Cup. He had played a rugby union game while based in Germany when he injured his knee. He didn't have an operation immediately, and an Army doctor advised him that for rugby "I was finished," but – through Martin Coyd's Warrington connections – he went to see their club surgeon, who advised him to have the operation. Unfortunately due to overseas commitments with the army he had to deploy to Bosnia where his knee condition worsened. He was returned to UK and was able to have the operation to fix his knee. He did rehabilitation for a year before he could play again, although this was more time than the surgeon, Dr Dai Rees, had expected it was understandable with all the trauma that the knee had gone through. Darrell had to change his playing style to being a more defensive centre, although he was not really fit, and his knee still troubles him to this day.

Darrell enjoys all sports. He played football at school. His dad was in the Army, and when "I was 9 or 10 we moved to Dorset and I played football more seriously, at county level. I played a couple of times for the AFC Bournemouth Youth team, which included a young Jamie Redknapp. His dad, Harry, was the club manager. But I did not get signed for them, so I joined the Army, which had always been part of my life plan anyway. It allowed me to play sport, and meant that I got a trade – I am a qualified electrician.

I also did fencing at that time, and then got involved in rugby union, initially through a trial for centennial match for the Royal Engineers versus Royal Artillery. I then picked up to play for the Army Colts side, then the Army and Combined Services at under-21 and under-23 levels, including a match against the New Zealand under-21 team."

Darrell then played rugby league for the first time, in the seven-a-side tournament at Chepstow that was the basis for selection for the first match at Leigh. But he missed out on this: "I was on a career course, and they wouldn't release me to play. The players from both sides were then training before a joint services squad would be chosen to go to play in Morocco. I was in the camp where they were training on a Saturday, so Martin Coyd said 'Come and train'. 'Who are you?' everyone was asking. But I went to Morocco, got in the team along with Paul Jones and Andy Sanger who was the other centre, and my first 13-a-side game of rugby league was against the Great Britain Students side, the day of our arrival. We trained on the beach in the morning, then played the match at 4pm. It was very tough.

I was born in Bolton, but had no background in rugby league. I have always been a sportsman, but thought 'this is for me'. I think I am better at league than union. It suits me; I can attack and defend, and enjoy the physical challenge of the game.

After that, I kept my place in the Army team for around 10 years, I had the privilege of playing alongside great Army players such as Andy Sanger and then Sean Fanning at centre. I also played for Combined Services. One of my best memories though is of the first Army Cup Final, 1 RSME against 1 PARA. It was a phenomenal match. I played in our first Challenge Cup campaign, and Paul Jones and I had to drive from Amsterdam, where we had been playing union, to Rochdale."

Darrell never played club rugby league, and after the World Cup, found his opportunities to play more limited – primarily due to Army commitments, first in Oman and then Iraq, but also when he tore the ligaments in his left knee, and injured his shoulder. Overall, he had five operations, and missed about six years of rugby. He did play some rugby union in this time, and still plays, when available and fit, for the rugby league Vets side.

He recalls that "Early on, there were six or seven of us who took to rugby league. Guys who were good at the game were given a chance. There was no prejudice about whether you had played before or not, and within a year, we were better than players who had played all their lives. I found that my skills from union and league worked well together. I believe that sport is very important in the Army, and that rugby league is about producing your best, working as a team and fighting for one another – as is the Army."

Darrell did tours of duty in Bosnia, Kosovo, Iraq and Afghanistan. At the time of writing (July 2012) he has just left the Army, as a Warrant Officer 2. His future career involves training soldiers in how to find roadside bombs, and he expects to be working in Jordan and the USA for some of the year. He still plans to play for the Vets when available, but does not have any other links with rugby league.

His selection for the 200 Emerging Nations World Cup, along with that of Lee Innes, was a huge step forward for Army Rugby League, and another indication of the sport's development. Martin Coyd said at the time: "It is not just credit to the lads, but also to the hundreds of hard working people who are involved in Services Rugby League, without them this would not be possible."

Anthony Cowburn

For someone who did not play rugby of either code until he was aged 21, Anthony Cowburn has achieved an enormous amount in rugby league, and is the most decorated rugby player, captain and coach within British Army Rugby League. His preferred position was loose forward, but he also played hooker, stand-off and scrum-half many times for all levels of service rugby.

At school, he captained the football team, competed at county level in gymnastics and cross-country running, and was the West Yorkshire Schools 800 meters champion. He recalls being "highly competitive". He joined the Army at 16, in 1987 and was in the Junior Leaders Regiment in the Royal Engineers, based at Old Park Barracks in Dover. He has always served in the Royal Engineers, and in July 2012 was promoted to Warrant Officer Class 1 Senior Adviser, and is a Sergeant Major Instructor. He recalls "I always wanted to join the Royal Engineers, and wanted to do something that would give me a trade for life, was professional and made a difference." He has been on active service in 17 countries, including two tours of duty in the Falklands and two in Afghanistan.

He first played rugby union "in the Falkland Islands. I ran around and tackled a lot. My first rugby league game was at the age of 23". At Regimental level he captained all the regimental sides he played for − 1 RSME, 35, 38 and 39 Engineering Regiments. He played for three winning teams in the Yeoman Cup, and was runner-up three times. At Unit level he was also involved in winning the Unit-9s three times, and was a runner−up twice. In the Sapper Games, he was in seven winning teams from 1997 to 2004, and four 9s winning teams from 2000 to 2003.

At Corp level, he captained and coached the Royal Engineers team, the most successful Corps team in the Army. From 1997 to 2011, he was involved with Royal Engineers teams that won the competition 11 times, and were runners-up twice. There were also eight successes in the Inter-Corps 9s between 1999 and 2006.

He says that to play for the British Army a player "must earn the right by producing the form and skills required at Regimental level first, then be selected for that person's particular Corps team."

Anthony played for the Army first team from 1996 to 2010, and was captain from 2001 to 2006 before being posted to Africa for a year. He has many memories from those matches, but says that "A couple spring to mind: receiving my first man-of-the-match award against the Navy in 2001 after a hard fought defensive win against an ever improving Navy team; also, when I won my second man-of-the-match against the Navy in 2003. This was without doubt the best year for me. I had captained my Regimental team to Yeoman Cup, 9s and Sapper Games victories, captained the Royal Engineers to victory at the Middlesex International 9s, Lawson Cup winner and Inter Corp 9s winner, captained the Army first team to the Inter-services title, with the man-of-the-match award and captained the Combined Services. Not a bad year..."

He says that "Playing against the other services is a test; the best against the best. You are playing not only for yourself, your Corp but for the rest of the British Army. You have a lot of responsibility; the passion, pride and pressure can get to the most seasoned of players. It brings out the best in a person, beating your opposite number, dominating them mentally and physically then been humble in the bar afterwards. The Inter-Services brings out another level in physicality. I have seen some very strong and big men be destroyed because they have not prepared themselves mentally. It's about looking at your mates next to you when you have just made three tackles on the trot and saying 'one more tackle mate... come on'. It's about finding that last breath to support your mates when he breaks through at 19–19 with a minute to go. It's about finding the heart when you are losing with three minutes to go to make that try-saving tackle and your team wins. It's about winning!"

Anthony has played against professional sides in the Challenge Cup, and had a spell with Gateshead Thunder, along with a couple of Army colleagues. He says that "I found playing against professional teams not physically hard with regard to the tackles been harder. The pace of the game and how technically superior these teams are compared to us was the difference. These teams taught us a lot about been more technically prepared rather than just physically strong."

Other great memories, along with many of his team-mates, are from international tours, with the Royal Engineers, Army Rugby League and the Combined Services side. He discretely says that "what happens on tour stays on tour". His first tour was with the Royal Engineers to Sydney in 1999, when they played the Australian Engineers team. "It was my first time as captain and we won all three games. I remember abseiling from Sydney Harbour, the Sydney 5 [key attractions] and being coached on Coogee Bay beach." Anthony's first tour with the Army side was to New Zealand in 2001 (see tours chapter). The following year he travelled with the Royal Engineers side to Philadelphia, to play two matches, including beating a team that included seven American internationals. He recalls "visiting Ground Zero and one player being chased by the police. Also, at one match players stuffing their bags with cans of Red Bull, not realising that they were complimentary anyway."

In 2004, Anthony captained the Army team on their 10th anniversary tour to Australia. He recalls it as "an amazing professional tour, the whole experience as Army captain was unforgettable... even the early morning PT that Sean Fanning introduced. We had our photo taken on the Penrith Panthers pitch with [Australian international legend] Laurie Daley, that picture takes pride of place on my wall. We watched a State of Origin match live, met the New South Wales team and had photos taken with them. We saw Adrian Morley play, and sat on the grass verge at Manley watching an NRL game with a cool beer. Great memories and there were 11 sappers on the tour."

Two years later, Anthony was back in Australia with the Combined Services team. He recalls that "This tour was hard for me because I had captained the Army the week before the tour against the GB Police team and broke my hand. I played in the third game, which was probably the hardest game of the tour. I had been on for three minutes and was 'big hitted'. Lee Innes turned to me and said 'welcome to the game mate'."

In 2009, Anthony was on the Army Rugby League tour to South Africa. He recalls: "We went there with a very balanced squad of old and young, we had great support and also managed to run coaching clinics and official courses for our hosts. I was on the tour as a defensive coach but managed to get on the park for two of the games. I was definitely starting to feel old now and my body certainly could not keep up much longer. Luckily we were there while the rugby union Lions tour was on and got to see the second Test at Johannesburg. Great experience, thanks Nobby Pocock and Ginge Windle for sharing the day with me."

Anthony believes that "Taking part in sport contributes to the operational effectiveness of the Army. It promotes self-discipline, esprit de corps and raises standards of fitness and endurance. It brings out the best in people and stimulates the hunger to win both on the field

and on the battleground. Sport is critical to the welfare and morale of the Armed Forces. It contributes to the physical and psychological rehabilitation for all soldiers who have been in combat. For many, sport forms a touchstone of normality as they prepare to go back to the stresses of the front line. And for the wounded, sport can provide the inspirational goals that help them move beyond their disability to regain confidence and return to active life."

Away from Army rugby league, Anthony also set up the South Dorset Giants, based at Weymouth. He explains: "The club allows the local rugby union teams in the county play the great game during the summer months and has attracted much support into the area. I brought the Royal Engineers team to play them as a charity match and raised not only the sport in the area, identified new talent and also raised money for worthwhile local charities."

Anthony has also enjoyed playing for the Army Veterans team, and is also involved in coaching with the Army Ladies team, Army Vets and Royal Engineers. However, he says that "I am now finishing my time. 2013 is to be the last involvement I will have with Service teams. I will be head coach of the Royal Engineers and Army Vets before bowing out to become just a keen supporter of the sport I have dedicated so much to. I will miss it but I will never forget it. Playing, captaining, coaching and being a part of something special. I have met a lot of great people along the way, special people who I will share memories for the rest of my life; friends that have shared the ups and downs, on-and-off the pitch; friends that are no longer with us; friends for life."

Anthony – or 'Pud' as he is known to his friends and team-mates – has certainly made an enormous contribution to rugby league for the Combined Services, Army and the Royal Engineers teams. If he does retire from active involvement at the end of 2013, he will be much missed.

Martin Coyd

Martin Coyd was Army Rugby League's first official – he was elected as secretary after the first Army seven-a-side tournament in 1992 at The Army Apprentice College at Chepstow, before the sport was given official recognition. He did not organise that event, the credit for that goes to Major Martin Morris RE, but he was at the centre of developing rugby league in the Army until the end of 2000.

He was born in Warrington, and grew up watching the Wire, as they were known in those pre-Super League days. Welsh winger John Bevan was one of his early heroes. He went to Lymm Grammar School, and played rugby union there. He remembers: "I played union at school and league at weekends in the park. There was no organised junior rugby league of either code in the town at that time, rugby union beginning to play juniors in the late 70's"

He spent a short time after leaving school in the construction industry, but his career started when he joined the army and the Royal Engineers. He joined as a Sapper, and was a plant operator mechanic – "a digger driver" he recalls. He was based in Ripon and was part of a group of rugby league fanatics in the 38 Engineer Regiment.

"We used to go to watch midweek professional matches and play at weekends – without permission from the army – for, amongst others, Gateshead Panthers in the North Yorkshire League. To play any sport outside the army a soldier had to get permission from their commanding officer, and of course we wouldn't have been given permission to play rugby league."

After the first Gulf War, he was posted to the Royal School of Military Engineering (RSME) at Chatham to teach there: "I was now a Corporal in the Royal Engineers and was in the plant training section. I was teaching soldiers how to drive bulldozers, operate plant machinery, specializing in explosives and quarrying."

Then came an event which would prove to be a major turning point for his future: "A Sergeant Major, WO2 Mick Rimmer, came up to me holding a signal – a military communication – saying that there was a rugby league seven-a-side tournament being held at Chepstow. He said that he knew I liked rugby league and gave me the bit of paper. We talked about it – we didn't have a rugby league team then of course – and decided to get a group together to play.

161

"Because the sport was not recognised we couldn't use taxpayers' money to travel there. So no vehicle was 'officially' available, but we were given one, and warned not to draw attention to ourselves or get into trouble. And the winners of the inaugural Army Sevens were 12 RSME Regiment. The tournament was held at Beechley Barracks, which was under the old Severn crossing bridge. Major Martin Morris, who was also in the Royal Engineers, and was from Wigan, had organised the tournament.

"Tom O'Donovan from the RFL had been involved behind the scenes, and Martin Morris was prepared to organise it. There were teams from 30 Signal Regiment at Bramcote, 399 Signals Unit from RAF Digby, and the Duke of Wellington's TA regiment. That threw up another issue – the territorials shouldn't play against regular soldiers [under Army regulations], and the 'Duke of Boots' was a real bastion of rugby union, so there was big trouble."

After the tournament, a meeting was held, and Corporal Martin Coyd was nominated to be secretary of Army Rugby League by Sergeant Nigel Rigby from the Medical Corps. Martin was thrown in the deep end – secretary of what was still an unofficial sport in the Army: "I arrived home and said to my wife 'We won the trophy and I'm the secretary' – I had no idea what this meant. Three weeks later an Army team was going to play the RAF. They had a team called the Blue Bombers, who were based at RAF Finningley near Doncaster, which is now Robin Hood Airport. They had been playing for some time, also without authority. We had no money or authority to organise anything, and this match was to be held at Leigh RLFC's then home, Hilton Park."

A training weekend was held at Chattenden Barracks in Kent. Brian Chambers, who had coached Martin in Warrington, helped identify prospective players for the team. But there was also the problem of where 30 soldiers would stay. It was time to call in some favours: "We stayed in a disused Royal Women's Army Corp block for the weekend. We kept quiet and were fed by sympathetic chefs at the barracks. We selected a squad for the game, but then had to ask their regiments for our players to be given time off to represent the Army against the RAF. I didn't even have a typewriter, so I used a pen and wrote on the straight edge of a ruler to ensure it was neat, and sent off faxes, having asked for permission to use this high tech piece of equipment. We could not claim our travel costs."

"Then the problem arose of where we were going to stay. There was a BARLA School of Excellence at Leigh, but that was a building with weights in it. Fortunately, I owned a house in Warrington then, and some of the lads stayed there, crashing out where they could. I got a box of bananas to feed them!"

Leigh gave some help with the kit, and a big crowd, including BARLA's top officials, people from the RFL and Wigan stars Phil Clarke and Ian Lucas as guests of honour, saw the Army win 26–22 with a try in the last few minutes. Famous referee Fred Lindop, who had recently left the RFL, was the man with the whistle.

The RFL gave the old Division Three Trophy to be presented to the winners; Martin recalls that it had "presented by Batley FC" on it. BARLA presented Major Martin Morris with a STAG GB shirt, although the event was run by the RFL.

It was well covered in the press, in particular in the *Daily Telegraph* by John Whalley, and six days later, Jeremy Hanley, the Armed Forces Minister, announced that rugby league was to become a recognised sport in the Armed Forces. This happened immediately with The Army, but the RAF and Royal Navy would have to wait.

While there had undoubtedly been long-term opposition to rugby league by union supporting senior officers, there had been an administrative problem to overcome. Being a recognised sport meant that food, travel and accommodation were provided to soldiers participating in the sport, all the things Martin had needed when organising the first match against the RAF. But it was laid down that each of the services could only have 20 recognised sports. And martial arts were also pressing for recognition. In the end the Army solved the problem by merging the winter sports into one, allowing league to finally achieve recognition. In the RAF it took three years to resolve this problem, because model aircraft flying and fishing were recognised, which they were not in the Army. It was also an issue when league got going in the Royal Navy. But by 29 April 1994 everything was resolved for the Army.

Martin believes that Lieutenant Colonel Mike Bowman, who became chairman of Army Rugby League in 1995, "was very important. He had no baggage about league or union and came from Durham. He could see the potential."

Even though the sport was now recognised, there were still problems. He recalls: "There were some regiments who wanted to play league, but they only had one pitch, and the union team would say it was 'ours'. Also in some places there was only one set of rugby kit. Sometimes our players would play in kit that had just been used by the union team."

In 1995, the sport was racked with divisions and controversy as Super League was introduced, with the professional arm of the game moving to a summer season in 1996. Martin had the Luddite view at the time that "we can't possibly play in summer. The pitches are too hard and it will be too hot", but Mike Bowman saw it as an opportunity to reduce the conflict with rugby union. People would be able to play both codes, there would be less conflict over the use of kit and equipment, and rugby union would feel less threatened.

Another great supporter of Army Rugby League was Lieutenant-General Sir Scott Grant, who became ARL's President. Martin says that "he was the Army's Quartermaster General, and used to tell all his colleagues at the top of the army how great rugby league was. Again, he had no conflict with rugby union, and used to say that 'Rugby league epitomises all of the qualities required of a soldier – skill, fitness, courage, teamwork, determination and a strong sense of discipline'."

As secretary, Martin used to attend meetings with other sports in the Army. For a young Corporal, dealing with very senior officers could be nerve racking: "There was a quarterly meeting of all the Army sports, the DASCB. Major General Alan Yeoman, who was a Royal Signals Officer, made me stand up at my first meeting and said 'Welcome to Corporal Martin Coyd'. He also noted that I wasn't wearing shoulder pads! [Martin is over six feet tall and well built]. We named the Yeoman Cup after him, and he used to come and watch some of our games. It was important for people to see that senior officers were supporting us. He was a rugby union man, but made us welcome. He was then replaced by General Simon Lyttle, who had no ties to any sport, embraced Army Rugby League, and accelerated our progress even more."

Another important development was the Army Rugby Stadium at Aldershot, which was developed in the mid-1990s, and "it was made clear that it was for both codes from the beginning."

Martin and his colleagues running Army Rugby League realised the need to build a base, and have an intermediate competition: "A successful businessman, who had done national service, wanted to donate a Cup, so we named it after him, and that's how the Lawson Cup started."

Martin's approach to rugby union was "to let them behave badly" and not act in the same way. He says there are many examples of people, including officers who supported union, trying to obstruct the development of rugby league, or intimidate players not to play. On one occasion a Colonel said to a team that "playing rugby league could harm your chances of promotion."

After an epic Yeoman Cup Final at Chatham, when the RSME beat 1 Para (1st Battalion) 16–12, a senior officer told the players that "You're all banned for life from playing rugby union." By this time there had been 'free passage' for amateur players between the two codes for over 10 years. Martin believes that these attacks rebounded on union: "Soldiers just wanted to play sport and would think 'No one's telling me what to play...'"

If players were refused release from their regiments for important matches, which Martin would say was at the request of the President of Army Rugby League, he would ask the regiment to telephone Lieutenant-General Grant to explain. Not surprisingly, this never happened and the players were allowed to play.

Martin eventually took redundancy from the Army, but was allowed to continue in the same role as a civilian, and was able to continue his involvement in Army Rugby League. He recalls that the players came from a mixture of sports backgrounds: "Some, such as Sean Fanning, came from league, others from union. 10 per cent would only play league, maybe 20 per cent preferred league, but played both codes, while a majority saw union as their main sport, but would play league in the summer. It was important for us to develop our own identity, and find players who were loyal to rugby league. Of course, in some cases we developed players and union would take them."

He believes that in union, for the big matches, a soldier's rank could influence selection: "In the early 1990's, the Army union team played the Navy, and 13 players were officers. The ordinary soldiers played in other matches. But in league it didn't matter what rank you were, we always selected on merit."

Martin left the Army at the end of 2000. In his time he had seen Army RL develop enormously: "At one stage we had 32 regiments playing, 10 Corps teams, including the Infantry and Logistics. We had an Army under-21 team and the open age side. We got wonderful support from people such as Ray French, Dave Hadfield, Tom O'Donovan, John Kear, Andy Harland, Dave Ellis, Kevin Tamati, Rick Rolt, Kevin Langer and Henry Mason from the Referees' Association. I had a wonderful time, and the game realised how important we were for the development of the sport overall."

The success of Army RL also helped establish the sport in the Navy. In 1997 a Navy team, organised by Wayne Okell and Chopper Smallbone were invited to compete in the Army 9s at Chatham. They beat the Paras in the final, but their commanding officer demanded the trophy – he couldn't understand how the Navy could win the Army 9s!

The establishment of the sport in the Navy lead to a full Combined Services side being organised, and Martin was the first secretary of Combined Services Rugby League. The development of the sport in the Navy saw the establishment of an Inter-Services Trophy, and to all three services entering the Rugby League Challenge Cup. Martin remembers being very insistent that all three services should enter, not just the winners of the Inter-Services trophy. Despite the difficulties of organising the teams, with players potentially all over the world, they have regularly beaten amateur teams, and on occasions given the professional sides a match.

The Army's first Challenge Cup match saw more publicity for the sport. Martin was interviewed in *The Times* by Christopher Irvine, their rugby league correspondent. Martin had told General Grant that all three services teams would win their matches, and the General had repeated this in an interview by Ray French as part of the BBC's coverage of the match. Fortunately for Martin, all three teams did win.

Another aspect of rugby league which opened up for Army RL in Martin's time was international matches. He recalls: "Louis Bonnery, from the French RL, phoned me to challenge the British Army to play the French Army. A match was arranged in Germany, for the Grant Cup." However, as Martin discovered, it was not really an even playing field: "The French had conscription, and they would select professional players who were doing national service. For example, Freddie Banquet (formerly with Wakefield Trinity and Paris St Germain), Laurent Luchesse, Fabian Devechi played against us, and on another occasion there were four Super League players on their bus. In the first match they beat us by four points."

When he left the Army, Martin joined Skanska, a major construction company. He was their national health and safety manager, but in 2013 moved to become Regional Head of Environment, Health & Safety – Europe, Middle East, Africa for Lend Lease.

He had a break from active involvement in rugby league, but in 2002 his six-year-old son wanted to play rugby league, and there wasn't any in Chatham. So Martin took him to the local rugby union club, wearing his Combined Services Rugby League jacket. He said he wouldn't get involved, but was soon coaching the primary school age players at Medway rugby union club. The team were successful, and Martin acknowledges how much he learnt from the likes of Ray Unsworth, Kevin Tamati and Dave Ellis.

In 2007, Kent Ravens RLC started a junior section, and Martin took 24 children from Medway RU to join it. He had tried organising a rugby league section of Medway RUFC, and had won the 'Mighty Quins' festival under-9s tournament wearing Medway RU kit. But it hadn't really worked so he walked away from the union club.

However, he recognised the potential for a local rugby league club and on 30 November 2007, 12 people met to set up the Medway Dragons RLC. The club started with under-9 and under-11 teams, and now, four years on, have 13 teams. As well as the junior sides, there is an open-age team, women's side and girl's side, and a wheelchair team. Over 230 players and 60 volunteers are involved, and they recently held a dinner to recognise the work of their volunteers. They have achieved the ClubMark Gold level, and have had support from the local council, who funded 12 sports wheelchairs for the club. The club play at the RSME in Chatham. Martin is also chairman of the London RL Junior League, which plays an important role in the development of new clubs in London and the South east.

Martin was recently added to the RFL's Roll of Honour, a well-merited award that reflects the huge amount he contributed to the development of the sport in the Army and in Kent. He has also been appointed to the RFL Community Board in November 2011. He has also worked with London Broncos RL in their junior development. His work at Chatham shows the potential for rugby league in the south east and hopefully Medway Dragons will develop further in the sport.

Jamie Doig

Jamie Doig first played rugby league in the Army. He recalls: "I played rugby union at school from the age of 8, at full-back; and then when I left school played football at semi-professional standard for Harrogate Town, from 1990 to 1992. I joined the Army in 1992, aged 18, and played rugby league for my Unit team, 38 Engineer Regiment in Ripon. A particular highlight was winning the Yeoman Cup twice, in 1998 and 1999. In one of the finals I scored the winning try in extra time with a breakaway 60 metre sprint. I played for the Royal Engineers Corps team for two year to gain my colour, from 1999 to 2000. Another special memory is my first start for the Army first team against the GB Police. But then I dislocated my knee playing on a wet pitch against the Infantry and thought I would never play again. However, I have managed to play for the Army Vets. As my age has grown, my playing position has crept forward from full-back to playing for Army Vets at prop, but I still have full-back in my heart."

Jamie also played football in the Army, in defence for the Royal Engineers FC for four years. In rugby league, he is now also involved on the management side: "I am now the assistant manager of the Army first team and also the Army Vets manager, along with having a role within the Soldiers' League management." Jamie is also involved with the Royal Engineers RL set-up.

When it comes to playing the other services, the Vets games are taken seriously: "Putting on the Army Red is something special, but playing with some quality players that work hard together and achieving the 2011 Inter-Services title was something very special as it was my first Inter-Services with the Vets. In management, trying to get the best out of your players in the build-up; but once you cross the whitewash, it's all about playing hard, but enjoying the time out there."

He also thinks that the Challenge Cup is important for Army RL: "It is one of those fixtures that make part-time players in the Armed Forces test themselves against the might of civilian clubs. It is different from Armed Forces rugby league; fitness is always on our side, it's just the rugby league brain we need to develop." Jamie believes that links with the professional game are important: "I have been able to link up with a couple of Super League teams with my contacts and have taken both the Royal Engineers and Army teams to Castleford Tigers and Warrington Wolves for training sessions. This is great for the Army boys as they get to see the dedication and training that goes into being a Super League player."

Jamie says that "Sport is always important in the Army, the team ethos and work ethics provides all soldiers with the basis of team moral. The Army is great at producing elite level soldiers in sport and without the backing of coaches and managers these players may not get seen." He has not toured with Army RL, but hopes to in 2014. However, he says that the toughest place he has visited for rugby league so far is "Fryston ARLFC. It was that tough even the dogs walked around in pairs!"

Jamie was born in Woolwich, but with his father being a soldier as well, he grew up mostly in Ripon in North Yorkshire. He joined the Army in 1992: "I was originally going to join the Airport Fire Security team at Leeds Bradford Airport. But when I had completed the test I was then told that they were not taking anyone for three years, so I found the Army appealing.

I have had a varied career in the Army, learnt many skills and gained a lot of qualifications. I have been based in Hameln in Germany, Ripon, Nottingham, Minley (near Aldershot) Stoke on Trent and now in Wimbish in Essex. I have toured with the Army to Bosnia (twice), Kosovo, Sierra Leone, Iraq, and Afghanistan, I have been on exercises in Poland, Canada and Romania and various UK sites." Jamie is now a Staff Sergeant with 33 Engineer Regiment (Explosive Ordnance Disposal), and is looking forward to continuing to play an active role in Army Rugby League.

Katie Garside

The current captain of the Army Ladies Rugby League team is Katie Garside. Katie joined the Army in September 2001, aged 16: "The Army was always a career that I wanted to do since a young age", she recalls. "I have always been an active person and played various sports from a young age. I knew the Army supported that so I knew that it would be an ideal career path for me."

She completed her first year's training at the Army Foundation College in Harrogate, and then moved to the School of Artillery at Larkhill, in Wiltshire her phase 2 training. She then joined the 1st Regiment Royal Horse Artillery, part of the Royal Regiment of Artillery. She has seen active service twice in Iraq, had a tour of duty in Cyprus and been on exercises in Canada and Belize. She has achieved the rank of Bombardier. At the time of writing, she works in the quartermaster's department, but is being posted to Larkhill to train new recruits.

She says that since the age of 13, "I have played rugby league; it was my main sport when growing up. My brother Liam was into rugby league, and we joined Crofton Cougars. I also did a lot of long-distance running and swimming, but rugby league took up most of my time." Katie was selected for Yorkshire against Lancashire in an open age match when she was 15. Her school did not play rugby league, but she recalls that "Crofton had a women's structure, but there weren't that many teams then; we often played the same ones. It has grown now. We used to train on Mondays and Wednesdays, and then have a game at the weekend."

Liam has also represented the Army rugby league team, and played the sport at semi-professional level. They must be the first brother and sister to represent Army rugby league. All her family follow the game – "My mum and dad have a box at Wakefield Trinity. I support Leeds Rhinos, Liam prefers Castleford and my other brother Craig supports Wakefield!"

The highlight of her rugby league career so far "was to be picked as Army Rugby League Ladies captain." Her main position is loose-forward, but this season (2012), she also played at scrum-half. She is proud to represent the Army and says that "It's a massive honour to go out and represent your service against the other two services. We have never lost against either of the other services and that's a massive achievement in itself." In 2010 and 2012 the Army beat the Royal Navy comfortably at Aldershot, but Katie remembers a closer match in 2011: "We played at Portsmouth. They were winning 14–8 at half-time, and it was only in the last 20 minutes that we got control."

The number of matches the Army RL Women's team plays each varies. Katie commented: "This year we only had two matches before the Inter-Services. One was against Guildford, and I didn't play to allow the new players to get experience. Then we played a Yorkshire Select team; that was a very good standard, and they beat us by two points. It was disappointing that the RAF did not play this year, but we had a training camp instead. For 2013 we already have five matches organised." Women's rugby in both codes is not that strong at Corps level, and many players play both codes.

She has also played for the Combined Services Ladies side against the England Ladies team and against France. She recalls: "I was picked to captain the Combined Services for both these fixtures and am still at present the Combined Services captain and that's a massive honour in itself." The match against France was particularly significant: "We played at Belle Vue. My dad sponsored the match. We used the first team dressing rooms, came out through the tunnel and the national anthems were played. It was a very good experience for us." The match was a warm-up for the French team before they played England. The Combined Services team have an annual match against the England Students team. Katie captained the team in a 18–8 win at RAF Cranwell in 2012, and won the player-of-the-match award.

She is one of the most experienced rugby league players in the Army. As captain she tries "to lead by example. A lot of the girls have more experience in rugby union. I try to share my rugby league experience with them. There are very different standards in the team, and it's important that players progress. League is different from union and they need to develop."

Katie was one of the participants in the recent Army Rugby League coaching course, and achieved the Level 2 qualification. She explained: "Rosie Haigh and I were the first two women in the Army to do the course. It was very good, but a bit intimidating at first because most of the other people were experienced instructors. But I passed and got a good report."

Many of the Army players are based in the south of England, and only one, Sarah Roper, has played for the full England team so far. Katie feels that "We need to play more regularly" to have a chance of being selected, but hopefully in the future the England coaches can look at the undoubted talent that exists in the Armed Forces teams. If the Army play some of the teams in the north of England that will help the players become more prominent.

Katie says that "Sport is massive within the Army and is a major part of my Army life. My unit supports me in it so that makes it easier to juggle sport and Army life." Having established her place in the Army Ladies Rugby League team, she was spotted by the Rugby Union officials and was asked to attend the union trials. She has now represented both the Army and Combined Services in both codes. In rugby union she plays at full-back or any of the back positions.

For someone who is clearly very active, one of her best rugby league memories is of a match when she was not playing: "After the Royal Navy match I was selected as the Army female player-of-the-year. I got a telephone call from our coach, Jace Grant. He asked if I wanted to represent the Army at the 2012 Super League Grand Final. He said I had to wear service dress." Corporal Casey Shaw also represented the Army, along with two players from the Royal Navy and two from the RAF. "I'm a massive Leeds Rhinos fans and it was a great honour to represent the British Army in carrying the Super League trophy onto the pitch just before they played Warrington. The players had a chat with us before the game; we had really good seats and went into the VIP areas. And Leeds won – it was a brilliant day. That is one of my best memories and something that I won't forget."

Dave Goddard

Dave Goddard achieved all the honours in Forces Rugby League, being part of the Royal Engineers Corps side, as well as playing for the Army and Combined Services, but also had the rare distinction of being part of two BRALA Great Britain international tours, to Russia and Australia.

At school he "played all the sports – swimming, cricket, volleyball and running, but mostly rugby union." He joined the Royal Engineers "In 1990 as an apprentice, and trained as a fitter. I have always played rugby union, which was part of the reason I joined the Army, but made the move to rugby league in 2001. I still play both codes." In rugby league, Dave has played in the pack, at loose-forward, second row and prop. The highlights from his time are "playing with some outstanding players and having some great wins. In the Inter-Services, it was pure hard work and team work, some amazing skills and the life on the line – never say die attitude. Another special memory is Sly being knocked out – Bambi!"

Dave has toured Australia three times and "Beat the Aussies every time – the best thing ever." Another great experience was touring in the USA with the Royal Engineers and "an outstanding performance in Philadelphia, playing rugby league on an American Football pitch, posts and all, in front of 500 young offenders, who loved us by the end of the game! But my biggest moments in rugby league were being selected for the BARLA tours, and all my best memories in the game have been with the Royal Engineers, the Army, Combined Services and BARLA. And it's great that rugby league is growing in the Army and getting better and better."

In his Army career, Dave has been posted in England, Germany and Northern Ireland, and has done tours in Northern Ireland, Canada and Bosnia. He is now finishing his career as a MT Staff Sergeant.

(This interview was conducted via Facebook, because Dave was overseas at the time of writing).

Jason Grant MBE

Jason Grant has been involved in rugby league for almost all of his time in the Army, and was one of the founders of the game in Germany in the early 1990s.

He comes from Millom in Cumbria, a strong rugby league area: "We lived two streets away from the Millom RFLC ground. They are the oldest rugby league club in the world, and I played there as a junior. My mother's side of the family were enmeshed in the club, with past players, committee members and club officials among my relatives. I played rugby union at school, but also played league for the Town team, at under-15 and under-16 level."

Jason joined the Army at the age of 16 as a junior soldier in January 1987. He found that the only rugby available was union: "I didn't take to it, even though I had played a lot at school. I switched to playing football." Jason was in the 5th Royal Inniskilling Dragoon Guards, and was posted to Germany in February 1988, where again he found that union was all that was on offer. "I didn't do any sport for a couple of years. In 1992, after a regimental amalgamation that created the Royal Dragoon Guards (RDG), he played some regimental rugby.

However, the prospect of rugby league being played in the Army was now being debated in the rugby league press. Jason recalls: "There was a lot of stuff being written about rugby league and the army.

There was a Corporal Smith in REME who had written about it in *Open Rugby*, and a Warrant Officer 1, RSM Paul Southworth, had raised the issue and was starting to pull things together. I was interested, and started to put a game plan together to start the sport within the regiment, although everything had to settle down after amalgamation." The RDG recruited mainly from the north of England, so there was a lot of potential for the game. Jason was still in Germany, and recalls a rugby league match taking place between the 4th Armoured Workshops and 3rd Battalion Light Infantry: "I had been hoping to speak to my CO before we went on an exercise about a plan I had drawn up to start rugby league. I was at a 'Smoker' (a social evening during a stand down on exercise) on exercise, and he pulled me to one side, said he had read my 'plan of attack', asked a couple of questions and said 'Go ahead, make it work'. So when we returned from the exercises, I started some training sessions and got a regimental team on the go. We played our first game in October 1992, and carried on playing in the 1992–93 season. There was a small ad-hoc cup competition. The eventual winners were the 2nd Light Infantry. We did get a bit of friction from the regiment's rugby union stalwarts. We couldn't train on the regimental pitch, but we could play on it. They were allowed to train on it." All this, of course, had started 18 months before the sport was officially recognised in April 1994.

Jason's initiative continued to develop: "To cut costs, we were told to order the same kit at the Regiment's rugby union team. That didn't go down well. Their concept was that the rugby union team was a club, with the first team having a different kit. But the Regiment's second in command said to go ahead. At the back end of 1993, we organised a tour, and took the Regiment team to Cumbria. We played three matches, against Roose [near Barrow], Millom and Ulverston. We got thumped in all of them, but what we learnt we put into the preparation for our next season. As a learning experience it was fantastic. For the 1993-94 season, we were much better and were untouchable in Germany. We beat all the other teams. There had been six sides in the first season, now, we had about 10."

As well as the game becoming established in the Army, the RAF were playing as well: "We were sent on a long exercise towards the end of the season. Two days after we got

Photo: Jason receiving an award from Andy Gregory.

back, we played in the inaugural British Forces Germany Cup Final against RAF Bruggen, and lost. There were two RAF teams as well as those in the Army."

The RDG team continued to do well, but then the regiment left Germany in 1996, and was deployed to Northern Ireland. Once back in the UK, Jason continued to be involved with the Regiment team, but concentrating on coaching. One particular memory was playing against the Queen's Lancashire Regiment at Wigan's Central Park in the Shield Final – "a fantastic experience. We had a good club atmosphere in the team. We would organise dinners, with professional players involved. We hosted the Leeds Rhinos at Tidworth; Dean Bell was their head coach at the time, for a team bonding exercise. The next year he was the academy coach, and brought them – many of the successful Leeds first team were there, including Rob Burrow, Chev Walker, Keith Mason, Richie Mathers and Danny McGuire. We gave them a good training session, although they needed a bit of shouting at."

Jason's squadron was posted to Bosnia for a time, and he had a break from the game while on duty there. However, he did become involved on the coaching side, with the Army under-23 (development) team as assistant coach.

In 2000, he returned to Germany; and more success on the pitch. The RDG team won the Shield in the Army 9s, and won the BAG (British Army Germany) Final, beating the Royal Regiment of Wales, in 2001. He recalls: "Eight months later, we played the UK champions, the SEAE. It was a fantastic match; we were well ahead, but it was a draw at full-time, and we won it in extra time. This was the first unofficial Champions of Champions match, which was organised by Brian Stow. The next year we were knocked out in the semi-final by the Duke of Wellington's Regiment."

However, changes to Army structures and operational commitments, followed by service in Iraq, weakened the game in Germany. However, Jason does recall being part of a team being flown to play in a 9s competition at the RAC sports tournament, held at Hodgson's Horse: "We were one of the better teams, and our CO wanted us to win. In fact, I was under strict instructions to make sure we did win!" The tournament was for teams in the RAC and was held at Bovington every year."

Jason was then posted back to the UK, as a Permanent Staff Instructor for the Territorial Army in Devon. He became involved in student rugby league, and for three years coached the Exeter University team, who he made into a 'formidable force' in the National South competition. By now there was no domestic competition in Germany, but there was a link with a civilian club, West Leeds, who went to Germany to play the regiment's team, and gave some players the chance to play in civilian rugby league.

His main involvement at Army level has been as coach to the Army Ladies team, and the Combined Services ladies team. He comments: "That has been my main role since 2005. I enjoy coaching the teams; there are no preconceptions and no egos. Neither team has lost a match.

I did my coaching qualifications off my own back, and have also worked for the RFL as a coach educator. I was asked if I was interested in applying to be the coach for the full England Women's team. I didn't get it, but it was nice to be interviewed. At Corps level, I became head coach for the RAC team since 2004. In my first year, we won the Plate competition, then we had a poor year, but in the next two seasons, we reached the Lawson Cup Final, only to be beaten by the Royal Engineers. With only 6 per cent of the Army to choose from, this was a massive achievement. Since 2008, the regimental team has mainly entered one day tournaments, and have tried to continue our link with West Leeds. It has been difficult due to operational commitments."

Jason is now involved with organising the Catterick Crusaders: "This team is a mix of some players from the regiment, some from other regiments within the garrison, and some civilians. We also run some kids teams. We play in the North East League. The team used to be called the North Yorkshire Stallions, and we won the league in 2011, and reached the national final." Jason is currently a Level 2 coach, but is working towards his Level 3 qualification. His MBE was for services to Army and Regimental Rugby League, which he received as part of the New Year Honours list in 1998. He was only 28 at the time.

Jason was involved in the armed services' first international tour, when a combined Army and RAF team went to Morocco in July to play in a tournament to celebrate the King of Morocco's birthday. He recalls: "Some players were from the Army and RAF in Germany, others had played in the first Inter-Services match at Leigh. I was a sort of assistant coach and kitman. We met up at Hounslow Cavalry Barracks for a day's training. On the plane, we had to fill in immigration cards. We were not in uniform, and apparently there had been problems when a military band had tried to enter the country. So we were told fill in the immigration forms with equivalent civilian occupations. So 'Signals' became 'telecommunications', civil engineers etc. One infantryman put 'Ram Raider' on his form; we thought this might cause a problem, so he had to fill in another form!

I remember that we trained on the beach in Casablanca, and the local kids rubbed our arms, because we were so pale white. Some of the squad were converts from union, while there were a few experienced league players. We played the GB Students, and there were a lot of casualties. No holds barred, they played a hard game, and it was a great match. The two matches against Moroccan teams we won easily.

We had a guided tour round the local 'bazaar'. Everyone wanted to sell us stuff, but we were told not to buy anything by the tour guides. Someone tried to sell me two watches, one apparently Christian Dior, but I already had my fake Rolex, so I didn't need them. But one of the RAF players bought them, after bargaining, for £7. On our way back we stopped over in Gibraltar. He showed them to a watch shop there and one was worth almost £1,000!"

Another great international trip was going with the RDG team to Australia in 2003: "We spent three weeks there. We raised a lot of money to do it, and it was a great experience. We were staying near South Sydney, and went to their Leagues Club [social club] where we met Ricky Stuart and Brad Fittler. I'd had a few drinks, and decided to phone my dad so he could talk to Brad Fittler. 'Wait there' I said to him while I made the call, woke my dad up at 2 in the morning, and then had to convince him that I was really with Brad Fittler. But he was pleased that he got to speak to an Australian rugby league legend.

In 2006, I went with the RAC team to Australia, which was also a brilliant experience. We stayed at a hotel in Darling Harbour and trained at an Army Camp near Sydney, and played three games against civilian sides. One was the Paramatta Eels third team, and we played at Cabramatta Stadium. We lost 32–10. Some of their Polynesian supporters were very hostile because we were British. It was one of the physically hardest games I have ever experienced. We then beat the Portuguese RL side (composed of Australians of Portuguese origin) in a very tough match at West Tigers Stadium. Then we beat the New South Wales Academy team. It was a fantastic achievement to win two out of three matches, and great experience as a coach."

To Jason, sport is "massively important" in the Army: "The team we had in Germany, when we beat the Royal Regiment of Wales, typified what the Army is about. The camaraderie we developed helped our work off the rugby pitch. 200 people would come to watch the matches. The discipline for rugby league is also important for soldiers."

Jason joined the Army "because it was what I had always wanted to do". After his first year's training, he was posted to Paderborn, and eventually became a Tank Commander, and then a Troop Sergeant. He has also been a Regimental Quarter Master Technical, a Training Warrant Officer and an Intelligence Warrant Officer, which he did for three years.

He is now a Warrant Officer 2, working in the RDG Welfare Office in Catterick: "My role is providing welfare support needs for the regiment while they are in Afghanistan. This has included being a casualty visiting officer, but now my main role is to deal with people's problems, not just in Catterick." At the time of being interviewed for this profile, he was planning to take a group of Army wives on a mountaineering trip to Scafell Pike.

Another recent activity was hosting the Hull FC under-19 squad, to show them some life skills for a weekend. "They had a hard time," he outlines, "but they did very well. We used Army values and standards to teach them about leadership, and to show what's expected of them, and linked this to what they learn from their coaches."

Jason has given a great deal of service to Army Rugby League, mainly in a coaching capacity, and continues to enthusiastically spend time developing the sport. MBEs are fairly rare for people involved in rugby league, and it is very positive for the sport that his work was recognised in this way.

Dave Groce

Army Rugby League has been fortunate over the years to have some very capable administrators. The current Executive Secretary is Major Dave Groce, although he says that he "does all the jobs no one else wants". In fact, his role is central to running of Army RL: "I'm responsible for the general running of Army RL, ensuring all teams are consistent in their approach. I'm the inter-face between the RFL and Army RL, and the Army Sports Control Board and Army RL. I organise the Inter-Services home fixture, have responsibility for liaison with the media, and run the AGMs and Executive Committee meetings. I do all the central bookings for accommodation; liaise with Team Army and our sponsors. I'm also responsible for any corporate aspects of our organisation, including sourcing suppliers and sponsors. Finally, I also am the executive manager for the first XIII, with responsibility for liaison with units for the release of players for fixtures."

Dave grew up in Beverley in East Yorkshire. He played all sports at school, but mainly cricket and rugby league. Apart from representing his school, he also played for Beverley Panthers. He then went to Welbeck Army Sixth Form College, and played rugby union for the first time, as well as captaining the cricket team. He stayed in Yorkshire to go to university, at Leeds, where he played union for the First XV, and played for West Park Bramhope in the North 2 League. He continued to play for the club until he went to Sandhurst in January 2003.

He says that "Rugby league has always been my main passion" and he played for the Royal Logistics Corps side from 2004 to 2010. He mainly played in the second row or at centre, but now he has graduated to the Army Vets "I play on the wing – mainly because I'm quicker than the centres." He soon became involved in the administrative side of the sport, and was secretary and team manager of RLC Rugby League from 2006 to 2011. He was Army RL public relations officer from 2007 to 2008, and took on his current role in 2008. That year he also completed a referee's course, and now referees military and civilian matches. He is also chairman of the Combined Services Referees Society.

Dave organised tours of Australia and Malta, but "I couldn't go due to work commitments. Typically I could attend the RLC tour to Cumbria, which was wet and cold. I was able to attend the RLC tour to Cyprus, which by contrast was hot. The rugby was not great although we did convincingly destroy the Akrotiri team which was loaded with players from 2 LANCS. I did manage to get to the Bahrain RU 10s with 3 LSR in 2005, which we won. It came at the end of our six months in Iraq, so it was great from a social aspect also, having been "dry" for the whole 6 months"

Dave joined the Army in January 2003, and was commissioned from the Royal Military Academy Sandhurst in December 2003. He joined the Army "to follow my father's footsteps". He was a Troop Commander from 2004 to 2006, including tours to Canada and Iraq. He was then promoted to Captain, and was Regimental Signals Officer. From 2008 to 2010 I was SO2 Training, then from 2010 to 2011 Adjutant [a staff officer who assists a commanding officer] for 9 Regiment RLC. In 2011 I was promoted to Major, and for a year worked at the Staff College. From 2012 until the present time I am writing the Strategic Logistic Policy for Defence."

Dave believes that "Sport is integral to Army life; the characteristics required for team sports, especially rugby league are synonymous with those required on the battlefield: courage, selfless commitment and physical robustness. However, the parallels between Rugby League and the Army run further than the values it imbues. On the battlefield every individual has a slightly different role, and despite acting a part of a unit, is doing something individual to achieve a collective aim, which for example may be the defeat of an insurgent position. The rifleman, the grenadier, the mortars, the support gunners, the signaller and the section commander all want to defeat the insurgent, but each is contributing to it in their own unique ways. This is the same on the rugby pitch where each player has their own responsibility, be they stand-off, centre, hooker or second-row, all doing something bespoke on the pitch, driving toward the collective aim of defeating the opposition.

Dave does not have any involvement with civilian rugby league, because – not surprisingly – "I have no free time. However, he is a "lifelong Hull FC fan, and love to watch any standard of rugby league."

Highs and lows

Dave recalls: "It was by pure chance that I was introduced to rugby league in the Army, I had just turned up at my first unit in Abingdon and my Troop Sergeant played for the RLC, he had suffered an injury and LCpl 'Dancer' Kenway came into the office to see if he had recovered. He hadn't and I stepped into his place in the Corps side. That season of rugby league was one of the Corps's most successful and it was unique for me as far as Army Rugby is concerned as I was simply 'one of the boys' without any responsibilities. It was truly eye opening, I'd played some tough rugby in the past, but I'd never experienced a Fijian tackle. I remember my first game against the Royal Engineers, we went in with high hopes and I received a somewhat painful lesson in rugby league from Lee Innes.

Having turned 35 and qualifying to represent the Army Vets, it was a honour to take the pitch with Dancer, Billy Bragg and Bob Byers again, and play alongside some of the "nemeses" from other sides such as Sean Fanning, Pud Cowburn and Ryan Swindale. I'm hoping this will continue for many years.

A very recent memory, seeing Great Britain defeated in the semi-finals of the 2013 Armed Forces Rugby League World Cup, is one of the lows of my experience of military rugby. Having seen a group of individuals put so much effort and hard work into something and bond to form a cohesive unit was fantastic, but to see them fail to fulfil their potential in the competition, despite being the fittest, strongest and most talented side, was devastating. After the match I had the unenviable appointment of doing the post-match speech and man-of-the-match presentations to each side. I, like the Great Britain players, was feeling empty and gutted. It was difficult to find the correct words, the Kiwis had deserved their victory and their plaudits, but my heart was going out to the Great Britain players who were dejected and inconsolable. But winning and losing is the essence of sport, and why we love it, if it was a forgone conclusion, it wouldn't inspire the same passion and emotion.

I did take away one high from the tournament, and that was witnessing the spirit of the Serbian Army RL side, in spite of suffering enormous defeats against all sides, they showed an amazing strength of character and bounced back from each defeat with a smile and a took the positives from each game. To me this is the essence of rugby league is about, a group of guys, putting their bodies on the line, having fun and playing the greatest game in the world."

RLC boys turning out for the Vets team: Mark 'Billy' Bragg MBE, John 'Dancer' Kenway, Akuila 'Maz' Masere, Craig 'Bob' Byers, Dave Groce.

Rob Hinton

Rob Hinton has the very rare honour of having represented the Army at three different sports. The crossover between rugby union and rugby league has been done by a number of players, especially since league switched to the summer. However, those two sports combined with Bobsleigh Racing is probably unique.

Rob joined the Army in April 1987: "for the challenge, excitement and opportunity to better myself" he recalls. His main sports up to then were rugby union, where he had played for Northampton Saints for three years in the first team, and Bobsleigh Racing, where he had represented Great Britain. He got involved in Bobsleigh Racing "after trying out for a mate's team, Sean Olsson, who was himself a paratrooper who later went on to win an Olympic bronze medal. Being successful in being a brakeman I went on to drive the sled, with my best moment being taking Jeremy Clarkson down the Olympic track at Innsbruck while making one of his television programmes. This can be found on *You Tube*."

He played for the Army Rugby Union team "for a few years" and then when rugby league became a recognised sport got involved with that code as well, playing at full-back. Not surprisingly, given the barriers between the two codes up to 1995, he had not played league before. Rob says that "One of the highlights of my rugby league career was being made captain of the Army side in 1996. However, the greatest highlight was having the privilege of meeting and playing alongside some of the finest, funniest and hardest men I have ever known; a lot of whom I am still in touch with some 20 odd years later."

The 1996 match against the RAF was dramatic one for many reasons. Rob recalls "One of my best memories of rugby league was watching Nav accidentally collide with Oz Hicks, the RAF full-back, himself a very tough player. Oz woke up 20 minutes later in need of about 20 stitches to sew his ear back on. In the same game, the RAF coach sadly suffered a heart attack before the game, and we heard that it was fatal at half time. The RAF players bravely came out for the second half and played for a very hard fought 24–24 draw. Afterwards, the camaraderie was apparent as we all put rugby to one side and drank to the memory of their coach." Rob scored two tries in that match which preserved the Army's unbeaten run against the RAF.

Rob says that the Inter-Services matches were like "Great Britain versus Australia, State of Origin, the Challenge Cup Final – need I say more." He believes that "Rugby league encapsulates all those qualities that are good in a soldier: robustness, courage, teamwork, skill. It embodies that ability to push yourself just that little bit further that you know you should. It makes you believe in yourself and those in your team and you would do anything not to let them down." Rob retired from playing in 2010, having played for and captained both the union and league Veterans teams. Although no longer directly involved in rugby league, Rob is now the Ice coach for the Army Bobsleigh team. He also coaches a local rugby union side in West Mersea, who he says "often get 'beasted' in training".

Rob joined the Parachute Regiment, and "During my time there I was a Physical Training Instructor, member of the anti-tank Platoon and a Recruit Instructor. I transferred into the RAMC after 12 years. I did operational tours in Northern Ireland, Iraq, Afghanistan, Bosnia, Macedonia and Kosovo." He is now a Captain in the 144 Parachute Medical Squadron RAMC (V).

It is actually incredible that Rob managed to do all this sport as well as parachuting. He recalls: "In 1994 I broke my neck in a car accident fracturing C2 and C3 in what is called a hangman's fracture. I had halo traction drilled into my head for four months and was told I would never parachute or bobsleigh or play rugby again. I went on to do all three at full Army level afterwards and won the Parachute Regiment's 'top soldier of the year' and 'athlete of the year' awards in 1996."

Finally, he says that "I think it important not to forgot the guys who remain in the respective units while all the 'sport billies' go off and compete in representative sport.

These guys, without complaint, step up and complete the duties of the sport playing soldier. This again demonstrates that the Army is more than just sport teams. The top military sporting representatives never forget their comrades back in barracks and I know, from long term experience, that their help is always very much appreciated."

Ben Hughes

Since rugby league became established in the Army, and started playing in the summer, there has been considerable cross-over of players and coaches between the codes. One great example of this is Ben Hughes, who is the most capped Services player in history in

Rugby Union. He retired having made 38 appearances for the Army in Inter-Services and international matches, having beaten Rory Underwood's 32 appearances for the RAF. He is also one of a handful of players to have played union and league at Corps, Army and Combined Services level.

Rugby union was one of the main reasons that Ben joined the Army in October 1994. He recalls: "I joined because I was playing a decent level of rugby union at the time in my local town Weymouth, for my county Dorset & Wiltshire, South West of England, and then England Under-19s. Because the game wasn't professional the Army offered me a career playing almost full-time rugby and would support my ambition to play a higher level of rugby union." Incredibly, Ben did not play rugby until he was aged 17: "I started late in age in the rugby world. My school didn't play rugby and if it wasn't for my dad's influence I may have never even looked at a rugby ball. My first game was for Weymouth Rugby Club at the age of 17 and I scored a hat-trick of tries. I enjoyed the feeling that much I never looked back."

Ben played in the pack in both codes, at loose-forward or in the second row in league, and in union in the back row at number 8 or 6, or in the second row at number 4 or 5.

He says that the highlights of his time in rugby league were " Inter Services, playing with some quality players who not only had a great skill set, but a passion and desire to play like you represented your country; achieving my Corps colours, Army colours and Combined Services colours, and then of course the same in rugby union helping me join a very small group of players, of around eight who have only ever done this."

Forces rugby union has a much high profile than rugby league. The highlights are: "Playing every year against the Royal Navy at Twickenham in front of 60,000 people; also winning the Defence World Cup in New Zealand against the Australians." Other great memories include "Playing against the Barbarians RFC – smashing heads with some players at the top of their game, another time in New Zealand in which I got man-of-the-match (the hardest game I've ever played in); in the same game Andy Evans broke his forearm. I mean it snapped and went floppy, but he insisted that they tape it up so he could play on!! He did for about 10 minutes until he nearly fainted with pain, but like he said 'I still did 10 minutes'".

The Inter-Services matches in both codes were always tough encounters: "Winning more than losing and always, whether it was winning by one point or 10 it didn't matter, it was just about winning.

I remember in a league match Darrell Cooper tackling a massive Navy player called 'Whisky', a man mountain of a guy. Darrell threw himself at Whisky's legs in a last ditch attempt to stop the Navy scoring. He got tangled up in Whisky's boot laces and Whisky fell like a huge oak tree right on top of Darrell. All you could see were two hands and feet and a little voice saying 'help'. It looked like something out of Warner Brothers Cartoon. I could only laugh and then slowly peel what was left of Darrell's pancake body off the pitch – but he did stop the try!"

To play the other services means "EVERYTHING and MORE. The best of the Army versus the Best of the Navy or RAF. Blood, sweat and tears doesn't come close once you pull down that jersey, you fear no man and no matter at what cost, you will win that game for everyone. I became a very well established rugby union and rugby league player, and in my rugby union circles would be called upon to say a few words on match day at Twickenham. I would say this: "The Navy hate us that much that they breed hate in their ranks, you could take 15 supporters from the crowd on match day and they would run us close for 15 mins on hatred alone, so before you go out there remember the only friends you have are the ones that are stood in this changing room with you now."

Apart from rugby in the Army, Ben also played semi-professionally with Ballymena in the All Ireland League, including having sabbatical to play full-time. He has also been involved in coaching rugby union.

Ben has spent his Army career in the Royal Engineers: "I have worked at various camps and regiments within the Royal Engineers from the North of England (Ripon) for roughly 3 years as well as 5 years in Northern Ireland. I spent nearly five years on the Royal Engineers recruiting team travelling nationwide selling the Army and the sport and opportunity's it can give you. Most of the regiments I have worked at are Armoured Engineer Regiments including my current Regiment 22 Engineer Regt (Tidworth)." Ben was promoted to Sergeant while with 21 Engineer Regiment. His work with the recruiting team included planning and organising the Royal Engineer Display Team, while his work in Northern Ireland included liaison with the Police Service of Northern Ireland on crowd control. He has also been involved in training troops for service in Afghanistan.

Ben still plays rugby union, now for the Army Masters (veterans) side. He can look back on a remarkable career in both codes, and hopefully will retain his links with rugby league as well as union.

John and Julie Hulatt

Rugby league is one of those sports that draws people in. Particularly at the lowest levels of the professional game, and throughout the amateur side of the sport, volunteers play a vital role. This is true in Army RL as well, where many people give up their time voluntarily to ensure that rugby league functions at different levels.

What is different about John and Julie in Army RL is that they are, and always have been, civilians, and had no previous connections with the Army. John is a vehicle inspector for the local bus company, while Julie is a housewife, and looks after their two youngest grandchildren two days a week.

Julie recalls: "In June 2006 the Army came to play the British Police in the Skanska Cup at Castleford Panthers ARLFC, where John was the physio. He was asked if he could help out with cover for the game by Richard Naivalurua. He said 'Yes' and has been helping Army RL ever since. Everyone made us very welcome. Teams have changed along with coaches, but we're always made to feel like we're part of the set-up and we now call them our second family."

Julie's main role, apart from supporting the team and taking photos at matches (including some in this book), is with Soldiers' League: "I became involved with Soldiers League by becoming a member at its launch in November 2007 and from then on been an active member to this present day by selling SL kit and other items at all the Army RL representative games.

I'm also a webmaster of the Soldiers League Pitchero website. Our aim is to raise money for our chosen armed services charities: Blesma, Combat Stress and The Royal British Legion; and to support Army Rugby League. Soldiers' League is run by volunteers." Julie is also a board member of Soldiers' League, and runs the Soldiers' League stall, most recently at the Ladies' and Vets matches at Chorley RLFC. She enjoys "being an active member of Soldiers League and being on the committee working alongside a fantastic committed group of people all trying to raise the profile of Soldiers' League and Army RL."

The couple have a lot of good memories from their time with Army RL, and they have made many friends, "especially Sean and Clare". For Julie, a particular highlight was going on the Army RL tour of South Africa in 2009: "My best memory is of the games and training sessions, with a relatively small squad which we had to keep turning round at very short intervals between the fixtures. Also, we went on a safari to Pilanesberg National Park with some of the team and support staff on our 'R&R'."

She also recalls: "We met Barrie McDermott, Terry O'Connor and Robbie Hunter-Paul who have been guest speakers at Soldiers' League dinners. Also, one of our dinners was filmed by the BBC for James Mayes's Man Lab. Watching it back on television was very funny."

John's highlight of his time with Army RL was the recent Armed Forces World Cup in Colchester, where he worked with the Great Britain squad as one of their physios for the whole fortnight.

John and Julie at Colchester for the Armed Forces World Cup Final. (Photo: Peter Lush)

When not at Army matches, Julie has supported Castleford Tigers for 47 years, and John has supported them for over 50. She says that the Tigers have had their "ups and downs" but is now optimistic for the club with a new coach and more sponsorship coming in. However, their main involvement with the game has been with the amateur Castleford Panthers club.

John retired from being the physio with Castleford Panthers in 2010, after 30 years involvement with the club. They have both been heavily involved with the club. Julie recalls that "Castleford Panthers ran from the back of a pub in a Portacabin until they got a Big Lottery grant to build their own clubhouse, but by the time the plans had been sorted out, the cost had more than doubled. We became part of the development committee, and along with 10 other couples we all put our homes up as collateral against the building costs. It was a bit of a mad thing to do, but the Panthers was our life! After the first 12 months, the club got a friendly society loan and we were released from the commitment. John became the steward at the club, and in 1999 I assisted as stewardess. I did the job for four years while John still had his permanent job. We've stepped down from the club now, along with the other couples who backed the building programme, because it's time for new blood and fresh ideas to move the club forward! We're all still there in the back ground just in case they need us for anything. If we hadn't done what we did to get the clubhouse built, they never would have had anywhere of their own."

John and Julie plan to stay involved with the team for "the next few years", and certainly both play an invaluable role, one helping keep players on the pitch, the other supporting a campaign that potentially can help everyone in the Army. And all this despite having no previous connection with the Army until that match in 2006.

Lee Innes MBE

The school Lee attended did not play rugby league, despite being in Bradford. Rhodesway School was different – it was a pioneer boxing establishment. Fortunately, it was a sport he grew to enjoy and Lee was good enough in the ring to represent Bradford, Yorkshire and England schools. Football was also on offer and Lee played for Bradford Schools.

Lee joined up as a boy soldier, aged 16, in 1987 and while stationed at the Old Park Barracks in Dover he continued with those two sports from his school days – boxing for the regiment and playing football for the Army youth side. Perhaps not surprisingly, when it came to the passing out parade Lee was awarded best at physical training and best sportsman. Lee then went on to phase two training with 1&3 TRG Regiment, where he completed the combat engineering course

His first posting was to the 22 Engineer Regiment based at Tidworth, where his love of boxing was soon recognised and he was quickly drafted into the Army boxing team. Lee spent five years on the Army boxing team and won four Combined Services Boxing Association titles, reached three Amateur Boxing Association (ABA) quarter-finals, one ABA semi-final and was ranked number two in Great Britain at one time.

Boxing alone was not enough and Lee continued to play football. During this time he was also playing football for the Royal Engineers, the Army, CSFA as well as a number of civilian teams – Camberley Town, Chatham Town, Yeading, Kingstonian and Harrogate Town. Along the way Lee picked up a number of football honours: Royal Engineers player of the year, UK Army Cup winner's medals, Kent Football League's top goal scorer and was looked at by Arsenal. He was also in the team that won the Kentish Cup, which is a tournament played between the British, Dutch and Belgium Armies.

It was a most enjoyable period: "During this time my Army career was all just based around sport and doing a couple of physical training courses, but I managed to reach the rank of Corporal quite quickly thanks to my sporting achievements."

After such a successful sporting career, Lee wanted to put something back into those sports which had given him so much enjoyment. It was boxing that gained most: "I passed a judging course while I was on the boxing team and when the chance came I grabbed the opportunity to attend a boxing referees course, which I passed with flying colours. I've been a boxing official since 1991 and I'm currently a one-star international boxing referee and judge." Needless to say Lee is still officiating to this day.

Having never even been to see a game or played in one while he was growing up, Lee took up rugby league at the relatively late age of 28 and says "if it wasn't for a guy called Tony Cheadle I wouldn't have played the game. I quickly got the grasp of rugby league and worked my way through the ranks of the rugby teams and it wasn't long before I was playing for the British Army. 20 months down the line I was representing the Combined Services in a trial to represent the British Amateur Rugby League Association (BARLA). Darrel Cooper and I were the first serving solders to ever represent BARLA when we turned out against Morocco at Featherstone in November 2000. It was great experience especially memorable as I scored two tries and kicked two goals that day. BARLA went on to win the Emerging Nations World Cup. I played in every group game, but didn't get picked for the final even after being the top try scorer."

Having come to the game so late, Lee grabbed the unexpected chance to prolong his sporting career. Lee's fierce, but fair, athleticism found a natural home on the rugby pitch and it allowed him to assemble a remarkable playing record; representing the British Army and the Combined Services for nine years, captaining the British Army in 2007, representing BARLA five times, Great Britain Community Lions six times and serving as vice-captain on the Community Lions' tour of France.

In addition, Lee was on the winning side in the Army Yeoman Cup three times, the Lawson Cup eight times and the Inter-Services four times. He was chosen as the Combined Services' player-of-the-year in 2002.

In a long and varied Army career Lee has certainly seen the world; "I toured New Zealand, Australia, South Africa and Philadelphia with rugby league, Austria, Canada, Sweden, France and Cyprus with boxing and Cyprus, South Africa, Nepal and India with football.

Top:Rob Smart and Lee Innes with the Cheltenham 9s trophy in 2008, having beaten the Royal Navy in the final. (Photo: Courtesy Richard Naivalurua)

Left: Ben Hughes leads out the Army Rugby Union team at Twickenham.
(Photo: Courtesy Ben Hughes)

After being posted to Ripon, Lee got involved with the West Bowling club, members of the National Conference League, in Bradford, with more success. Having moved from wing to full back, Lee finished 2001–02 as the National Conference League's leading points scorer and in 2005–06 he was chosen as that League's Division One player-of-the-year.

When he finished playing, Lee's background made coaching and conditioning the natural next step and it brought further recognition: "I was fortunate to accompany the Great Britain Community Lions under-18 team on their tour of South Africa as a coach in 2011. The lads did really well, winning all three tests against what was really open age opposition."

In recognition of his commitment and dedication to Combined Services sport, Lee was awarded the MBE in the Queen's Birthday Honour's List in 2010. Lee received the award from Her Majesty the Queen at Buckingham Palace in August. That same year, Lee left the Army after 23 years of service. It is hard to believe that his remarkable multi-sport record will ever be matched.

Andy Kershaw

In January 1989, Andy Kershaw decided to take on a new challenge to his life and join the Army. During his time in the Army he played both codes of rugby spanning over a very active operationally committed career of 22 years active service. He initially played rugby union at Priory school in Barnsley – "the gym instructor was a union man" – he recalls, although he did play rugby league as well. He joined the Army on 17 July 1989, as a Trooper in the Royal Armoured Corps, in the Regiment 13th-18th Royal Hussars (QMO). He was soon playing union for the Regiment and Corps showing his qualities as a player, and he played for the British Army Germany between 1993 and 1998, including various tours. He remembers playing against the New Zealand side in 1997, on a tour of Fiji and New Zealand.

His introduction to organised rugby league came in 1994 and 1995, when he was based in Germany. "I remember that I started playing for the Garrison side (Hohne Hawks), and then there was a big profile tournament in Germany between teams from the British Army UK, the British Army in Germany and the French Army which consisted of many Super League players and professionals. Martin Coyd got me involved in the Army rugby league team after spotting my skills, talent and speed of the game and I played fairly regularly between 1997 and 2004."

In 1998 Andy was posted back to the UK after eight years in Germany. With Army rugby league mainly played in the summer, he was also able to play union. "I was posted to Harrogate, and played union for Rotherham in 1998 and 1999, although I didn't make the cut to play in the Premiership. So I moved back to the rugby code I loved the most rugby league. In league I played for the Sheffield Eagles academy side, I also played for East Leeds between 1998 and 2000 and was known as the super sub scoring nearly every time I was brought on."

In 1999, the services teams entered the Challenge Cup for the first time: "In 1999 we reached the third round of the Challenge Cup and played Rochdale Hornets. I'd watched the

Challenge Cup on television as a kid, and it was special to be part of it. There was big coverage of the Army team, which was good for us and the game. We only got together a couple of days before the matches, and faced teams who played together regularly. Had we been playing together regularly and for longer, maybe we could have beaten Rochdale."

Another great experience for Andy was playing in the Inter-Services matches: "Playing in those games was like a big derby match. We knew some of the other players through the Combined Services side, so it was a reunion as well. It was always a big challenge to come out on top. I was nervous as well because the Combined Services side was selected from the Inter-Services matches, and I always wanted to try to get into that as well. I would play above my normal level. One match I particularly remember was when we played the Navy in Hull. Sky Sports covered the game and my mum, dad and friends saw it on television me scoring a try."

Going on tour is another fond memory for Andy. "I went on tour to New Zealand in 2001, and scored a vital try in the final test to clinch the game which hasn't been done often on New Zealand home soil. I also went to Australia in 2004 which was the Anniversary of Army Rugby League. I also played rugby union for the Army Select Operational tour side in Iraq, and played in the Bahrain 10s. That was mostly forming from Army RL players – playing rugby union. We narrowly missed out losing in the final. In 2006 I played in Dubai for the Army rugby union Vets side which was a tour to remember as it rain like you never seen it rain before but the ruby was hard and good."

His last game with the Army first team was in 2004 Australia tour, but still plays Vets rugby league: "I thought about retiring in 2010, after scoring a hat-trick against the RAF, but then played against the Navy at Portsmouth in 2011 and scored two tries. I also played for a BARLA Vets side against the Yorkshire Vets – mainly ex-pros – and that was very tough and took several days to recover. I also played for the Combined Services Vets against a BARLA team in Cumbria."

Andy spent the whole of his army career in the Royal Armoured Corps. He left the Army on 17 July 2011, as a Warrant Officer Second Class, but kept his links with the Army by joining the TA, and is doing the role of Recruiting Warrant Officer. He now works as a facilities manager in a school at Bovington Garrison in Dorset, and helps out with the rugby league side for the Royal Armoured Corps and with the school.

He recalls: "I played for the Armoured Corps in the Inter-Corps tournament in the Army. There are more tours and opportunities for players now, but we still need to recruit more if we are going to compete at a high level. The game of Rugby league has come on leaps and bounds compared to when I first started. Not many people from the Armoured Corps represent the Army in sport due to Operational commitments, but I did and I was very luck to represent the Royal Armoured Corps at rugby league and rugby union, and in athletics with 400m time of 50.14 sec's against the Germany Army team."

Sport was always there for Andy during his Army career between Operational tours and busy Regimental commitments, but he also had a wide-ranging career in the Army, including as a crew commander and support troop section commander with CVR(T), Regimental

Signals Warrant Officer(RSWO) as well as working as a Physical training Instructor (PTI) with his Regiment and at Harrogate training recruits during his earlier years of service.

In rugby, Andy mainly played on the wing in his younger days, but "as I got older played at centre and full-back. For the Vets I even played in the second-row and in the backs, anywhere I'm needed I would play." Looking back, he "will always remember playing in the Challenge Cup against top amateur and professional teams and beating them!! Also being on television and being in the press. I still have a match report from September 2000 when we beat the RAF. 'Kershaw clinches it for the Army' was the headline."

Richard Naivalurua

Major Richard Naivalurua (known as 'Nav') has made an enormous contribution to Army Rugby League, first as a player, but also as a coach, manager and administrator, at every level.

His father was one of the 212 Fijians who were recruited into the British Army, in 1961. His mother was English and the family finally settled in Bristol. He played rugby union primarily as a centre, at Clifton RFC in Bristol from 1976 to 1984, where his three younger brothers also played, before he joined the Army in 1985. He had a break from playing rugby when he joined the Army, primarily due to a serious knee injury not being conducive to soldiering. He got back involved playing rugby in 1992 with the Queens Royal Irish Hussars RU team, whilst based in Germany, who had a great Unit club who played hard, both on and off the pitch. On returning to the UK to complete his REME Artificer course followed by a posting as an Instructor in the School of Electronic Engineering he continued to play RU at Unit level and also at Corps level for the Royal Electrical & Mechanical Engineers (REME).

Most players, especially in the forwards, move from rugby league to rugby union as they get older. Nav did the reverse, and played his first game of rugby league in 1995. He vividly recalls his first game of rugby league; "The first ever game played in the REME, was played by the School of Electronic and Aeronautical Engineering (SEAE) against the Prince of Wales' Own Regiment of Yorkshire (PWO). It was a bloodbath. I had my collarbone broken within five minutes of kick off, after the tackle had been completed. John Sheriff, a great character who I later got to know well, was the culprit. He was a very funny guy from Hull who turned into a maniac once he took the field. Welcome to rugby league! Rugby league had a different element of violence compared to union, but it suited me".

His first Corps game was at centre against the Royal Engineers, in the first ever game played at Corps level in the Army, which was between the Sappers and REME in 1996, with the Sappers contributing the majority of the Army team at the time. This time he lasted 80 minutes: "Our captain Curley Airey, who was an Army player, was sent off and our vice-captain Tim White, who was also an Army player, was sin-binned. We were still winning at half-time, but we just lost. The pitch was next to the Mess where I was accommodated, so I was in my room after having a shower and went to eat a bowl of cereal as I felt a bit peckish. As I went to spoon the cereal into my mouth my arm started shaking and I threw cereal all over the place. This was a different type of game. I had never experienced an energy debt like it before and I had played a lot of rugby union to a fair standard, but this was something different."

Nav first played for the Army team in 1996: "It was a great honour for me. We played the England Students, as a curtain-raiser before the Warrington versus Workington Town Super League match at Easter in 1996, the first year of Super League. I had previously been booked on a skiing trip to Whistler, Canada over the Easter break. To play, I missed the flight I was previously booked on and had to pay personally to catch another flight from Heathrow and pay for the parking at the airport. It cost me over £300 to play my first game for the Army, but it was well worth it. It always meant a lot to me to play for the Army Rugby League team."

His first Inter-Services match was against the RAF in 1996, which ended in a draw after a last minute drop-goal by RAF skipper Clacker Clayton. He mainly played in the second row, but also played at prop, centre, stand-off or loose-forward on occasion as the need arose. He has fond memories of winning the first full Inter-Services tournament in 1998.

He was selected at second row in the first ever Combined Services Rugby League team that was selected immediately after the first Inter-Services in 1998, playing in the first four Combined Services matches in 1998 and 1999. He was the Combined Services player-of-the-year in 1998, which was chosen by the Combined Services coach, Ray Unsworth. His final game was against the French Combined Services side in 1999, at RAF Uxbridge. "We won by 30 points [42–12]; it was our first win against a French side. I remember that Dave Ellis was our coach versus the French. We played against Redhill who were the BARLA Cup Champions in the first match in RAF Uxbridge, which ended in a draw, a Southern Conference select side in Portsmouth and the touring Australian Police in Camberley. I formally retired after the French game having had another knee operation just prior to playing that last game. I was 33, a Warrant Officer with a chronic knee injury and young son. I formally retired, but have probably played another 50 games over the following years, primarily as a coach or manager taking the field when the team was short, in Veterans games for the Army RL RATS, charity games or end of season type games, and on Rugby Tour. I even played a couple more games for the Army Team first Team when the manager, on tour in Australia in 2004."

A posting to Germany followed. Nav had done a Rugby League Club Coach course, run by the RFL in 1997, for Army coaches: "Sean Fanning was on the same course. I coached the SEAE team from 1996 to 1997, and did some coaching at Corps level. In Germany, I coached and managed the 2nd Royal Tank Regiment Rugby Union team from 1999 to 2002 and in 2002 was posted to 1 Battalion REME again in Germany where I coached the Battalion Rugby League team."

One memorable event of Nav's time in Germany was the visit of the Leeds Rhinos squad in November 2002: "They were there for pre-season training. They were beasted which they loved and we finished with a black tie dinner in the Warrant Officers' and Sergeants' Mess for them. I sat next to Mal Reilly who was the first ever Army RL Veterans (RATS) Team

Coach in 2004, with initial contact made between Brian Stow and Mal that night. Rob Burrow, Kevin Sinfield, Barrie McDermott, and Jamie Jones-Buchanan were all there. Look how well Leeds have done since then. Rugby league was strong in Germany in 2001 and 2002 driven by Major Brian Stow as Secretary who ran a great 9s tournament in 2001 and 2002 which kicked the season off.

I took on the role of Team Manager and Head Coach of the British Army (Germany) (BA (G) RL Team in 2002 and we really produced the goods in a short rep campaign. We hosted and played both the English Students and Scottish Students teams, fielding two teams on each occasion, playing both teams twice. It was a World Cup year for them and they wanted warm-up matches playing their whole squad. Against both the Scots and English we fielded two teams, winning one match and losing the other. The England Students side had five players at Super League clubs and we beat them in a cracking game, which was very much a coaching highlight for me. On both occasions we trained for a single weekend then put two teams out. We also took a tour back to England beating the Royal Marines and narrowly losing to the touring New Zealand Army side in Aldershot in the first match on their tour in 2002. I was the Tour/Team Manager, Head Coach and one of the mini bus drivers. It was a mad trip with a great bunch of lads. I think that BA (G) team would have beaten the full Army team at that time."

In 2003 Nav returned to England, on commissioning as a Captain, posted to Andover where he took over managing and coaching the REME Corps Rugby League team. In 2004 he became manager of the Army Rugby League first team, a post he held for five seasons with Sean Fanning as Head Coach until 2008, with his final season of involvement with the first team, being as Head Coach in 2009. During this time he was also running rugby league in REME.

One of his first tasks for the Army team was to organise and lead the tour to Australia in 2004. He recalls: "In 2004 there were some really memorable games. In Australia we had 10 players injured, so I came back out of retirement and played in the second and third games, against the New South Wales Combined Services side and against the Australian Army. There was also the first ever Army RL Vets match; as the Army Rugby League RATS (Race Against Time & Senility) which I played in, the team coached by GB legend Mal Riley against a Leeds Rhinos / Tykes side. Mal was a delightful bloke. Very quietly spoken, but you could definitely still tell what a hard nut he was and no doubt still is. We went from strength to strength. In 2005 the highlight was when we beat the BARLA under-21 team at Whitehaven on a Wednesday evening in an incredible game which we won by 40 points. We had never beaten a BARLA team before."

Playing for the RATS team is something Nav has enjoyed, but also thinks is important for Army RL: "Brian Stow was brilliant in getting the RATS started, and I supported him just as a player. We only played once or twice a year, but raised between £3,000 and £5,000 for charity each time. The rationale and the ethos of the Army RL RATS set by Brian attracted me, in that it enabled older guys to still play and have fun, but originally the idea was that all players must also contribute something else to Army Rugby League in the broader sense.

It Keeps Army Public Eye (KAPE) and shows the Army in a positive light. Just being a RATS player on its own in my view has very limited value. However, it's getting a bit serious now – there's even training. I played for the RATS from the start in 2004 up to the first Inter-Services match against the RAF in 2008 and the first full Inter-Services tournament in 2009, when all three services fielded Veteran sides and we won it. It then seemed a good time to formally retire from Vets/RATS rugby. I was also coaching the Army first team at the same time as that last game."

Nav stood down from his roles with the first team at the end of the 2009 season, but was still involved in the REME set up. He recalls 2009 as "a mad year! I was the Director and Head Coach of Army RL, Director, Team Manager and Head Coach of REME RL and Head Coach and Team Manger of SEME RFC; the unit in which I was based. Another highlight was our tour to South Africa in 2009 where I was Team Manager and Head Coach. We played three games in six days; beating the National side; the South African Rhinos and Rhinos 'A' team. Against the National team, our first half execution of the game plan was the best as a coach I have ever seen. We were winning [24–6] at half-time, but once they stopped trying to kill us and played rugby, coupled with the Army team not keeping to the game plan it was a great relief to win a very tough game 36–34. They're relative novices at league, but huge blokes, really tough and very good rugby players.

As well as playing, we ran a workshop for South African coaches and referees. We took Jase Grant and Ian Curzon over to deliver the workshops as well as Jase being my assistant coach and Ian referee for a couple of games. We didn't impose on them at all, we were self-sufficient and organised everything ourselves. The British Lions Rugby Union team were touring at the same time and most of us went to the second test match at Loftus Versfeld in Pretoria, which was another great experience. We had a couple of days 'R and R' at the end of the tour and some of us drove down from Pretoria to Durban, to see the country. It's a stunning place. We were given fantastic hospitality and I really recommend it as a tour destination. We had a lot of new young guys, with over twenty players not available to tour, but we also had some of 'legends' of Army RL, in Sly Silvester, Sean Fanning, Darrell Cooper, Lee Innes, Pud Cowburn, Rob Kama and Nobby Pocock. Some people who primarily originally had support roles ended up playing, but 'class is permanent' and the mix of 'young guns' and the 'old guard' delivered a highlight of my rugby experience."

Nav has also been heavily involved in the Army's Challenge Cup campaigns: "One of our most memorable performances was in 2005. We played West Hull away, and were given no hope. They were a top team, but we went there and battered them. Sean's coaching was targeted against a particular team and it worked a treat." But the Challenge Cup is always difficult for the Army: "In each game we have five or six first team debutants. We play a team who are 20 games into their season and we haven't played for four months and usually only have two days training. The hospitality we receive is always fantastic. There is a big connection between communities in the North and the Army. Often they know people who have joined up and are very supportive. Another highlight of our Challenge Cup matches for me was playing Oldham at Aldershot, where our winger Ben Seru so impressed Oldham they signed him".

The ongoing Army Rugby League connection with the North is also shown in the Craig Hopson Memorial Trophy. Nav outlined: "Craig Hopson was a Gunner from Castleford who was killed in Afghanistan in 2009. The Royal Artillery (Gunner) team have played a Castleford Select team, at the Stoop, home of Quins RL, and up north. Craig had played for the Army Rugby League Academy side. Another great and moving experience was to be present in Hull as Army Rugby League representatives with Major Brian Stow when the Jack Harrison VC memorial was unveiled outside the Hull FC ground."

Another very memorable occasion was being involved in the first Tom Sefton Memorial Trophy match on Saturday 18 September 2010: "There was a strong link between Warrington and the 1 MERCIAN, in particular through Sergeant Alan Boyle, a big Warrington fan. The Army first team had an Inter-Services match two days before the Memorial game and were effectively not available. I led on putting the team together with less than 10 days notice to ensure the massive event had suitable representation from Army Rugby League. Cpl Mags Marangon played in the Inter-Services game and backed up on the Saturday. We also had some other first team players who had not been available for the Inter-Services match and five of the Academy players who backed up with a couple of RATS. It was one of the biggest crowds ever to watch an Army Rugby League representative team play."

Almost 2,000 people were at Crosfields ARLFC to see an Army XIII beat a Crosfields Select XIII 32–30. All the Crosfields players had played with Tom Sefton at the club. A report on the links between Warrington RLFC and 1 MERCIAN commented: "Special thanks must go out to the Director of Army Community Rugby League, Major Richard Naivalurua, as his help and tireless support made this match possible." Nav recalls that around the same time, Sergeant David 'Bob' Monkhouse Royal Dragoon Guards had been killed in Afghanistan, and it was "quite an emotional time." Bob Monkhouse had been the 'strapper' for the Army first team during much of Nav's time as manager.

The match was also significant for Nav because he supports Warrington: "In the late 1980s I went home with a mate and he lived in Warrington and took me to watch the Wire play." He has followed the club ever since.

In 2010, Nav took on his current role as the Director of Army Community Rugby League. He leads on running and developing the Lawson (Inter-Corps) Cup, the Yeoman (Inter-Unit) Cup and Army RL 9s competitions. He has taken a step back from the first team and now concentrates on bringing new people through, for example by organising a Level 2 Rugby League coaching course in October 2012 for 19 new coaches, including the first women coaches to qualify in the Army and another Level 2 course in May 2013 which qualified another 19 coaches, who will hopefully deliver effect and get soldiers onto the field of play.

As Secretary of the Lawson Cup completion since 2011 a really strong Corps competition currently is now in place, with the most ever Corps Teams taking part for the last 2 successive seasons with 9 Corps Teams taking the field in 2012 and 2013. For Unit rugby league: "We have turned the Yeoman Cup and Army 9s into single day festivals run by my right hand man in Community Rugby League; WO1 (ASM) Andy Franklin, with no cost to enter or for insurance, where all costs are covered by Army RL as part of my initiative to get soldiers onto the field of play at the grass roots levels, by removing as many obstacles as possible."

At Unit level, "the most successful side have been the 3 YORKS team – 'The Dukes'. They are a very famous rugby union regiment, who are now also playing rugby league and formed the core of the BA (G) RL team in Germany in the 2002 season. They won the BA (G) RL Cup in Germany and then beat the reigning UK based Army Yeoman Cup champions in 2003–04. Last year they won the Army Cup at the one day festival, a great days' rugby, where they were competing from the Rear Operations Group as the Battalion was deployed in Afghanistan. Immediately after winning the Cup five of the players had to drive to Castleford to be pall bearers for one of the Duke's soldiers who had been killed the previous week. That shows the operational pressures we are under. It is important to remember that there have been huge operational demands on the Army since 2003. We had four Army players who were not available for the 2013 Armed Forces World Cup due to operational commitments."

Another connection Nav has with Unit rugby league is that his brother Joe played in the Army Rugby League Yeoman Cup winning 38 Engineer Regiment side as a 'young Sapper'. However, he was killed while on duty in Northern Ireland in 2000. Joe also played rugby union, along with Nav and his other brothers Rob and Pete, at Clifton RFC. Joe and Rob were then staunch members of Southmead RFC in Bristol. A pre-season memorial tournament in his memory is played at the Bristol-based club, and attracts Fijian-dominated Army rugby union teams including the DUKES, 1 RIFLES and 17 Port & Maritime Regiment. In Southmead, they are still talking about one of the teams which took the field as "The Bristol Navs" with Nav coming out of retirement again, with his brothers Pete and Rob, brother in law Andy, Army RL old boy Richie Yeomans, several top quality local Bristol lads and Army RL stars Noxi Veikune, Naca Nacamavuto, Ben Seru and Stew Butters captained by Lee Innes. It was some team.

The Royal Engineers have dominated Corps rugby league which has maintained an intensive Lawson Cup competition since 1996. Nav reflects that "In Armed Forces sport, they have been the most dominant side in any sport, and have been champions for 13 out of 17 seasons so far. In 2012, it was only the second time that the Royal Engineers had not been in the Lawson Cup Final. The Gunners are the current Lawson Cup Champions"

Nav has not had any direct involvement in the Army Ladies team, but did ensure that in 2011, the women's team players were awarded caps for playing in Inter-Service matches, something which had been introduced for the men's team in 2010. However, he believes there is huge potential for the Ladies' team: "We can take them to the highest level, because women's rugby league is amateur. In the men's game we can beat the best amateur teams, but then we face the pros. We could beat a semi-professional team, but we would have to be at our best and usually it's a step too far for us. But our women players are ideally suited to rugby league at the highest level in the country. We need more senior guys to come through and lead the way for the girls. They have the most potential."

Nav still currently has one coaching role – he is sometimes assistant coach for his son's under-14 rugby union team at Cleve RFC in Bristol. He is pleased that there is a good relationship between the two codes in the Army and players can now play both without problems. "People will have their own priorities and prejudices. The key thing is that we play sport for the benefit of the soldiers. A good proportion play both and should be enabled to play both to the highest level, within personal priorities and the requirements of the Army".

Nav joined the Army in 1985. He joined REME, following his father's advice: "I was in the Royal Marines Reserve Bristol for two years, joining when I was in the sixth form at school, my formative years in the forces where I was moulded. I planned to join the regular Royal Marines, but there was a one year waiting list at the time, so I decided to follow my Dad's advice 'get a trade' and joined REME. I have never regretted it. My first posting was with 29 Commando Regiment Royal Artillery, in support to the Royal Marines. Thirty years on, I'm now a Major, based in Portsmouth in Navy Command Headquarters providing engineering support to Royal Marines Command. I've spent most of my career working on Armour and Main Battle Tanks (MBT), from Chieftain, Challenger 1 to Challenger 2. I've also been an instructor and project manager in our trade training schools, a Systems Engineer in support to Artillery Regiments, worked in Defence procurement and spent eight years in Germany. My next, and probably last job, in the Army is as Officer Commanding 29 Explosive Ordnance Disposal & Search Group Workshop REME"

Not surprisingly, Nav believes that sport is very important in the Army: "Sport is integral to the British Army ethos in terms of character development and team building, balance of life and development of the core values and standards of the British Army. It also plays an important role in recruitment. I am a rugby union man by descent. Rugby in general is the ideal team sport for the British Army. The key thing about rugby league is that you have to be physically brave to take the field as there is nowhere to hide. The operational pressures we have had over the last 10 years in particular have made it a difficult time for sport in general, but with "competent enthusiasts" leading the way and willing to do the extra required on top of their basic work duties, we need to continue to facilitate people playing rugby league, because it delivers great value".

Finally, at the time of writing this profile, January 2013, Nav had just been appointed as Officer-in-Charge for the 2013 Armed Forces World Cup. In 2008 in Australia, when GB beat the Australians in the final at Aussie Stadium Sydney he was team manager, but now, despite a heavy workload, has agreed to take on leading the Great Britain Armed Forces team organisation for the tournament.

He concluded: "I get energised through contact with the players. My work in rugby league is a real 'labour of love'. We need to put sustainable structures in place, to develop players and give them the conduit to play at the highest representative levels, make it easier to get coaching qualifications and develop administrators. Development of grass roots rugby

Richard Naivalurua at Colchester during the Armed Forces World Cup 2013.
(Photo: Peter Lush)

is critical which in itself will build the game and the crowds that watch our representative teams. The first team isn't my primary concern anymore, but I hope I left a good legacy.

I'm proud of the British Army; for me it's not just about winning, the style we do things, how we are viewed and our reputation is everything. It's all about setting and maintaining standards. In rugby league; the players are the most important elements and we must maximise their potential. It was a massive honour and privilege for me to play for the Army Rugby League Team. Some of the best people I will ever meet have been involved, with the most fun, laughs and memorable experiences. I see it as my duty to enable other soldiers to have the opportunities I had. I want soldiers to be able to look back and realise how good it was playing rugby league in the British Army."

Andy Sanger MBE

Andy Sanger has been heavily involved in both rugby codes since joining the Army as a 17-year-old in 1985, although he says that "My military responsibilities have always come first". At school he "played most sports; rugby union and football and did athletics." He decided to concentrate on rugby union, and was "in the Wales School system; and I played for the Welsh Schools team." He also played club rugby union for Bedwas, who at that time were a feeder club for Newport.

When he joined the Army, in the Royal Engineers, he played at under-19 and under-21 levels for the Army and Combined Services sides at centre or scrum-half. He also played for a time for London Welsh. Two major shoulder injuries saw him play very little rugby for a couple of years, but he played for the Army Rugby Union side, which in the days of union being a solely amateur sport, was a very high standard: "We had five or six internationals, and were probably at Premiership standard. We used to play all the big clubs. I remember we went to play Bath at The Rec. They had nine internationals or British Lions, but we won 27–9. The Army was a strong set up then, with international players in the team."

Andy got involved in rugby league by chance. He had watched the game on television, but when he was growing up, the divide between the two codes was huge, and there was little opportunity to play League in South Wales. He recalls "Martin Coyd and Major Martin Morris were starting to establish rugby league. A question had been asked in Parliament by David Hinchliffe MP about why rugby league was not played. I was an established rugby union player, but the question put was why 'Corporal Sanger wants to play rugby league, but can't?' I knew nothing about it, and had not consented to it, but it never did me any harm. I played in the 9s tournament at Chepstow before the first match at Leigh, the RFL coach chose me as 'Player-of-the-tournament' and I was chosen for the team. I was new to rugby league, but was a decent rugby player. They put me on the wing, and I wanted to get the ball, then they moved me to centre, and I finished the game at stand-off. It was very fast and very physical. At that time union was not played at the same pace as good quality rugby league."

After this, Andy played both codes: "I first played for the Army against the Royal Navy in 1994, and I scored a try. It was great to run out at Twickenham in front of a big crowd. I was the only Welshman on the field. I played regularly for the rugby league team for six or seven years, and captained the side. But I always had to balance my rugby commitments with my work as a soldier. There were career courses and operational commitments, which is why I only toured once in rugby league. But I was never on the losing side as a player in an Inter-Services match.

The Army were dominant in the early days, I think we drew once. By the mid- to late-90s, we had a core of really good players. Shaun Knott had played professionally with Hull KR, Sean Anders, and then Sean Fanning and Wayne Braddock got involved. I think our full team could have competed with some of the semi-professional teams. I remember in the Challenge Cup that we beat Dewsbury Celtic and Oulton Rangers, two strong amateur sides, and then lost to Rochdale Hornets when we didn't have our strongest team out. Participation and organisation has really developed since those days."

For Andy, playing in the Inter-Services matches was very important: "It was more than just a game. You were playing for your Corps and your Service. You would go back to work on the Monday after a game and could say that you'd put one over on the RAF or the Royal Navy. We had the bragging rights. It was like a local derby, but more intense – there was only one chance a year."

The Challenge Cup was another highlight: "I remember we were on *Grandstand* in the first year. I had watched the Challenge Cup Finals on television when I was young. It would have been great, if we'd had all our players available, to have got to the fourth round and play a Super League team. They would beat us of course, but it would have been great."

Andy has always been involved in both codes since first playing League, and was interviewed by Ray French, then the BBC rugby league commentator, on *Grandstand:* "He asked me about the differences between the codes, then asked me which I preferred. I said there were merits to both, and I enjoyed playing both. League is faster and more physical. Union at that time was developing as a professional sport, with better conditioning and nutrition coming in."

Andy only went on one rugby league tour: "I went with the Joint Services side to Morocco in 1994. We played the Great Britain Students side and two Moroccan teams. Hussain M'Barki was involved. It was all a bit surreal. We met members of the royal family, and visited the Palace. We were treated very well. However, the playing conditions were horrendous – incredibly hot. Stuart Campbell and Russell Smith were the referees. It was great having professional referees; they built up a rapport with the players and were well ahead of rugby union referees at the time.

In union, I've toured all the major countries, Australia, New Zealand South Africa, Fiji, the USA and Canada, and played in Europe. I coached the Army team that won the Defence Forces World Cup in New Zealand. We beat the Australians in the final, thumped them. Some of the teams had a broad definition of who could play, and we played a Tongan side with full internationals."

Andy retired as a player in 2000: "I was a Staff Sergeant in Northern Ireland, working on the EOD and search teams. Work came first, but I would have liked to have carried on playing rugby league. One of my last games was against the full Tonga side before the 2000 RL World Cup. They were incredibly fast, and beat us overwhelmingly. We only had a couple of weeks' notice of the match, and gave them a physical encounter, which was what they wanted."

After playing came coaching: "I did my rugby league coaching badge in 2003; and did some coaching with the Royal Engineers team. In rugby union, I was fast tracked through the system, and have a Level 3 badge, which means I could coach at Premiership level. In 2005, I became assistant coach for the Army RU first team, and then became 'A' team coach. But I also had service commitments abroad at that time. Then I got involved with the Royal Engineers RU team, and we were unbeaten for three seasons.

In 2010, I became first team coach for the Army RL team, who had been going through a hard time. We beat the Royal Navy and the RAF, and then I went straight onto coaching the Army RU team for their season. I had to stop doing the rugby league side because of the Defence Forces World Cup. I was the first person to play for the Army first team in both codes, and I am still the only person to coach the first team in both codes. When I was coach of the league team, I did 'cherry pick' some of the union players, which apparently annoyed some of the union senior officers!

In rugby league, ball skills and physicality are important. Players need a good rugby brain and ball skills. I try to have teams that are disciplined, well drilled and have a simple game plan. In union, there are more technicalities in different positions, and players need more experience, especially in the forwards. Overall, union is a bit more technical."

Not surprisingly, Andy is a big advocate of sport generally, and sport in the services, especially rugby: "For rugby league, players need physical fitness and discipline. For a soldier, in rugby league someone can run at him, and smash him. He must get up and take the physical aspect of the game, and have mental discipline. These are all qualities of a good soldier – to face physical and mental challenges. For the last 10 years there have been huge operational demands on the services, and less time for 'fun'. Sport can be a release, but it also builds camaraderie and being part of a team. The ethos of sport gets to people. I think in society generally we need to play more sport, and competitive sport."

Apart from a spell with London Welsh, Andy has never played for club sides due to lack of time. However, he did have the chance to train with the Welsh Rugby League side in 1996. The Army had played the Welsh Student side, and Welsh RL manager Mike Nicholas had spotted him playing. "I was part of an extended training squad, including Jonathan Davies, Scott Gibbs, Jonathan Devereux, Allan Bateman and Gerald Cordle. I got involved in the training, but then I was posted to Germany, and then Bosnia. League didn't have a high profile in those days."

Andy doesn't support a particular team in rugby league, but enjoys watching St Helens and Wigan "especially Saints with their adventurous play."

Andy joined the Army "at the time of the miners' strike. I was doing my 'A' levels and was planning to go to Swansea University to a sports science course. But I went with a friend to the recruitment office – he wanted to join the RAF – and a Welsh Guardsman signed me up. The Welsh Guards were big in rugby union. South Wales was devastated at that time. I had no military background in the family, and my father would only allow me to join if I got a trade, hence me joining the Royal Engineers. Twenty eight years on, I'm still here and have gone through the ranks to be commissioned as a Captain in 2009. It's been tremendous." Andy trained as a mechanic, but has done very little of that work, and has mainly been involved in 'close support' work for the Army – facilitating for the troops through road and bridge construction, water supply and generally 'enabling the army to move around and fight'. He now works in EOD and bomb disposal. He has fought in all the major campaigns over the past 20 years, and was awarded the Accumulated Service Medal for service on Operations.

Andy was awarded the MBE in the 2013 New Year honours list. "It was a great surprise; I am very fortunate and feel very humble. It was for coaching in rugby union and rugby league, with the 'headline' the Defence Forces World Cup win. I felt it was very much a team award for the coaches and players. Also, I must stress that my military role came first. I was the first Army RU coach for 10 years to both continue a military role and coach the team.

I was presented with the MBE by the Queen. She asked what the highlight of the Defence Forces World Cup was and I said 'Putting one over the Aussies' and she laughed. There is always a senior military person in charge of the awards, and it was the Air Vice-Marshall. There was consternation – what had I said that made the Queen laugh? After the ceremony his ADC came up to me. 'What did you say to Her Majesty' he asked. I explained and all was well. I suppose I will be the one who was lucky enough to make the Queen laugh!"

Andy stepped down as rugby union first team coach because he was due to go to Afghanistan in April 2013, and he was not prepared to let his rugby commitments interfere with operational duties. That trip in fact has been delayed to September 2013, and he ended up commentating on the Army versus Royal Navy union game for Sky Sports. But he will stay involved in union in some capacity, and hopefully will be involved in league again in the future once his current operational commitments are completed.

Mick Scholes

One of the challenges that faced rugby league when it was becoming established was to set up administrative and management structures to develop the sport within the Army. Army Rugby League has been served over the years by some very dedicated and capable people off the pitch.

Mick Scholes was involved in Army Rugby League from when the sport was recognised in 1994 until he left the Army in 2012. He was first team manager for two spells, secretary for four years, and ran all the cup competitions. As team manager, he was involved in winning the Inter-Services trophy, gaining entry to the Super League 9s, taking the team to the Challenge Cup third round for the first time and winning the Public Services Cup. Within the Army, he managed teams that won the Army Cup and the Army Cup Challenge Trophy (UK against British Forces Germany), Army 9s, Lawson Cup, Corps 9s and Middlesex 9s (with the Royal Engineers). He played rugby union in his younger days, before rugby league was a recognised sport in the Army.

Mick became first team manager in 1999, and had a very successful first year. He recalls: "In 1999 we beat the Great Britain and Ireland Students in the final of the Scottish Courage (Public Services) Cup at Knowsley Road. We also reached the third round of the Silk Challenge Cup, having been invited to participate for the first time by the Rugby Football League." The Army played Rochdale Hornets, having beaten Dewsbury Celtic and Oulton Raiders. "In those days we had to play away at the professionals' ground. Typically, due to player availability, we put out our weakest team out of the three rounds, but it was a great experience. It created a lot of media attention with a big spread in the *News of the World*. Rochdale had some class players including a young Danny Sculthorpe who ripped us apart playing at centre."

Another memorable event he was involved in was in 2000: "In my second year we played Tonga at AFC Harrogate in a warm up game in their preparation for the World Cup. My lasting memory of the match is when our most dynamic prop, Sly Silvester, caught a pass on the Army 20 metre line. Our coach Rick Rolt and I were behind the sticks watching directly as Willie Mason left the ground like Superman in a horizontal position and hit Sly about chest height... my God!! Sly hit the deck, jumped up, and played the ball immediately to his credit and then continued to look around for the number of the bus that just hit him. It seemed like he was in conference with his whole family at the time because believe me he didn't have a clue whether he was in Harrogate or Plymouth at that moment!

The match was followed by a celebration dinner when Army Rugby League hosted Tonga and the likes of Tevita Veikona and Willie Mason who were absolute gentlemen taking the time to mix and chat with our players."

The Inter-Services matches were an important part of Mick's activities for Army Rugby League: "These games are what we are judged on – everything else is about getting this right and nothing else matters. It is usually the culmination of your season's efforts. As always the Navy holds a special meaning, but in rugby league the RAF game is special as well. We used to have a real social event playing against the RAF in the early days based around the Challenge Cup Final weekend at RAF Uxbridge, London. We played on the Friday in very competitive, close and hard fought matches and then everyone jumped on the tube and went to Wembley on the Saturday – great times."

One particular inter-service match that stands out for Mick is the September 2000 fixture against the Royal Navy: "We had commissioned the Jack Harrison VC Trophy for the annual Army versus Royal Navy fixture. We played the game at the Hull FC ground and watched the Navy run onto the pitch like rabid dogs; they were massive, looked fitter and stronger than I had ever seen them. We had a youngster on the wing on debut who was our X Factor, he scored a hat-trick and we beat the Navy 28–18. Bruno Green was the man-of-the-match and went on to represent the Combined Services Team, one of those talented players who achieved a double in both rugby union and rugby league. It was important to us that the first name on the trophy was 'Army'."

As well as working for Army Rugby League, Mick was also chairman of the Combined Services team in 2008. It was a very important time for the side: "Combined Services competed in the inaugural Defence Forces World Cup, which was played in Sydney. The RFL had granted approval for the team to play under the banner 'Great Britain Armed Forces Rugby League' and to play in the national playing strip. It was a daunting schedule with five matches in 12 days, having travelled halfway around the world and playing in tropical conditions. The team never, not once, went behind on the scoreboard and were the outstanding team of the competition." This was truly a daunting feat made possible by the combination of the best people in Services Rugby League being together at the right time:

President: Air Marshal S.W. Peach CBE (RAF) (Ex Officio)

Chairman: Major Michael (Mick) Scholes (Army)

Secretary: Chief Petty Officer Clive (Perry) Mason (Royal Navy)

Team manager: Captain Richard (Nav) Naivalurua (Army)

Tour manager: Flight Sergeant Colin (Col) Davies (RAF)

Head coach: Mr Ray Unsworth (RFL)

Coach: Warrant Officer Class 1 Wayne (Wayno) Okell (Royal Navy)

Captain / players' representative: Sergeant Sean Fanning (Army)

Physiotherapist: Captain Nicola Rush (Army)

Support Manager: Flight Sergeant Dave ('Shippers') Mortimer (RAF)

Mick believes that rugby league fits perfectly into Army life. He says it "embodies everything a soldier should be: professional, courageous, strong, brave, a team player, decisive, morally mature and selfless." He says that "sport plays a great part in service life. It is part of the covenant that ensures we work hard and play hard supporting that team ethic and strive for ultimate fitness – being strong, agile and durable."

One final highlight in his Army Rugby League time involves the people he has met and worked with who have kept the sport alive in the forces; players and management alike have had a huge impact. These include: captains of his teams: Wayne Braddock, Andy Sanger, Sean Fanning, Tim White, Nellie Nelson, Sly Silvester and Pud Cowburn; fellow management: Martin Coyd, Richard 'Nav' Naivalurua, Jimmy Aspinall, Rick Nolan, Beef Betham, Nobby Pocock and Nic Rush; the Executive Management that remains crucial to show the game as a serious player in services sport; the Chairmen: Mike Bowman, Jeremy Bethell and current Army RL chairman, Brigadier Frank Noble.

Mick recalls: "As Army RL Executive Secretary, I invited my Commanding Officer in Northern Ireland at the time to consider taking over from Jeremy Bethell as the Chairman of Army Rugby League. I gave him my pitch about staying involved with soldiers (he was leaving on promotion to Colonel) and that he could shape and help a vibrant sport. After some consideration for a couple of days, he accepted. Brigadier Frank Noble has been nothing short of outstanding for the sport. I think people underestimate the Chairman's importance to the game, I know he does and would never accept any platitudes, but he deserves great credit for keeping the sport alive through difficult and operationally challenging times. Like me his playing days were rugby union, but we both have an affinity in being total converts and lovers of the great game of rugby league. I remain indebted to Frank for his friendship and support.

Further it would be remiss not to mention Martin Coyd who was and is an unbelievable achiever and leading light of the sport. Without his ability to singularly drive the sport in its infancy, setting up all of the structure and competitions including Combined Services Rugby League, we would not exist today! This is embodied further by his vision to start the 'Medway Dragons Rugby League Club' opposite Brompton Barracks in Kent... you will hear a lot more about this club nationally very soon I am sure."

Mick joined the Army on 6 January 1980. He says that it "was what I always wanted to do since childhood. I was the five-year-old with a box of toy soldiers under my bed. I ended up in the Army Cadets and then joined the Royal Engineers as an adult soldier as soon as I could after my 17th birthday (6 days to be precise!). At school, Mick played a lot of sport, including captaining the football and rugby union teams. His favourite – and best – sport was rugby union, and he continued to play in the Army.

Having joined the Royal Engineers as a Sapper, he left the Army on 31 August 2012, as a Major, after 33 years' service. He says that until May 2001, he had a "regimental career typical of a soldier in the Royal Engineers who are successfully awarded the Queens Commission as a Late Entry Officer." Since then, he held a number of management positions, including Second in Command for 36 Training Support Squadron, Echelon

200

Commander for 25 Engineer Regiment in Northern Ireland, Regimental Career Management Officer for the same regiment, also in Northern Ireland, which took him up to 2007. Since then, he was Staff Officer (Training) at the Headquarters Royal School of Military Engineering, then Regimental second in command with 1 Royal School of Military Engineering Regiment and finally was the Officer Commanding UK Trade and Investment, Defence and Security Organisation Export Support team at Bovington.

He is now a lecturer for Mid Kent College Training Services, working at the Royal School of Military Engineering. Away from Army Rugby League, Mick supports Wigan Warriors, and says that he "will never admit we were beaten by the better team; in my opinion either the ref is blind, stupid and inept (or all three) or the opposition were lucky". All of you who know Mick will smile and nod, knowing never a truer word was spoken! A truly balanced Pie Eater!

Stuart Silvester

Stuart Silvester has been one of the key players in the development of Army Rugby League. He usually played at prop, but says that he has "a very good pass, and in my younger days had good footwork as well," so has also played at half-back, loose-forward and second-row. However, some of his best memories come from playing in the front-row, especially in international matches. One particularly notable match was against Tonga in 2000 in a warm-up match for the World Cup: "My life flashed before me when 6 feet 8 inches, 18 stone Willie Mason – now a formidable Green and Gold Kangaroo – decided to ruin my day with a hit on me that I can only describe as stepping out in front of a fully laden arctic truck."

Another hard-fought game was for the Great Britain Armed Forces (Combined Services) in Australia in 2006. The match against the Australian Defence Force was played as a curtain-raiser to a Sydney Roosters match on ANZAC Day. Stuart recalls: "There must have been 40,000 in the ground watching as I found myself in the centre of a brawl. I tried to extract myself, and be blameless of the whole event when the referee, Russell Smith, called me over. The big screen was showing a number of swift uppercuts to my opposite number. Nothing worse than receiving a yellow card, but in front of 40,000 abusive Aussies I hung my head in shame. It was all put right for me when I returned to the action – I scored two tries in quick succession, which contributed to our win over the Aussies."

Stuart also played against an Australian-based Portugal side on that tour. For the Army, he recalls: "I had the honour to be captain when we beat the South African national side in Pretoria, a momentous victory." Stuart was also on the Army Rugby League 2001 tour of New Zealand and the 2004 tour of Australia. He says that he has "travelled the world while in the Army playing rugby league and rugby union."

The inter-service matches were another great highlight for Stuart: "I captained the Army to a number of inter-service victories." He says that the matches against the Navy are "like the Aussie State of Origin – it's fast and intense, with no love lost. I particularly remember running a ball into the opposition. I had a clash of heads and on the way down a sure fire short arm finished the job; knocked me unconscious and broke two of my back teeth.

Stuart Silvester tackles a BARLA player in 2006.
(Photo: Courtesy Richard Naivalurua)

The next thing I remember is getting up to try to play the ball the wrong way round and playing to the Navy side, then running aimlessly like Bambi with my legs buckling. My eyes were trying to fix on Nav, our coach, who was yelling all sorts of orders at me. All I could fix on was the smelling salts to get me back in the game." He says that "It's just an honour whatever the code you play to represent your Service and to ensure that you represent all personnel who are deployed and unable to play at that level."

In the Challenge Cup, Stuart played in the Army's first season, including against Rochdale Hornets and against Oldham in 2008. Overall, he has been involved for around 14 years, and was a mainstay of the side for many years. He first played rugby league in 1996.

Rugby union was his first sport "I played from the age of 5, starting in Coventry, my home town. I joined my dad and my brother at a club called Kersley. It was in a rough mining village, but still ran six teams and a full mini and junior set up. I also played for my school, Coundon Court."

He has played for the Army Rugby Union first team, and at under-18 and under-21 level: "I have played Inter-Services at Twickenham for the Army against the Navy. I am also the first ever Regimental Sergeant Major (RSM) in history to play in that fixture at Twickenham. I was part of the Army team that won the first inaugural International Defence Rugby Competition (i.e. Armed Forces World Cup) in Australia in 2011. All the group games were played in Australia and the final was played two days before the Rugby World Cup Final in Auckland. We played the Australian Defence Force which we won 67–17."

At club level, he played for London Scottish and remembers one particular local derby: "Not to brag about, but I have one of the quickest sending offs in rugby union while I was playing for London Scottish in a local derby against Richmond I think within 10 seconds of the game beginning."

Stuart with Air Chief Marshal Sir Stuart Peach, Vice Chief of Defence Staff. (Photo: sbsphotos.co.uk)

203

He is currently player-forwards coach at Bracknell RFC. They are aiming for promotion to get back into the national leagues.

Stuart joined the Army at the age of 16, in 1991, to fulfil a "childhood dream." He is in the RAMC, and has completed 11 operational tours of duty, "from Bosnia to Afghanistan" and at the time of writing is about to embark again to Afghanistan in April 2013. He is currently based at Fort Blockhouse in Portsmouth.

He believes that "Sport and rugby league has all the same core values that we want in our soldiers. Now I am a RSM I encourage sport whatever they maybe to be played as often as feasibly possible, as it provides the 'Espirit de Corps' that soldiers desire."

Finally, on rugby league outside the Army, he says that "I always keep my eyes on the results, but in particular St Helens."

Kevin Tamati

Kevin Tamati had a distinguished rugby league career in New Zealand and Great Britain, including 22 test matches for the Kiwis. After playing in New Zealand for Wellington and Auckland, he joined Widnes in 1982, aged 29. After three seasons with the Chemics, which included a Challenge Cup Final winner's medal in 1984, he joined Warrington in 1985.

He is fondly remembered by Warrington supporters. Lifelong supporter Gary Slater recalls: "At Wilderspool, he became a key part in one of the finest and fiercest front rows in the club's history – Boyd, Tamati, Jackson – with the proud Kiwi hooker flanked by two Australian props, Les Boyd and Bob Jackson.

The three of them lined up together in the 1986 Premiership final against Halifax at Elland Road and all three scored tries as the Wire scored a resounding 38-10 victory to give Warrington their first trophy for almost four years. Kevin just missed out to Boyd in the voting for the Harry Sunderland Trophy as man-of-the-match.

The following season the trio joined forces again against Wigan in the John Player Special Trophy final at Bolton, in front of a 21,000-plus crowd; although on this occasion they had to settle for runners-up medals.

Kevin captained the side in the 1987-88 season when he was named "clubman of the year" by the directors and the supporters. He also began working for Warrington Borough Council as a rugby league development officer, encouraging hundreds of youngsters to take up the sport, and coaching Warrington's 'A' team.

In October 1989, after making 105 full appearances for Warrington and 11 more as a substitute, Salford recognised his leadership qualities by appointing him as their player-coach."

Warrington's finance manager Neil Dowson also has good memories of Kevin's time at Wilderspool: "I am the same age as Kevin and played against him at Vets rugby union level a number of times and we always enjoyed a good tussle and a drink and a chat afterwards. He worked as Warrington rugby league development officer for many years even when coaching other clubs. He taught many youngsters the basics of rugby league, including my two sons. He continued to live and work in Warrington until his return to New Zealand around 10 years ago. Kevin is a great bloke, fondly remembered by many and is missed in Warrington."

It was quite a coup for the Army Rugby League team to have such an experienced coach. Kevin recalls that "In his capacity as British Army Rugby League secretary Martin Coyd contacted the Rugby League office in Leeds asking for assistance and was passed on to me. I was asked to facilitate a rugby league coaching course at Chester Army Camp in 1996 after which I was approached by Martin who asked if I would be interested in coaching the army team.

We talked about a forces tournament in Germany, the British Navy, RAF and the Army were invited. The tournament was organised with the Navy, Army and RAF playing each other, and whoever finished highest on points would play the French Army team. My original involvement was just to run coaching courses for the Army at Chester.

The players came from rugby league and rugby union backgrounds; I think some of them came along to get a free trip back to Germany. Most were very green and wouldn't have stood out on any BARLA field, but as time passed some of them came to understand the game and its requirements and could have done quite well in the professional game. We won the tournament in Germany and played the French Army who then showed the boys how rugby league was really played.

Kevin Tamati (Photo: Martin Coyd)

I became good friends with Staff Sergeant Taffy Jones who was my assistant. At most I was with them for a couple of years, but because of the nature of the beast we could never put the same side on the park in consecutive games.

I thoroughly enjoyed my short time with the boys at Chester and Catterick and then in Germany. At all times I was looked after very well; my accommodation was always in the officers' quarters which were very nice indeed. While in the mess at Catterick I read one of the plaques or it may have been on a dinner mat.

It mentioned that the unit served in New Zealand and was involved in the Māori land wars to which I quickly shouted across the table at Taffy, 'Your bastard mates killed my people'. He chuckled and replied 'the bastards killed mine as well.'

My stay with the Army was short, I finished up with Lancashire Lynx and Warrington Borough Council and moved up to Whitehaven for a couple of years coaching then dropped out of the game altogether, got divorced and two years later moved back home to New Zealand." Kevin still lives in New Zealand.

Kevin's work had a good effect on the Army team. In May 1997 they beat the RAF 26–19, and in April had beaten the more experienced Civil Service team 46–14. *Open Rugby* reported that even this score "did not prevent some serious after-match comment from Kevin. 'They're a good amateur team' he says, 'but they've got to build the individual's understanding and responsibility for the game and then concentrate on putting that into a team context." In August that year, the Army beat the Great Britain Students side 18–16, "one of their most impressive performances to date" according to *Open Rugby*.

Having a coach of Kevin's experience clearly helped rugby league develop in the Army, and he set standards from his experience in the professional game that helped the team progress at an important time.

Eugene Viljoen

Rugby league in Britain has always, from its earliest days, had many different nationalities playing the game. And Army Rugby League is no different. One of the team's South African players in recent years was Eugene Viljoen, known in the Army as 'Bokka'.

Bokka joined the Army, aged 25, in 2002, "to travel, play sports and possibly as a career. I enjoy working outdoors, meeting new people and seeing new places. It was an adventure." He joined the Royal Engineers, and at basic training was the best recruit, winning three of the five awards, including best shot and PT. He then went on Combat Engineer training, and then did trade training at Chatham, as a building and structural finisher. He was then posted to Northern Ireland, and finished his service with 18 months at Waterbeach, near Cambridge, in air support.

In South Africa, Bokka played in his school first team at rugby union, cricket, tennis and hockey. When he left school he played first class club rugby, trained with the Natal Sharks under-21 team and played with junior clubs in Natal. He enjoys all sports, and says that "Sport is very much a way of life for me". He is now involved with rover canoeing, trail running, mountain bike trails, and enjoys playing golf. Since he left the Army in 2009, he has set up a tour company in South Africa, Sport n
Safari (www.sportsnsafari.com) and sport is a major part of their work.

With his rugby union background, Bokka initially played union in the Army, including the Army team and the Combined Services side, at full-back. For the Royal Engineers union team, he played full-back, but later on switched to fly-half. He first played rugby league, which was a new sport for him, for the very successful Royal Engineers team, and recalls winning the London 9s one year and being runners up another time. He played a few games at full-back, but was mainly a half-back, with a few appearances at centre. He won every honour in both union and league at Regimental, Corps and Army level, and at the time was one of 13 players to represent the Combined Services in both codes. He says "I am very grateful for what the Army has given and done for me. I have learnt so much and been so fortunate due to the Army being exposed to rugby league. I would never ever have played the game if it was not for the Army and the people involved with Army RL. What an awesome family to have and be part of!"

He believes that the highlight of his time with Army RL was "Playing with a great bunch of guys, learning a new game (I think union and league complement each other), which most certainly improved my game. Playing in the inter-services was so intense and exhilarating! I was given the opportunity to play top class rugby and was exposed to a new level of preparation." A special memory is "beating the Navy and the RAF and scoring a few good tries; also I had the honour of skippering such a group of outstanding athletes in the toughest competition ever, the Army team in the rugby league inter-services. Every time you run onto the field you know it's going to be 80 minutes of sheer power, cuts and glory to win. Putting on that red jersey in the inter-services for the first time I will never forget; I left it till the last moment to put it on and the night before battled to sleep. I thought about the game and what I was going to do where and when on the field. It's like going into battle, but this time with great friends instead of comrades! I was part of Army RL winning teams against both the Navy and the RAF, but unfortunately missed out on winning the RL inter-services by one point."

Another special memory of his Army Rugby League days was playing in the Challenge Cup: "Just to be part of the Challenge Cup and possibly ending up playing against the likes of Leeds. The best for me was when we played Oldham in the third round at Aldershot in 2008. There were interviews and we were also on television. I also enjoyed playing against the professional teams in the York 9s, and a definite highlight for me was playing at Headingley in the Leeds 9s, and captaining the Army RL team."

Bokka never got to tour with the Army Rugby League team, and missed out on the Combined Services World Cup win in Australia in 2008 because he was playing rugby union – "Boy do I regret that because they ended up winning the Cup." However, he played a major part in organising the 2009 tour to South Africa and was honoured to play in the last game. Although he missed out on rugby league tours, he did play union in a wide range of international venues: "I counted the other day and I was very fortunate to have gone on about 15 rugby union tours around the world. Tours that stand out to me is the Cyprus 10s where we were in the Final as a tiny Regimental team against the full Navy team, Barbados and Estonia of all places stand out, we won like 110-0! France was also good; we played a curtain raiser for Toulouse and Brive."

He believes that sport is very important in the Army: "Absolutely, I think it is vital! Especially in the Army because there are a lot of similarities with going into combat for real and playing rugby. All the core value and standards are exactly the same. Nav, our coach, always reminded us of that and that is something I apply to everyday life still today and will do so till the end. Sport and being part of and playing Rugby League are extremely important in so many ways. As I mentioned before, the core value and standards are part and parcel of it and sport has no boundaries as far as background, upbringing, race, status etc is concerned. When you play sport in the Army at whatever level there is also no rank. It's an opportunity even if it is just for a few hours for everyone to play and socialise on the same level as team mates and friends, no 'Yes Sir' 'No Sir' protocols. In fact heavy fines are dished out. My best and closest friends are all guys I met playing rugby. Sport and rugby does not care where you come from, what you look like or what colour skin you got, how much money you have or what country you come from. It is all about your commitment, dedication, ability and then of course those value and standards. It's the same here in South Africa as I am sure it is around the world. Because of our past in this country, sport is one thing that has helped with our transformation and bridging the gap with the haves and have not's and in particular race. The players, supporters and ordinary South Africans, when it comes to supporting your team, nothing maters other than supporting your team and of course a winning team. So as far as I am concerned I believe sport around the world is important and most definitely in the Army, it's a must!"

Bokka says that: "My rugby playing days in the Army are some of the best memories I have and I seriously miss them and all my Army friends." He was very pleased to be involved with the 2009 Army RL tour to South Africa, and hopes that other teams will also visit and help develop the game in his home country: "Together with the games they had some good R&R days which Sport n Safari also arranged. Rugby league here in South Africa is still a very young sport and Sport n Safari wants to promote the game more internationally, and make South Africa a great place to come to for a training camp and to play some good rugby league. A lot of hard work still needs to be done but we are getting there."

The testimonials on Sport n Safari's website show Army RL's appreciation of the support and service they were given. Brigadier Frank Noble commented "Thanks to Mr Eugene Viljoen (Bokka) of Sport n Safari for the local in-country support to the planning and delivery of the tour. Outstanding advice, planning and organisation."

Major Rich Naivalurua commented: "May I again thank you on behalf of the soldiers of the British Army Rugby League for the outstanding service and support, you and your company, Sport n Safari, gave to the British Army Rugby Team when we toured your beautiful country ... Sport n Safari was critical in ensuring the success of the tour. You provided our link to the South African Rugby League and provided outstanding liaison at every level in South Africa. Your attention to detail and dedication to ensure our programme of activities was balanced with focus on rugby and enjoying the full experience of South Africa, was outstanding. The accommodation that you booked for us, the training facilities you organised for our benefit, and the travel arrangements you put in place were all first class. On behalf of British Army Rugby League, I would be delighted to recommend you and your company Sport n Safari to team who wished to tour South Africa."

Rugby league is featured on the company's website, and hopefully more tours by different parts of the sport can be organised, to help the development of the sport in South Africa.

The RATS in action

Left: Sean Fanning and Dean Lewis with former Great Britain forward Barrie McDermott in July 2009.

Below: The Army team, including Barrie McDermott.

(Both photos: Julie Hulatt)

9.   A soldier's life: Sean Fanning

Sean has been involved with Combined Services RL from the start. Three stalwarts of that team reflect below on his work, both for Army Rugby League and Combined Services.

From the Royal Navy, Wayne Okell said: "Sean Fanning has been at the forefront of the Inter-Services competition for a decade or more, we (Royal Navy) have come so close to winning on many occasions but it always seemed to be Sean who would come up with a special play to split the game or a try in the dying moments to earn another Army victory. He could seek out an opportunity where others couldn't, had an amazing step to break the line and knew exactly what was required to win. He has broken our hearts on several occasions when we thought we had the game won and been our nemesis for many years but the manner in which he conducts himself as an individual commands respect from all quarters, when we first won the tournament in 2004, Sean was the first person to congratulate us. That's the sort of bloke he is; a real true professional, a role model and revered. He's a great example for everyone.

We played in the first early years for Combined Services together and when I became head coach, it took me no time at all to appoint Sean as captain. Throughout the years he has been at the heart of all our great victories, BARLA, the Anzac Test in Sydney 2006, winning the Armed Forces World Cup in Sydney in 2008 particularly stand out for me, none of this would have been possible without his leadership; he has always been my 'Captain Fantastic'. He knew how to manage players through adversity and knew exactly how to deal with tough situations.

Sean is not only a very good friend of mine, but also my old man coached him when he played for Leigh. I grew up in Leigh and Sean was always in the local papers with his weekly performances, he was a star player when he was younger. For me, he's been the stand-out player in Armed Forces rugby league since it began. Its only when you scratch the surface and look a little deeper that you begin to understand why; he is a student of the game, he is also one of the fittest and strongest players that I have been involved with, he is a seriously tough competitor with an appetite for hard work, but most of all he is a seriously smart and classy footballer. He has without doubt been the most special player of our generation and I am immensely proud of my association with him and our friendship."

Damian Clayton from the RAF commented: "We had some tough battles in the Inter-Services matches. He's an honest guy, and it was a pity that I didn't go to Australia with him in 2006 and 2008. He epitomises the honest rugby league player from up north. He says the appropriate things, leads by example and is a tough, honest bloke. I have a lot of respect for him, enjoy his company and friendship.

Dave Mortimer (Shippers) said: "He's one of the nicest blokes I've ever met and one of the toughest. He'll put his body on the line, a total professional and a very good rugby league player. He will be missed from our sport. I remember we played the Australians at Hull KR; he brought the team together, toughened them up and we beat the Australians. He led by example, a top dog. One of my favourite photos is from the 2008 World Cup, I am with Nav, Sean, Wayne and Ray Unsworth from the RFL, who also was involved with Combined Services from the beginning. "

My first experience of rugby league was in my junior school, I must have been eight years old, and I seemed to quite enjoy it as far as I remember. I think I had developed some elusive skills playing a game called Skilio in the playground at break time. Basically we had to catch someone from the opposite team and put them on a base; then other team members could get them released by touching the base and shouting 'skilio', but obviously risking getting captured themselves while attempting the feat. The other game we played that might be an indication of where my love for rugby came from was 'run across', better known as British Bulldog. The object of this game is to select one or two individuals to try to stop everyone else from getting from point A to point B, another game where being elusive came in handy.

Mum and Dad: Tony and Catherine Fanning

Junior school rugby was great. We played against other schools in the area; I always remember coming out of the changing rooms to play at Merton Bank junior school and attempting to kick the ball onto the pitch. Unfortunately, I had my boots on and was on a concrete playground and basically nearly did a somersault and landed on my back winding myself in the process. Trying to gasp for oxygen wasn't the best match preparation as I remember; the teacher quickly got me on my feet and onto the pitch. "Stop messing about and get on with it" I think he said. No accident reporting or health and safety in those days.

At my senior school some of the teachers were former rugby players. Bob Prosser was a former St Helens rugby league scrum-half and Mr Hitchin was also a rugby man, another PE teacher, Mr Rawlinson, who was the water polo teacher, also liked his rugby. I really looked up to these guys and sport was one of the few lessons I looked forward to, but rugby was just one sport at school and I loved some other sports, even football although I hate to admit that now.

Playing at St Helens' ground as a schoolboy should have set me on a path to rugby league, but it didn't. I liked athletics, basketball, cricket and even tennis although we weren't allowed to play it at school, it was seen as a girls' game. No wonder with that policy we don't have any English champions, although maybe things have changed now.

My brother Anthony was always a better rugby player than me and seemed to be better than me at most sports. He is younger than me, but everything I did at school he seemed to do slightly better. He was the school rugby captain for his year; I was the basketball captain and cricket captain. He joined Blackbrook Amateur Rugby League Club, played for the town team in various age groups and was in the same team as Gary Connelly who went on to have a great professional rugby league career. I, on the other hand, went to Sutton Harriers athletics club doing cross-country and thought I was going to be the new Sebastian Coe or Steve Ovett. The 400 and 800 metres were my best races; I wanted to be in the 100 and 200 metres but there always seemed to be someone faster than me in those events.

Towards the end of school I seemed to lose a bit of focus as do many young lads. Even my love of sport couldn't keep me in school and although I didn't smoke, I did give into some peer pressure when it came to bunking off. I remember loads of times going over to 'the licker', an area of rough ground and fields, and playing football when I was supposed to be in maths. In fact, it got that bad in the end the only lessons I went in for were the ones I liked. Sport was obviously one of those and I attended most, if not all, of the classes.

It was then that some of the guys I was knocking around with started talking about the Army. The Falklands war was still fresh in the mind for all the lads at school. We had been interested when the war was going on. So this became our focus when we were wagging school. Off to the careers office we went to find out about joining the Army. There was absolutely no chance what so ever of finding an ordinary job in the early 1980s and when youngsters left school they were expected to take up a YTS (Youth Training Scheme), although there wasn't usually a job at the end of it.

The careers office was great. We just took our blazers and ties off and put leather jackets on, sometimes we even asked for the morning off school and told them we had appointments at the Army careers office. Obviously we then went on to take the whole day off, no wonder my maths and English are so poor. The guys in the careers office knew what they were doing; we were asked constantly what sport we did. "Rugby" I said, "Yes, but what other sports do you do", they said. 'This is great' I thought, 'it must be all sport in the Army.' So I left there thinking the Army was all sport and skiing with some adventure training thrown in. Soldiering and staging on weren't really mentioned; how naive I was then, aged just 15.

Most of the lads were already getting into trouble while off bunking off school, selling scrap was one activity I remember; lads would get on the roofs of the old factories ripping off anything they could sell. This included old wiring which they would roll up into bundles, burn the plastic off then weigh it in at the scrap metal yard. We remembered to take our school ties off when we were bunking off school. This was the start of bad times for most of my old school mates; a lot of them spent time in the old borstals or detention centres. So doing something different was very appealing and I jumped at the chance to get away and take the Queen's shilling.

Basic training

I joined the Army in 1985. Basic training was exactly that; basic. Anyone who was averagely fit and fairly robust was all right. Sutton Coldfield was the Army's testing facility. We were put through a 1.5 mile run and gym tests such as pull-ups and sit-ups on an incline bench with press-ups and a vertical jump. Easy stuff I thought and I ate them up. The academic tests were even easy although I had missed most of my final year climbing roofs. Then I went in for an interview with an officer. "Well done" he said, "You have done really well in your tests, you have got a place in the RAMC." This was a downer because I had put this down as my third choice, I was under the impression I was going to be flying helicopters, wonder where I got that from, thanks a lot guys.

After leaving school to join the Army I started to enjoy the physicality of rugby when we had our inter-company sports, even though it was rugby union, and I felt I didn't know what I was doing. Still, it started to appeal to me, although I was in the College football team as well. It was as if I couldn't make my mind up about which was my favourite, similar to when I was at school.

I left the junior Army to join the regulars, and more rugby union. I found that the Army loved rugby union; nearly every unit had a team. That's when I started to realise how much I missed and enjoyed rugby league. So I started to go home regularly at weekends and tried to play for any team that would let me. The Hare and Hounds would let me play even though I wasn't able to train with them. I met some nice lads there, who took me out for a few good nights on the town. On the next day I would then go and watch my home town team, St Helens RLFC.

I think the pride in where you are born that comes out when you move away. As I have got older sport still makes me proud of St Helens.

Doing this every weekend made me want rugby league even more. The fact was that I enjoyed going home and playing rugby league there, and was starting to not enjoy the Army. I wanted more to get home, see my family, play rugby and socialise with my mates.

23 Para Field Ambulance (23PFA)

My first proper unit was 23 Para Field Ambulance (PFA). It turned out to be my only unit for my first six years in the Army. Looking back, it was a great unit. This is where I met some people who became lifelong friends, lads who I am still in touch with even though they have left the Army. Being an airborne unit it was busy and in the field quite often. Obviously this didn't help me to get involved with rugby union; rugby league didn't exist in the Army at this time.

The only rugby I was able to play at this time was for my unit, and even though we didn't play often, there were some good quality players in the team. Even the players who didn't have much of a rugby background were very fit. As an Airborne unit, I found that the mentality suited rugby. Some of the guys couldn't play the game, but they still wanted to rip the opposition's heads off, which helped the team. Most of the unit rugby was against other units in the medical corps, so our unit did very well.

The PFA team always did well in the AMS tournaments and often made a clean sweep of the trophies, winning the Harris & Mullins cup and the 7-a-side and 10-a-side competitions.

Running the team at the time was a Falklands vet called Dave Wilson who was also my pre Para DS staff. He was also into tug-of-war and I think liked everything which was a physical challenge. The great thing about being in the unit rugby team in those days was that we turned up on a Monday for a game on Wednesday and didn't need to shave, although most of that has changed now. There is no way players today would turn up on a Monday for a Wednesday unit game because the Army is much busier.

PFA also did well in the Army Cup (Minor units) and got to the semi-final and final on numerous occasions. This showed we weren't a bad team because we were pitched against teams with a lot more players to choose from. Playing unit sport was a great way to bond with the other guys in the unit and the social life after the games was great. I started to myther (pester) other mates of mine to play rugby, Eddie Bryan, Geordie Evison, Tim Ducket were all non-rugby players who started playing after a bit of persuading. We had some great socials after the games.

AMS Corps rugby union

The AMS Corps rugby union frustrated me; my point is this and I won't labour it. I felt that some good players didn't get picked, even though they were good enough. I remember lads scoring loads of tries in the AMS competitions and going along to the Corps training and not getting a look in. In the 1980s and early 1990s the AMS team was a decent side with some good standard players, including doctors who had played university rugby and one or two officers who had played at a decent level. I didn't feel I got a look in with this set up and never returned. The AMS as a team now are struggling, although to be fair they have suffered because the AMS obviously recruit more women than probably any other Corps now. I'm not being derogatory to women because the AMS women's rugby team could be one of the best in the Army. Also, the AMS is without doubt one of the busiest corps because of its size.

Some of the good players I met in the Corps set up turned out to be from rugby league backgrounds and later in my Army career when league was going strong linked up to form a great AMS rugby league team, including Shaun Knott, Tony Thornhill, Paul Desborough, Nigel Rigby, Loll Wood, Chris Jenkins, Pat Hoyte, Tim Ducket, Roger Dussard and Woz Kerr. They all played a part in the success of the AMS rugby league team.

Every now and again rugby had to be put on hold and a little work had to be done. I was due out of the Army soon and the last place I wanted to spend time then was Northern Ireland; nevertheless when the RSM insists you are going, off you go. I was on tour there in 1990, attached to 3 Para.

Within a week of being told I was going, I was out there and within 48 hours I was down at Woodburn RUC station doing top cover in an armoured land rover with a weapon system I hadn't even been trained on. ['Top cover' is providing the security for a vehicle – being on top and stopping it from coming under fire.] I remember sticking my body armour over the

215

top of my smock and getting laughed at. I hadn't realised it had to go under the smock. It was different to today's body armour of course.

The weapon I had been trained with was the SLR (Self-loading rifle 7.62) and my personal weapon as a medic was the SMG (submachine gun). Unfortunately for me they had just changed over to the new weapon system and used the SA 80 rifle. This wasn't a problem, or so I thought, because I believed I would get the opportunity to test and adjust when I arrived in the country at Palace Barracks Belfast. I thought I could familiarise myself with the new weapon and have a go at using it on the camp ranges.

This was, however, not to be. After being laughed at putting the body armour on wrong I was now in danger of looking like a right Muppet with my slick drills with the SA80. It turned out to be not too bad and it wasn't until getting back and looking dreadful with my unload drills that the CSM (Company Sargeant Major) saw me and rightly told me off. He told me to get a grip of the handling drills before he got a grip of my body. Time passed quickly and before I knew it I was back in the base at the Palace Barracks. To my surprise there was an opportunity to play rugby again, albeit union. The battalion team were training for an Army cup match back in the UK, so I turned up at training.

'Great', I thought, 'even on Op tour and I'm getting the chance to play rugby', even though it was union. The first game was against an Irish battalion stationed in Northern Ireland and the whole battalion turned up to watch. It was great to play in front of a noisy crowd. However, the game was very stop-start with penalties all over the place, there was no open rugby and this disappointed me. The most exciting part of the game was a big scrap which had the crowd very excited to say the least. We won this game so were through to the next round. This meant a trip back to the UK; an added bonus – a trip home. Parachute Regiment had some big monsters and aggression and fitness weren't really in short supply, however rugby talent was. When we played back in the UK we were turned over in Bordon by a REME outfit who were a bit too well drilled for us. There was no chance to visit friends or go out, we went straight back to Northern Ireland, which was disappointing.

Some work did have to be done in between my rugby escapades. When I was at the RUC station at Woodburn, after an early morning start I was on top cover again with HQ, setting up a security cordon round an estate that reminded me of 'cement city' in Derbyshire Hill in St Helens. It was strange to see soldiers knocking about in a place that just looked like a town in the north of England. This was probably the worst part of the tour really, the kneeling position was murder in those days without the pads that are used today. I had to stay in position in the freezing cold while some of the other guys were getting to kick down someone's door searching for weapons or explosives. My medical abilities were also put to the test with my first attempts at stitching; I dread to think of those poor guys who have scars that have had my handy work all over them.

We did get the chance to get a social drink in Bangor though and I remember going out with some of the 3 Para medics, one of whom later transferred to the AMS and I'm still in touch with him. Mark Shanley was a prop who switched from rugby union. We went down to town, only to legal places, not out-of-bounds ones of course.

My next tour was Operation Granby in 1991, in the first Gulf War. We were attached to 33 Field Hospital. This was a tour everyone wanted to be on and I just managed to jump onto it having not long returned from Northern Ireland. Not everyone from my unit managed to get on it, and some had to remain, do rear party and cover standby duties. It was also an opportunity to see my then girlfriend who I not seen for six months because of my Northern Ireland deployment. While I was away she had been deployed to the Gulf attached to 33 Field Hospital.

This was a war that nobody seemed to know how it would go. The briefs we were given warned us that Saddam would definitely use his chemical and biological weapons and there was a massive NBC drive to get everyone up to speed. This turned out to be a false alarm. The RAF were the busiest and each briefing we got was about detailed air strikes and bombardments. I do, however, remember one of my mates jumping for cover when we heard the first air raid siren go. It was the same as a Second World War siren, and by the time he had hit the deck he had somehow managed to put on his NBC (Nuclear, Biological, Chemical) suit before he hit the ground. This turned out to be another false call as there turned out to be no NBC threat. We were lucky when we got there because we had some good accommodation compared to some of the guys, probably due to having Pat Donnelly with us. He was a man that could get things sorted for us. In close proximity to me, Jimmy Middleton and Taff Higgs was another guy who was a bit of legend in the unit for all the wrong reasons. He was a great lad who liked a good time and seemed to get in even more trouble than me. I think after serving some time at Her Majesty's pleasure he was discharged. I remember getting in some trouble over there before the war kicked off. They stuck me on Sanger duties as a punishment and when I turned up for duty, this guy was already on there for something else. The film *Jar head* was pretty much just like life over there, a lot of waiting and training, but not much at the end of it.

I do remember a lot of sunbathing, cards and attempts to make alcoholic beverages which turned out to be horrible. Other things that stick with me were not the casualties of war, but the ones that seem needless. There was a guy that came through with horrible burns of more than 80 per cent. I think anything over 50 to 60 per cent people don't normally survive. This poor soul had been involved in a heater exploding and survived for days, but eventually died on the way back to the UK. Another one was a suicide, all conflicts have incidents where soldiers lose their lives in sometimes stupid incidents. But some of the medics who got the call to go forward told me of some horrible sights from bunkers being burned out with flame throwing units and explosives. Everyone who went over there will remember the first scud missile sirens. My other memories are of when the day turned to night with the burning of the oil fields, it was certainly a weird experience.

I left the service in 1991, just after the first Gulf War and bought a house in Thatto Heath in St Helens. I was signed by Leigh RLFC who later became the Centurions with the advent of summer rugby league. This, however, was not immediately after I left the services. Before joining Leigh I had an unsuccessful trial for a few weeks with St Helens RLFC where I played under a coach called Frank Barrow who was a very successful player in his day, but a very 'old school' coach.

I wasn't signed by Saints, which was a massive disappointment to me at the time. I had built this up as a very important point in my life, I did, however, learn a great deal. But in the professional game I found myself well off the pace and way behind the curve.

Up until this point I had only played unit, corps, and Army under-21 rugby union. Although I was extremely fit from my days running about up-and-down hills, it didn't really stand me in good stead for the rigours of professional rugby league.

For a start, everyone in the 'A' (second) team was a few years younger than me. The average age was around 18 or 19, whereas I was 23. These were guys that I didn't recognise at the time, but that became very successful rugby league players. They included Gary Connelly, Alan Hunte and Sonny Nickle. There were other players in the dressing room who were more my age. I did recognise some players who the club had just signed and wanted to give some game time. Jonathan Griffiths was one such player; he was a Welsh rugby union international who the club had spent big money on. The 'A' team on paper looked great; however I played some games where we got spanked by Bradford and Wigan. This did not help my quest to try to sign for my home town team. Like I said, you have to take something away from every situation, and I learnt a valuable lesson in that thrashing by Wigan.

Wigan's 'A' team that day beat us by 90 points. Looking back, no wonder I didn't get signed by Saints. They had experienced internationals such as Dean Bell and Graeme West in their side who were coming back from injury. We were put to the sword. This was all new to me and I was just happy to be on the field with the Saints' red V on my chest, I threw myself everywhere, and dived at everything in a Wigan shirt. I was so passionate and I gave every ounce of energy I had, but I remember I didn't get the ball in hand at all. However, I felt that I must have made an impression with my fitness and effort and I thought my tackle count must be massive because I had dived at everything that moved. The trouble with a player who goes off their feet at everything and everyone is that he is likely to come away a high missed tackle count also, and that is exactly what happened to me. The bollocking and the stats came in the changing rooms at training in the week. Tackle selection in the professional game can be about stats. This was not the case for me in this game. If I got anywhere near a Wigan player I attempted to rip him in two, even if he was not quite in range or he was someone else's responsibility. However, these attempted assists were all put down as missed tackles; maybe it was just his way of firing me off with feedback stats. This was devastating as I remember not getting signed and it knocked me off my stride for a while.

This all led to a little too much drinking and I remember doing some serious partying with a few Army mates in Birkenhead.

Another unsuccessful rugby move for me was with Runcorn Highfield in 1991. The original Runcorn team had played after the 1895 breakaway, but this club was the latest incantation of Liverpool City, who became Huyton and then Highfield. They were down on their luck and were not doing well. It was a team of local players and a massive come down from Saints, but I thought I just need some game time to get some experience. They were being coached by another former Saints star, Chris Arkwright, who was one of my favourite players when I used to watch Saints. I completed all the pre-season training with these guys, but then they didn't give me an opportunity to play. There was a lot of former Saints players in the set up though; I was an unknown so they probably stuck with who they knew.

So things were looking quite disappointing on the rugby front. I was on the verge of calling it a day, but I thought I would give it one last go and spoke to Leigh RLFC who took me on trial and made me feel really welcome. I remember the coach there was really old school and another legend of the game. Kevin Ashcroft was the same generation as Frank Barrow and had played with Alex Murphy. Things went better at Leigh; I was signed on and received my first bit of semi-professional rugby league money. This gave me a chance to experience the rigours of professional sport, and it wasn't all a bed of roses as I found out. Training was hard and I used to travel with an old school mate, David Hill. I made my debut for Leigh on 26 April 1992.

Again I found myself slightly behind the curve; I wasn't the fastest of wingers and with Barrie Ledger on the wing I knew I was going to struggle to get in the team. Barrie Ledger was another big name in the game; he was well-known from his days with St Helens when he played in the same team as the great Australian Mal Meninga.

I remember for one game I was picking up Barrie up at Haresfinch because he lived in St Helens as well. I was on the panel, because I had just played in the 'A' team and been selected for the first team squad. This was great because even if I didn't play I got half the money anyway. So here I was, waiting for Barrie, and he didn't show up. I waited with Aide Earner in the car, but still no Barrie. So we were going to leave because we thought Barrie had been on a night out. We thought either he is not coming or he had made his own way. Anyway, when we got there Barrie was not there and the coach wanted to know where he was. "Not sure", we said, then the club got a phone call to say that we hadn't picked him up and he got a taxi, which isn't cheap from St Helens. Kevin Ashcroft was not happy and dropped him from the starting line-up. This meant that I ended up playing and Barrie was on the bench which went down really well with the lads. Obviously they thought I had done it on purpose to get my place from Barrie. I received a right ribbing from the boys, which Barrie loved.

I always wanted to play at half-back, but with Jason Donohue at scrum-half and a legend of the game, John Woods, at stand-off, there was no chance of that. If I am honest my ball skills and experience weren't up to it. This is where my commitment wasn't good enough either and what I should have done was work on the weaker parts of my game, but it was easy to come up with excuses.

Holding down a job in those days was usual with any semi-professional rugby player, so it's not a good enough excuse and that for me is the difference between someone who makes the top end of the sporting world and the player who just plays. A dedicated player will always make up for their inadequacies in commitment and dedication. This is what I never did and even though training became a big commitment, especially when Leigh were promoted at the end of the 1991–92 season and training went from Tuesday and Thursday with Saturday morning for a game on Sunday to almost every day after work. The sign of a true professional would be to put the extra hours in to climb above the rest. This would have meant giving up my job, and I wasn't convinced I had the talent and dedication to actually make it work. There were younger lads than me, faster and stronger in the gym, who seemed to be a little keener.

But like I said I enjoyed my time at Leigh and gained some great experience playing alongside some great players. I went to a dinner recently at Leigh Miners ARLC, and met up with some of the guys from those days, including Mark Sarsfield, John Woods and Jason Donohue.

What was great about being at Leigh was the opportunity to play against my home town club, Saints. I remember my old neighbour taking the mickey out of me when he knew we were playing Saints. Saints had just signed Jerrod McCracken to play at centre and Fred, a great bloke, loved to joke that McCracken was going to throw me about a bit. This just gave me an incentive to play well and motivated me to prove a point, and sometimes this is how the teams at the lower end of the league beat the ones at the top of the league.

This is exactly what happened on 11 November 1992; Saints were at the top of Division One and we were joint bottom. Wet and windy conditions suited us, and not Saints' free-flowing, exciting rugby that had got them clear at the top. Loads of former Saints players in our side were out to prove a point. We had two massive props that day: big Tim Street who could look after himself, and another robust lad, Lee Hanson – a giant of a man. But on paper we shouldn't have stood a chance. Ropati, Gary Connelly, Alan Hunte, Chris Joynt and Shane Cooper – Saints' side was just brimming with talent, but that day Leigh were up for it and we got stuck into them. This frustrated them and they tried to throw the ball about a bit, but the wet conditions didn't allow them to get away with it and they played into our hands. We won 11–6. Our fans were ecstatic and walking off the pitch at the end was great, especially because the Saints' coaching bench had Frankie Barrow sat there with McLennan - both down after a defeat. It turned out that this result cost Saints the title that year because they were piped on points difference by Wigan. I wish I had gone out that night with the lads, it would have been a great, but I lived in St Helens and Dave Hill and I use to shoot off most of the time. I do often regret not socialising more with the guys at Leigh, but I think in my first six years in the Army I had done enough socialising to last me a lifetime.

One of my memories from those days was a game against Leeds at the end of the 1993–94 season. In this game I came up against all the players I admired and had watched on television when I was in the Army. Their team was packed with stars including Ellery Hanley and from 1 to 13 all the players were well-known. Garry Schofield, Kevin Iro, Alan Tait and

Craig Innes were all playing that day so we knew we were in for a tough afternoon. But these are the games any player wants to play in and are the days when players get valuable experience. We were beaten 52–20 at Hilton Park and I remember chasing Ellery Hanley to the line as he scored. He was practically running sideways, handing people off as he went, and I still couldn't catch him. Another player who was very hard to put down was Kevin Iro. He was such a dangerous runner with ball in hand, and was very hard to get a shot on because his footwork always stopped him being lined up for a big hit. Leeds did well that year, but still couldn't wrestle the honours from Wigan even with Hanley in the side.

Second Division

It was good experience playing in the top flight of the rugby league world, but for Leigh it didn't last and we just couldn't quite get the results, some said it was because we had to many former stars on their way down, who were not committed, and not enough young guys, but I disagree. I don't think that is fair on the guys, the effort was there, but when early results don't go your way it's hard to dig your way out of trouble.

Kevin Ashcroft was hard done by, he was the one who got Leigh promoted and when they went up the club sacked him, and after that the club had four coaches in as many seasons as they struggled.

Another boyhood hero of mine was Alex Murphy. He was a legend in the game and everybody spoke of him at Leigh with fond memories because he was there as a player and coach. There were loads of stories about him, both good and bad. But what everyone did say was what a character he was.

My worst memory at Leigh was being booed off the field and spat on by the fans after a bad defeat. We were beaten heavily at Workington in the Challenge Cup on 26 February 1995. We had got through the early rounds against Swinton and Heworth, and been given some new blazers to look the part. We set off to Cumbria to face a side that had got into the First Division and seemed to have some funding behind them. They had spent some money and were doing well in the top flight. Des Drummond was on the wing against me and I had watched him play for Great Britain, he was a very tough player and I knew I had to be on my toes. They also had a big pack.

Anyway, things went really badly and it was a record defeat for the club, 94–4. Needless to say the lads were gutted; we got on the coach for a long drive back to Lancashire and the lads got a few beers down their necks as anyone would do after a horrible experience like that. I, however, was driving back to St Helens and wasn't drinking. This used to do my head in because it's nice to relax and get a few pints down after the battle of a game; it also lets everyone relax and bonds the team.

Having to shoot off all the time didn't do me any favours in regard to mixing with the guys. On their return to Leigh, the lads carried on and went out on the town. I got back to my car which had been broken into outside the club and my coat had been stolen off the back seat. A lesson learnt.

However, the lads had gone down town in their blazers. There were bad reports in the press and the next day the club was inundated with phone calls calling for heads to roll. People were talking about players not giving the right commitment and not caring about the club. A week later we all had the blazers taken back from us and had some hard training sessions.

We were being coached by a former Wigan player called Ian Lucas who had retired early in his career because of a nasty neck injury, but was a good prop in his day. I remember he wasn't happy after the defeat and we were on the end of his anger in training the following week. In the changing rooms after training he gave us his views on the game and told us what he thought of us. Some of the forwards took it really personally and it got quite heated to say the least. Two of them standing face to face nearly came to blows; this was the reality of professional sport, people's reputations and careers were on the line.

When results don't go your way it doesn't just seem like a game anymore, not when there is money involved. And when the team is losing the atmosphere can turn. This is why my mum never came to watch me play; she had turned up to one of my first games only to hear some guy slating me for fumbling a ball while trying to score a try. This was in the players' families' area where the players hope that their relatives are out of earshot of all the idiots, but it was too much for her and she didn't come again.

But usually the fans at Leigh were great and they are really passionate about their team. They have had some success and even as long ago as the 1980s they won the First Division title and have had success in the Challenge Cup, but now they are in the Championship. They have recently moved from Hilton Park and hopefully their new ground will bring them more success.

I will always have some fond memories from my time there, meeting characters like Allen Rowley and Stan Wall I'll always remember doing a runner from a taxi with all the lads from St Helens on our return after a night out in Leigh Marshy Meadows and Bungle.

While I was out of the Army I worked for the Merseyside Ambulance Service. I was part-time with the patient transport service, but that fitted in well with rugby. At one time Leigh were training almost every night.

I rejoined the Army in March 1996. I didn't see that I would continue to play rugby, playing part-time was difficult if you got injured and had to miss work. Maybe I was not quite dedicated enough. However, Tommy Frodsham − a former St Helens player − asked me to join Highfield. Another former Saints player, Geoff Fletcher, kept the club going as chairman and was very passionate about the team. I played for them for two years, and in the second season they became the Prescot Panthers, before the club disbanded at the end of the season. We had Maurice Bamford as coach for a bit. He knew his rugby league, but he was very aggressive in the changing rooms, which was not my approach as a coach.

We often seemed to lose by a few points. In 1996 we played the South Wales side. They had some decent players, Welsh international such as Andy Currier and Paul Moriarty. But some of the referee's decisions went against us. I felt that the RFL was not interested in a team like Prescot, although we had some good players.

222

I was based in Aldershot then, and used to go up north at the weekends to play. I got my expenses to go home, and my match fee.

Fort Blockhouse

Army Rugby League had established the Lawson Cup. This was anyone's chance to get involved in rugby league and a chance to bring the game to players who wouldn't normally get the chance to play for their Regiment or Corps teams. The Lawson Cup was about getting a bunch of blokes and starting a team. And this is what I wanted to do at Fort Blockhouse in Gosport.

I coached the rugby union team and started a rugby league side at the end of the union season. The lads loved it, and there was a social aspect as well.

Blockhouse was a tri-service establishment and a different world from the Army in Aldershot where I had just come from. It was a pleasant surprise. After serving with a bunch of guys with red lids on exercise most of the time and loads of testosterone knocking about, this was a far more pleasant place. I made a lot of friends down in Gosport service and civvies alike, mostly through rugby union. And I found plenty of people to convert from other sports to league when they realised how good the sport is. I remember watching the Blockhouse football team and seeing a guy who was good at the game, but kept getting sent off. I spoke to him, he was a Geordie lad, Dave Armstrong, and said 'You're playing the wrong sport mate, give league a try. He never looked back and has been part of our rugby set up ever since.

Working in the gym at Blockhouse gave me the chance to organise sport; I obviously concentrated on rugby and wasn't short of volunteers. It was mostly a medical environment with loads of nurses, medics, doctors and technicians. The submariners from the Navy were also based there, and they turned out to be great source of rugby talent to tap into.

Sammy Felfel was a great guy and already a good rugby union player; we got him playing league and he loved it. He went on to play for the Navy, although he sustained a bad arm injury in his first game. The gym had some talented rugby players on the staff in my time there. Most of the PTIs could turn their hand to rugby: Paul Bramhall, Pinch Martin, Ollie Burton, Harry Harrison and Rob will all look back on those days with fond memories, and the rugby wasn't bad either.

After a great rugby union season in which we went from the third division to winning five trophies, we were on a roll and I persuaded all the union guys to play rugby league. We had a great time in the union season and a few cracking socials, as you can imagine in a medical establishment. They didn't take much persuading to carry on into the summer playing rugby league. It was great to see union guys who had never played league enjoying it so much.

It may have a had a little to do with the social side, it was special, and it was that good I persuaded the Army team to train down there, obviously because of the facilities. The rugby league season at Blockhouse went well, although we were not quite as successful as the union team in wining trophies, but the enjoyment was just as good.

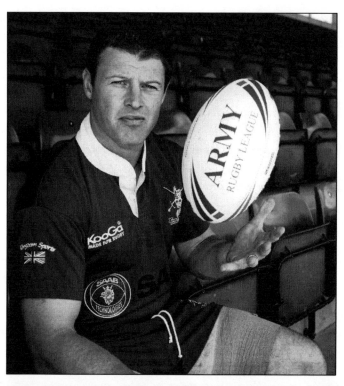

Top: Ready for action. Bottom: Running repairs from John Hulatt (Photo: Julie Hulatt).

Sean and Clare on their Wedding Day, 18 August 2007.

Clare and her work colleagues doing the Three Peaks Challenge to raise money for Soldiers' League.

After that season, looking back, we definitely influenced some die-hard union guys to look at league in a different way. I did my first coaching badge in rugby league when I rejoined the Army. The course was in Chester. I carried on playing as well, and did coaching with different units. I did my Level 2 course at Collingwood; Wayne Okell was also on the course. I did it again recently in Portsmouth to re-qualify; there were a lot of the Navy lads there.

Tour to Wales and St Helens

We had to do something to celebrate the success we had achieved with Blockhouse rugby, I think I didn't want it all to end, we had had such a great time, and looking back on those days they are probably my most enjoyable rugby memories.

We decided to tour. There wasn't much time or money so we sorted a mini tour to Wales, where my mate Taff Jenkins set up a game for us; and my home town of St Helens, which would be easy to get sorted. After getting some funding and an old minibus we set off, some of the lads were straight into the beer. We reached Swansea and booked into the TA centre. I took the lads down town; sometimes it feels like you are putting your career in your own hands when you organise socials for the lads, but I didn't worry. After I had dropped them I had to get the minibus back and get a lift into town so it took me quite a while; the lads were enjoying themselves. A great time, no trouble and loads of funnies.

The rugby union match didn't quite go so well. I had tried to match my bunch of tourists to a third team, but I think our opponents had misunderstood and thought the Army team was coming. What a horrible experience, most of my lads had spent the day in bed recovering from some serious abuse of the liver, and trying to get the team sorted in the changing rooms when at least two dropped out and another was unwell. The other thing I didn't want to do after going into the opposition changing rooms and seeing we were obviously not playing the third team and realising how up for it the opposition were, was perform a sort of good idea while we were drinking 'Hacka' that the forwards had devised. I won't attempt to describe it, needless to say we performed it to the delight of the sizable crowd that had gathered to see 'The Army'.

The opposition scored off the kick off, which pretty much set the tone for the game. We played most of the game with 14 men with some of our lads too ill to play. Spending most of the time under the sticks I asked the referee discreetly to call time early, but it defiantly fell on deaf ears as the opposition wanted a good run out. I'm not sure what score it was, but it must have been near a century.

The next day we were up and ready to leave after a great night out. St Helens here we come. I had booked us into a cadet hall with camp beds and we had a fancy dress night planned. I had lined up a game, not that I felt like playing after the last debacle, but I had chosen Liverpool St Helens 3rds, to play us on the Sunday before we returned. Everyone got into their fancy dress rig (Navy slang for 'Cloths') and we were off with Paul Bramhall leading with Fec and Scotty assisting. The game in St Helens was really good, we won by a couple of points. We had a good night out and everyone turned out on the Sunday.

The Army Medical
Service 9s competition that
was run at Fort Blockhouse.
Over 100 players
participated in this
competition, which started
in 2002.

Another great memory from my days at Blockhouse was the tour to Cyprus. This was again organised from the gymnasium and I decided to organise a joint ladies and gents tour, which some of the officers thought would be a recipe for disaster. It just seemed unfair at the time to sort the guys out and not do something for the girls even though they had only just started playing; they were very enthusiastic and I tried not to look at all the things that could go wrong. Instead it turned out to be really great, a tour that would be remembered and I still don't know of any other joint tours that have taken place since.

After all the organising the tour was nearly scuppered before it had begun because the coach driver got lost on the way to Brize Norton. Even though we got there an hour before the plane had to take off the RAF wouldn't let us go through and join the rest of the passengers sitting in the other lounge. The driver just shrugged and said he had got us there before the plane had taken off, but politely I told him to get on the phone and arrange with his company to get two rugby teams out to Cyprus. Great bloke that he was he did just that, his company must have loved him. Two days later after flights from Manchester and all over the place we were all in sunny Cyprus, it actually worked out really well for us as everyone who had flew out on military transport were all confined to camp, and because we had flown on civilian flights we could go where we wanted, apart from the out of bounds areas of course. The girls team proved very popular out in Cyprus, although outnumbered by the boys, but they really enjoyed it and even played some rugby. They won their 10-a-side tournament.

Future Mrs Fanning

This was also the place I met my wife Clare, and it just so happened she was a rugby player, they were great times in Gosport and a lot of the lads I knew then met ladies they settled down with and are still with today. Great weather, summer rugby with a great social side was a great combination for the some of my most enjoyable rugby.

My wife and I have some fond memories from those days and will always have a soft spot for that place. I am still in touch with many of the guys from there – Mark Wells, Oz, Fred Dougan and Marky B.

Clare and I have been together for over 12 years now and have two lovely children, Scarlett who is now five and Jack who has just turned two. Clare has supported me in my rugby and has kept me on the straight and narrow. She has played for the Army Rugby Union Ladies side and the Army Rugby League Ladies, being capped against the RAF before the Navy came into the competition.

Clare is also the Soldiers' League charity liaison officer for Combat Stress which stems from her job as a military community psychiatric nurse. She takes part in many fundraising events on behalf of Soldiers' League. Unfortunately, since the birth of our two munchkins I have been unable to persuade her to don her boots again.

Army Rugby Union

I was asked to join the Army Rugby Union coaching team as defence coach in 2008 by Andy Price, even though I didn't have any RU coaching qualifications. Andy was in the Welsh Guards and had gone through the coaching ranks of the ARU. He was a big man with an even bigger character and had been a prop forward in his day. He had assembled a coaching team of me as defensive coach; Lee Douglas as backs coach and himself as forwards coach. Lee was a northern lad who was in the PT Corps and in his last year in the Army. We worked well together, the squad was very strong and the lads were very successful on the park with a pretty much unbeaten first season and a big win at Twickenham at the end of the year. There was a load of guys that I knew in the squad from my RL squad such as Ben Hughes, Nacka, Ben Seru, Gerrard Wessels, Ceri Cummins, Kenny Downing, Taff Gittings, Sammy Speight, Gus Qasevakatini, Stuart Silvester, Gareth Slade-Jones, Joe Carver and Taff Evans.

I had explained to Andy that the Army RL had to come first because I was their coach. He agreed and was happy to still take me on board, but I remember missing the first Twickenham photo because the Army RL team had a game in Gloucester.

The success carried on with some cracking wins on the anniversary tour of Australia and New Zealand. The Fiji leg was cancelled because of a coup in the country which meant it was a risk travelling there. I remember staying in the Manly Pacific hotel on Manly beach where the Australian side were staying. The Great Britain rugby league touring side had also stayed there and I saw some pictures of them in the roof top swimming pool overlooking the beach, we were doing exactly the same thing, what a place.

The next season was much of the same. Lee Douglas left the Army and another northern mate of mine came on board as backs coach, Chris Brown, who also had a rugby league background. There was no change in the results and Andy Price had things going really well with further success and a really strong squad of blokes.

In South Africa there were more wins against strong opposition with fast flowing rugby. The Army RU guys got the red carpet treatment with really plush hotels in Cape Town. I remember thinking I wish I could win the Lottery and pay for the Army RL guys to get the same treatment. The hotel was amazing and the 'Kangaroo court' was special with Chris Brown coming in for more stick than me. Another win at Twickenham and it seemed like we couldn't go wrong. But as with all sports it all had to end sometime.

I remember we had trained well in South Africa and the camp had gone really well, but on the news the UK had the Ash cloud over it and the flights were all cancelled. This led to a massive delay getting back. At one point it looked like we would be driving back and there was talk of the tournament being cancelled. This didn't happen, but the RAF game was called off and the lads just got back in time for the Twickenham match against the Navy, no excuses but it did disrupt the preparation. The families of the squad must have been stressed with the delay. It's particular hard on them with the guys away for even longer than planned.

Army Rugby Union

The 2011 Defence Forces World Cup winning squad.

Celebrations after beating the Royal Navy at Twickenham.
(Both photos: Courtesy Ben Hughes)

Gosport Rugby Union club at Twickenham to play Halifax. Sitting next to Sean is Mark Wells, who was best man at Sean and Clare's wedding. Dave Goddard and Steve Emm also played for the team, along with other Forces union and league players.

We ended up at Twickenham for what would have been a fourth success for me, and a 10th for the team. But disaster struck for the team when the Navy turned us over with two of our guys getting sin-binned in the final 10 minutes. The beer didn't flow as well that night and it was a quiet affair. Andy, fair play to him, was a good sport and as a good coach should do, was able to man up and did the interviews and speeches. I thought that would be the end of my RU coaching stint.

This wasn't to be however, because Andy Sanger, another former rugby league player and coach, came on board and kept me as his defensive coach. We ripped into it for another season. We got revenge over the Navy at Twickenham and went on to tour Australia and New Zealand, including winning the RU Defence Forces World Cup. This was another great experience and although it is not quite the high of playing, it certainly give me some pleasure seeing the guys beat the Aussies in the final. The tournament was also played alongside the RU World Cup and this give the guys a wonderful opportunity to be at the World Cup final, which as you can imagine they took full advantage of.

I felt I had built some bridges with the other code, I had certainly made some good friends. I especially remember being 'beasted' on some of the 'Kangaroo courts' by Byron and Georgie Kemble. I also met some great players, too many to mention. App Satala and Damu both got international recognition; Appo for Fiji and Damu for England 7s. We also had Chris Budgen, who was playing in the Premiership for Exeter and Mark Lee who played for Scotland 7s. They had some talent in the squad and it was great to work with them.

This all came to an end in 2012 because Andy Sanger moved on and I went to Afghanistan, on my return I didn't jump back into it because my family deserves more out of me. I keep an eye on the results and wish the ARU boys all the success and thank them for my time with them, particular Andy Price for getting me on board and Ben Hughes for making the transition a little easier.

Who knows what the future holds? In a short time Army Rugby League has come a long way, having pretty much finished playing now my focus has changed to assisting the development of rugby league in the Army. Part of that development is partnership with Army rugby union, something unheard of in the not so distant past. Rugby league has been a professional sport for 100 years longer than union, but in the Army it's the other way round. The ARU has been around for 100 years longer than the rugby league in the Army and that time and experience can be utilised.

My first team rugby days have come to an end and my career in the Army is gradually coming to an end. I was posted from Salisbury (Westdown Camp) back to Aldershot, the home of the British Army were I have spent most of my days in the Army.

I have met some great people down at Westdown in the middle of the Salisbury plain training area, not just the squaddies, some of the training involved a company called Amputees' in Action (A@A) and this is where my eyes were opened to the courage of some great professional people.

The Army uses the company A@A to add some realism to the training and it certainly works, if you have a weak stomach it can be a testing when you first get eyes on. The guys and girls that work for A@A are from all different backgrounds' and it was an absolute pleasure getting to know them. Working with these guys' gives you a dose of humble pie, especially when you're having a bad day or just a bit fed up. Seeing them and how they lead their lives, I couldn't believe how proactive and positive these people are. One, pretty much a triple amputee through Meningitis was getting about with the use of prosthetic limbs. She told me about her horse riding and I was very impressed with the way she grabbed life and got on with it. Another guy was involved in a horrific motorcycle accident, is very committed and goes above and beyond the call of duty to make sure the soldiers get the best possible training. Someone else I met had lost both his legs.

In 2012 I was in Afghanistan for six months as a Staff Sergeant, mainly going out on patrol as a medic. I was based in Aldershot, but in 2013 was posted to the West Midlands.

I was looking forward to the Armed Forces World Cup, although due to military commitments and a knee injury I was not involved this time. It was a chance to show the Armed Forces in a good light, and to promote services rugby league. I would like to see the RFL link up with the forces more. There are very many young people in the armed forces who want to be involved in sport, and it's a great opportunity for the game. There are around 170,000 people in the forces; add their families and that's a big number. Rugby union put big resources into their services teams, and I think the RFL should help us build the game more. In Australia the league authorities give the forces teams a lot of support, and we need the same.

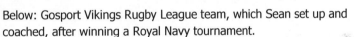

Top: Clare Fanning with Richie Yeomans, Mick Scholes and Richard Naivalurua when she received her Army RL cap.

Left: Clare when playing for Fort Blockhouse. Her coach (Sean) recalls being surprised at how tough and aggressive the tackling was in the Ladies' matches.

Below: Gosport Vikings Rugby League team, which Sean set up and coached, after winning a Royal Navy tournament.

Sean, Clare, Scarlett and Jack on top of the Wrekin Hill in Shropshire.

Sean presenting Tim Tamani with his shirt before the Inter-Services match against the Royal Navy in 2012. (Photo: Julie Hulatt)

Top: Sean with the 4 Medical Regiment Rugby Union team on tour in Germany in 2010.

Left: Sean visiting the tombstone for Anne Frank and her older sister Margot at Auschwitz on the above tour. They are believed to be buried in one of the mass graves which can be seen in the background.

Bottom: Reading RFC where Sean was coach.

From the top left, clockwise: Robbie Paul with capped Army players at a Soldiers' League dinner; Sean and Wayne Okell; The Veterans team (photo: Julie Hulatt); Sean and former England scrum-half Matt Dawson at an Army RU training camp; and Vets Dean Lewis, Anthony Cowburn and Sean attempt to stop former Great Britain international forward Barrie McDermott (Photo: Julie Hulatt).

10. Before recognition: The Army & Rugby League
By Graham Williams

This book focuses on the achievements and people of Army Rugby League since the sport's recognition as an official Army sport in 1994. However, we felt it was important to examine the period up to recognition. For all this time, rugby union was a solely amateur sport, and only went 'open' (i.e. allowing professionalism) in 1995; after rugby league had been recognised in the Army.

At times, the relationship between the two codes was difficult, and this is reflected in this chapter. Rugby league players beyond school age, both amateur and professional, until the 1980s, were not allowed to play rugby union by the rugby union authorities. However, today, with both codes having amateur and professional players, some of whom play both, and sharing stadiums and other facilities, the relationship is more cordial.

This is also true in the Army. Players play both codes, coaches have at times worked in both codes, and the Army Rugby Stadium in Aldershot is home to both codes. For one season, in 2010, Andy Sanger MBE was coach of both first teams, which is probably unique, and must have been exhausting.

The political work done by David Hinchliffe MP, Ian McCartney MP, and their colleagues in the All-Party Parliamentary Rugby League Group to help win recognition was covered in detail in David Hinchliffe's book *Rugby's Class War* (London League Publications Ltd, 2000) and is only covered briefly in this chapter.

When formed in August 1895, the Northern Union (NU), the forerunner of today's Rugby Football League (RFL), had been focused on establishing a senior competition, the Northern Rugby League (NRL). Over the next few years, circumstances dictated that the new Union had to widen its horizons and also take responsibility for a network of junior clubs spread across the northern counties of England. All this had been achieved in the face of the Rugby Football Union's (RFU) open hostility.

During that time, the NU appears to have made no significant effort to get its game played in the Army – not even in those regiments that drew recruits primarily from parts of the northern counties. This, in theory, should not have been too difficult as each of the infantry regiments had their own designated localities and so a number would have had a significant pool of NU players on which to draw. However, the regular Army at the start of the twentieth century was relatively small and around half of it at any time was to be found spread around the Empire – primarily in India and Ireland.

This was at a time when rugby football in the Army was poorly organised and not widely played. That changed at double quick time in 1906–07 after the formation of the Army Rugby Union (ARU) was approved by the Army Council on the last day of the year. Three weeks later the new body received the RFU's blessing and a trophy for inter-unit competition before finally an official Army XV met the Royal Navy (RN) at the end of February. There was a lot of ground to make up and the inaugural ARU Cup competition, held towards the end of 1906–07, attracted only 12 entrants. To help strengthen the teams, the RFU had granted a dispensation for former NU players to be used in the Cup competition.

The Great War

While the NU was not organising teams within the Army, a number of former soldiers were playing for its clubs at the highest level. Three of those former soldiers – Billy Jarman (Leeds), Jack Robinson and Walter Roman (both Rochdale Hornets) – were members of the 1914 British Lions tourists to Australia and New Zealand. During the five months the tourists were away, the assassination of Archduke Ferdinand in Sarajevo drew the United Kingdom into war. By the time the tourists arrived back in Plymouth on 27 September, the Army had been mobilised and those three former soldiers, who were still on the reserve list, were immediately recalled to the colours. Within days, Jarman had rejoined the Scots Guards and Robinson and Roman the Somerset Light Infantry. Both Jarman and Roman lost their lives in the ensuing conflict while Robinson suffered career-ending wounds.

While the tourists were waiting in Melbourne to complete their itinerary, Field Marshal Earl Kitchener, the Secretary of State for War, issued his appeal for 100,000 volunteers to fill up the first six divisions of his new Army. Within weeks, the first rugby union matches involving military teams were being organised as a way of encouraging men to join up and, in the process, raise funds for various wartime charities. One of the first of such teams was raised by the 4th Battalion of the Leicestershire Regiment, and took the field at Welford Road, Leicester after a military parade on 10 October. The Leicesters were very active throughout the conflict.

Four weeks later, a team representing Northern Command would take to the field in the same city. Regional military commands had not been particularly prominent in the rugby world prior to the outbreak of war, but Northern Command, which was based at York, and was responsible for military affairs on the eastern side of England, from the Scottish border to the east Midlands, would become very well-known over the coming years. Western Command, based at Chester, which held responsibility for a similar area on the western side of England, would not be quite so active.

One of the last of such matches, under Northern Union rules, took place at Birch Lane on Saturday 23 October 1915 when Bradford Northern took on a team from the locally based West Riding Brigade Royal Field Artillery (RFA). Although several of the Artillerymen had been connected with Northern prior to enlistment their team was not strong enough and lost 43–18. That weekend 68 men enlisted in the City of Bradford, 15 joining the RFA, which was considered a good figure, but not good enough as the war dragged on.

Even though by the end of 1915 over a million men had responded to Kitchener's appeal and joined the colours, still more men were needed and conscription had to be introduced for the first time at the end of January. The introduction of conscription practically ended the need for recruitment campaigns and changed many people's attitude to sport in wartime. As Britain struggled to train and equip the largest Army it had ever assembled and house the large numbers of Dominion troops that were also arriving in the country, occasional rugby matches became equally important both as a way of keeping the troops occupied and also for boosting the morale of the civilian population. At a time of extreme crisis for the nation, it seemed only common sense to many of the leading rugby unionists involved that the rigid peacetime rules setting out who could or could not play their game were divisive.

Responding to an invitation from Tom Crumbie, the honorary secretary of Leicester Tigers, to provide the opposition for a team he had selected, a Leicestershire Military XV, Bob Oakes, the honorary secretary of the Yorkshire Rugby Union, and himself the son of an Army sergeant born in the militia barracks at Hartlepool, raised his own Yorkshire Military XV. When some of his selected team failed to travel to Leicester on Saturday 12 February 1916, Oakes had to find replacements at short notice and he was prepared to confound pre-war sensibilities to make sure the match went ahead. Two of those drafted in were NU professionals serving with the West Yorkshire Regiment – Private Jimmy Sanders, Leeds's Welsh half-back, and Private Fred Longstaff, Huddersfield's international forward. A crowd of 4,000 watched the two teams finish all square, 16 points apiece.

When he returned home, Oakes worked to raise a new rugby union side, the North of England Military team, with the approval of Northern Command. Oakes made arrangements to play three friendlies in April and May 1916. For these matches, which generated great enthusiasm among players and spectators alike, Oakes determined not just to use NU players as necessary replacements, but to feature them as high profile members of his team.

Four leading players who had appeared in the NU test team, all members of Huddersfield's hugely successful 'Team of all the Talents' – captain and centre Harold Wagstaff, half-back Johnny Rogers, and forwards Douglas Clark and Ben Gronow – were featured in the side. Alongside them in those Northern Military sides were fellow test centre and former Welsh rugby union international, Willie A. Davies (Leeds), and the uncapped full-back Billy Seddon (Wigan).

The first match was held at Headingley on Saturday 8 April where Oakes's team beat the Australasian Forces 13–11 in front of 10,000 spectators. Four former Kangaroos – Viv Farnsworth (Oldham), Tommy Gleeson (Huddersfield) and Hull's Jim Devereux and Sid Deane – played for the Australasian Forces. Three weeks later, on Saturday 29 April, Oakes took his team to the Victoria Ground, Hartlepool, the home of Hartlepool United, to meet a Tees and Hartlepool Garrison XV. Finally, on Saturday 20 May, an Oakes XV met a Welsh XV at Anfield, the home of Liverpool AFC. The Welsh team, which it was stated was composed entirely of men in essential work, was raised by Captain Walter Rees, the Secretary of the Welsh RFU. A crowd estimated somewhere between 15,000 and 20,000 watched the match.

As a result of Oakes' activities, the RFU and the Welsh RFU agreed to suspend the professional laws as they applied to men in uniform for the duration of the war. The RFU issued the following statement on 4 October, supposedly clarifying the position as far as NU players were concerned: "Northern Union players can only play with Rugby Union players in bona-fide Naval and Military teams. Rugby Union teams can play against Naval and Military teams in which there are Northern Union players. Munitions workers cannot be regarded as Naval and

Military players. These rulings only apply during the war." The RFU's statement gave the go ahead for what was already happening in the ranks.

ASC (Motor Transport) team

The ASC (Motor Transport) team was the brainchild of Robert V. Stanley, a Major serving with the Motor Transport Army Service Corps (ASC) based at Grove Park in London, who represented Oxford University on the RFU committee. Recognising the benefits brought by the Service matches organised by the likes of Bob Oakes, Stanley assumed for himself and his unit the task of providing similar top-class rugby union in the Home Counties.

Through his many connections, Stanley's unit was able to both obtain the services of many internationals from both codes and also to arrange an extensive fixture list. Led by Malcolm Neale, the former Bristol and England union international, Stanley's team broke down barriers by fielding five leading members of Huddersfield NUFC – three of whom Douglas Clark, Ben Gronow and Harold Wagstaff had appeared for Oakes, plus Albert Rosenfeld (Australia) and Bill Trevarthen (New Zealand). Not surprisingly, their play had a major impact on the rugby game in the Home Counties.

Between September 1916 and January 1917, the ASC had played 18 matches, winning 17 against the likes of the Royal Engineers, the Public School Services XV, the Royal Flying Corps, a New Zealand Military XV and the Manchester Regiment, scoring 907 points while conceding only 32. While some viewed the ASC as one of the strongest sides ever seen in the capital, others pointed out correctly that a fair proportion of their opponents were scratch sides including convalescents, public schoolboys and a good number of average club players. Keen to see the ASC matched against worthy opponents, a Scot, Dr J.A. Russell-Cargill, assembled a strong United Services' team and arranged to use the Rectory Field at Blackheath. When the whistle sounded, ASC had suffered its first defeat, 6–3, largely as a result of the Services' pack gaining the upper hand. The ASC later won a return match against United Services 17--5.

In a review of the season's play, it was recorded in *The Tatler* on 28 March that the ASC had played and won 21 of their 22 matches scoring 1,046 points whilst only conceding 27. Single-handedly, Ben Gronow had contributed 106 goals and 20 tries to that points total. That same article rated two products of the NU's junior ranks, Harold Wagstaff and Douglas Clark respectively, as the best back and one of the best forwards seen in wartime matches. Sadly, it proved impossible for the ASC to arrange a match with either the Welsh XV or the RN Depot team from Devonport up to that point. That review contributed greatly to the break-up of the ASC team; within weeks, the players received their postings, many of them to the Middle East.

On some Saturdays when there was no scheduled senior opposition, occasional matches were organised between NRL clubs – Barrow, Bradford Northern, Hull and Oldham – and military units, mostly ones affiliated to the ARU like the Duke of Wellington's (West Riding) Regiment and the Leicestershire Regiment. Sometimes the matches were played under NU rules, sometimes under RFU rules. The receipts from these matches were generally donated to a war charity.

The   Battalion of the Manchester Regiment was raised in Oldham in August 1914 and was later designated as part of the training reserve. Many of the town's NRL club's players would pass through its ranks on their way to front-line units. Although the Battalion was stationed at Colchester, its officers were happy for a match to be arranged between their team and Oldham at the Watersheddings where the home side won 13–0 under NU rules on 30 December 1916. On the day, the Battalion team contained seven players – Jimmy Parkinson, the Australian Viv Farnsworth, Tom Grimes, Tommy Brice, Fred Wise, Charlie Waye and Tom McCabe – with Oldham first team experience.

While the Manchesters were stationed down south, they met amongst others the Coldstream Guards, the West Sussex Yeomanry and an Australian Services XV at Colchester on 25 March 1917, all under RFU rules. One of the strongest combinations in the south of England was the Public School Services XV (including A.L. Gracie and F.W. Gilligan) and it inflicted the first defeat on the Manchesters thanks to W.A. Stewart, the Scottish wing, who dropped two remarkable goals from near the touch-line and close to half-way.

At the start of the Great War, the ARU Cup was suspended but some of the Army's regional Commands continued with their own competitions. A Northern Command Military Cup was organised and the final held at the Boulevard prior to the Hull versus Hunslet match on Saturday 17 November 1917. Northern Command appeared ambivalent about which set of rugby laws should be used and the final was played under NU rules. Watched by General Sir Stanley van Donop, the final was contested by teams from the Leicestershire and Manchester Regiments. Despite the Manchester team including the recuperating Lieutenant James Parkinson, the Oldham full-back, in its ranks, the Leicestershire Regiment emerged victorious 10–3. Afterwards, a silver cup and medals were presented to the winners. General van Donop congratulated the players on a vigorous contest and went on to say that he hoped that the same spirit of earnestness would be shown in the sterner fight ahead.

The Victoria Cross

While Jack Harrison was the only active professional to be awarded the Victoria Cross, two other recipients in 1917 are known to have strong links to the game thanks to an article in the *Yorkshire Post* on Friday 22 December 2006.

Thomas Steele was born in the village of Springhead near Oldham on 6 February 1891. Just before the outbreak of war Steele joined up and found himself posted to a Scottish unit, the Battalion of the Seaforth Highlanders. Steele saw service on the Western Front in 1914 and 1915, but by 1917, he was to be found in Mesopotamia with the rank of sergeant. On 22 February 1917, the Highlanders were trying to break the siege laid by the Turks around Sanna-y-Yat, 500 miles from Basra. On that day, Steele's decisive action kept the trench line intact and prevented a successful enemy assault. After the war, Steele made three appearances for Broughton Rangers as part of a brief attempt to forge a professional career. Although in that he was unsuccessful, Steele regularly played for an Oldham amateur team, Healey Street Adults, which won the Standard Cup in 1924–25. Unable to settle back into civilian life, Steele moved to

Leicester around 1930 where he involved himself in the running of the Territorial Battalion of the Leicestershire Regiment. Towards the end of his life, Steele returned home to Oldham where he died in July 1978, aged 87.

Thomas Bryan had worked in the mines around Castleford and played for the town's original NU club in its last season, 1906–07, prior to enlisting in April 1915. By the start of 1917 Bryan was a Lance Corporal in the Service Battalion of the Northumberland Fusiliers' Brigade, known as the Tyneside Irish. The Fusiliers were part of the force taking part in the Arras offensive in April 1917. During that attack, near Vimy Ridge, on 8 April, Bryan, although wounded, single-handedly silenced a machine gun that was inflicting severe losses on his unit. Bryan survived the war, returning to the mines around Castleford and later Doncaster. He died in Bentley, Doncaster, aged 63 in October 1945.

The Armistice

Immediately the Armistice was signed, Lloyd George, the British Prime Minister, announced the end of conscription. Less than a month later it was clear that the liberal phase of relations between the two codes was truly over. On 11 December, Hunslet received a letter from the Royal Garrison Artillery Depot at Ripon informing them that the home and away fixtures arranged earlier would have to be cancelled. The Artillery had been forced to take this action, in the best interest of their players, as a result of instructions received from the RFU Secretary, Captain C.J.B. Marriott. It was naturally expected that the planned fixtures against Leeds and Halifax would also be cancelled.

After the Armistice, the New Zealand Expeditionary Force assembled a Rugby Union touring party drawn from the many regiments stationed in western-Europe. To make sure nothing untoward might be going on, the Welsh RFU in common with the other Home Unions refused in January 1919 to permit any game against the New Zealand Army teams without a guarantee that they were all amateurs. An irate service officer was moved to write in *Truth* "just as though it matters a damn whether they are amateurs or professionals when they have come all this way to fight and die for us". The magazine's editor added the rider that "the regenerating and purifying influence of the Great War is working in a mysterious way".

An Inter-Services tournament, for the King George V trophy, was organised by the ARU in March and April 1919 and involved a number of service teams. When approached about the use of its ground at Inverleith in Edinburgh for two of the matches, the Scottish RFU let it be known that no assistance would be offered if any professionals were to be selected in any of the teams appearing there.

After that tournament was completed, the New Zealand Service team continued to play matches around Britain. The last of the New Zealanders' fixtures, against Northern Command in aid of St. Dunstan's, was scheduled for Saturday 10 May at Headingley. As the day of the match approached, the ARU decided to ban the fixture on the grounds that Headingley was a NU ground. It was pointed out to the ARU that although the ground was the home of Leeds NUFC, its use was allowed because the professionals would gain no pecuniary benefit. With two days to spare the ARU relented and the match went ahead. A scratch Northern Command team took the field without any NU presence, many of the leading representatives having been either demobbed or allowed to rejoin their old clubs.

The Army Sports Control Board

One of the lessons learnt from the Great War was that the Army need a central body controlling the sports that were played. To meet those needs, the Army Sports Control Board (ASCB) was formed in November 1918 and brought together those sports' bodies that were already in existence. With practically no track record and no Army organisation, there was no place for the NU on the new Board. Without recognition and an organisation of its own, the NU was effectively stranded in no mans' land.

At its first post-war committee meeting on 14 January 1919, the RFU announced its major concession – any Northern Unionist remaining in the Armed Forces would be allowed to play Rugby Union so long as they did not resume playing or conclude any agreement with a NU club. Three months later the RFU prevented its civilian member clubs from playing against service teams containing any NU players.

As details of a letter reproduced in *The History of Army Rugby* make clear, the old ways were to be reintroduced immediately: "It has been brought to the notice of the ARU that cases have occurred during the war where Inter-Unit rugby football competitions have been held under NU rules for Cups or medals presented by clubs or individuals. I am directed by the Committee of the ARU to point out that soldiers taking part in any such competition in future will forfeit their right to come under terms of the amnesty granted to Army players".

As the book also outlines; "In the same year it was decided that unless absolutely unavoidable no NU player should be included in any trial match played with a view to selecting representative teams." Effectively, former NU players would be restricted to inter-unit matches. This had become more of an issue because the ARU along with the Royal Navy RU had decided to make its teams truly representative. The Army versus Royal Navy fixture at Twickenham on 28 February 1920 was the first time that other ranks were eligible for selection.

Despite the restrictions, some northern regiments, such as the King's Own Royal Regiment, worked around the great divide. The Regiment's depot at Lancaster happily accepted an invitation to spend a day at Millom RLFC on Friday 28 October 1927 and put out a team to meet and lose to the locals 41–0. Six months later, the Regiment's Battalion, stationed at Aldershot, not only entered the ARU Cup, but went on to reach the final where they narrowly lost to the holders, the Battalion South Wales Borderers.

Professional recruitment

While it may be true that the RFL had no official interest in Army rugby, that was not true for all sections of the professional game. NRL scouts were very active and following up tip offs from friends and acquaintances in the Army's ranks turned up some real talent for their clubs and the national team.

A good performance for their regiment, perhaps followed by an appearance in the Army XV, soon attracted the scouts' attention. If the serviceman was interested in taking up professional rugby then he had to purchase his discharge from the Army. With the assistance of his new club – to cover the cost which would be somewhere between £25 and £100 between the wars – the player was able to turn his back on the colours and pursue a new career. Some of them made it right to the top in their new careers.

Tommy Rees had been a collier in his native Pontyclun before joining the Welsh Guards. A full back, he made six appearances for the Army XV and won four Welsh caps, between 1926 and 1928. There would have been more had not a broken leg written off much of 1926–27. Rees made his debut for Oldham RLFC, aged 24, against Salford on 25 August 1928. He made a solitary appearance for Great Britain against Australia in October 1929.

Jim Croston, Wigan born but Dublin raised, made two appearances for the Army XV in March 1933. His play was noted and he was invited for a trial at Castleford. He appeared as 'A.N. Other' against Bradford Northern on 7 October 1933 and scored a try. That performance led to him being bought out of the Royal Engineers by Captain J.A. Pickles, the Castleford secretary. Croston appeared in the centre in one test for Great Britain against Australia in October 1937 and also made five appearances for England between 1936 and 1939.

Ted Sadler, who had made seven appearances for the Army XV between 1931 and 1933 and won two England union caps as a wing-forward in 1932–33, was bought out of the Royal Signals by Oldham in 1933. Sadler was almost immediately sought by Captain Pickles and his transfer to Castleford was completed in time for him to make his debut in February 1934. He won an England rugby league cap while with Oldham in December 1933.

Frank Whitcombe hailed from Cardiff and made two appearances for the Army XV at prop in March 1935. He was bought out of the Royal Engineers by Broughton Rangers later in 1935. Aged 23, Whitcombe made the first of his nine appearances for the Welsh league team in November 1938 and went on to make two test appearances for Great Britain on the 1946 'Indomitables' tour of Australasia.

The Second World War

Sadly, the Great War did not prove to be the war to end all wars. Just over two months into a new conflict, on 12 November 1939, the RFU passed a resolution allowing rugby league players in the Armed Forces, who had had no association with rugby league since their enlistment, to participate in union matches between clubs and service teams for the duration. That resolution accepted that:

a. A Rugby XV may play against a Service XV containing players who have played Rugby League football.

b. A Rugby Union XV may include Rugby League players belonging to His Majesty's Forces when playing matches against Service teams.

c. A Rugby Union XV may include Rugby League players belonging to the Forces when playing against another Rugby Union club.

As in the previous conflict, the Welsh RFU followed the RFU's lead whereas the Scottish RFU insisted that the ban on rugby league players taking part in any match against a team under its jurisdiction must remain in force. The pattern set in the Great War was set to continue. When he received the news of the RFU's decision, John Wilson, the secretary of the RFL, was quoted as saying he was "very glad. It is the proper thing that all men in the Army should be allowed to play football together without any restrictions."

And there was quite a lot of rugby to be played. Although the Inter-Service competition was not held for six years, the Army maintained a programme of high profile matches featuring the RAF, an Irish XV in Belfast and a South Wales XV at Swansea. Many servicemen enjoyed the chance to take part in some high quality rugby union – quite a number of them former or current rugby league professionals thanks to the dispensation agreed by the RFU.

Although transport continued to be a major headache for fixture organisers, the threat of invasion and acute shortages had eased sufficiently for a programme of wartime rugby union internationals to begin during 1941–42, under the auspices of the Inter-Services Committee. Those Service internationals, as they were known, created great public interest as well as healthy proceeds for Service charities. For many sportsmen, the war not only threatened to end their lives, but the possibility they may have had of a successful sporting career. Those unofficial international matches played a very valuable role in providing, at least for a few prominent soldiers fortunate enough to be billeted in Britain, the opportunity to represent their country in a uniform other than worsted.

Between March 1942 and April 1945, England played 16 matches against Scotland and Wales – while the latter two countries played only eight as they never arranged to meet each other. A number of serving rugby league players, many of whom were pre-war union internationals, were selected to appear alongside various past and future internationals for the English and Welsh sides. Despite their hostility to the whole idea, Scotland did agree to meet English teams containing league men. The Scots even allowed some professionals to set foot on Murrayfield's previously unsullied turf once it was released from its role as a supply depot by the War Office. Suddenly, a host of professionalised players with a strong union background were made available to the Welsh team, their English equivalents having had in most cases only a brief flirtation with the union game. For the record, the English Services included six Army rugby league backs – Stan Brogden (Hull), Roy Francis (Barrow), Albert Johnson (Warrington), Harold Pimblett (St Helens), Jimmy Stott (St Helens) and Ernest Ward (Bradford Northern). Some strange military logic must have been at work to push a Welshman into those English teams, but once done it could not be undone and Roy Francis just had to accept the decision and make the best of his time as an England threequarter. Only three Army professionals found their way into the English pack – Ted Bedford (Hull KR), Ned Hodgson (Broughton Rangers) and Ken Jubb (Leeds).

In every international, the Welsh Services proved to be a very effective combination; their outstanding backs enabling them to record seven victories over England from their eight meetings. So total was the integration that Gus Risman of Salford was even accorded the honour of captaining the team when his commitments to the Airborne Division permitted. Only one other Army professional took the field alongside Risman in the Welsh backs and that was Syd Williams (Salford). Included in the Welsh pack were six 'professional' soldiers – Emrys Evans (Salford), Trevor Foster (Bradford Northern), Doug Phillips (Oldham), Jim Regan (Huddersfield), Harold Thomas (Salford) and Gwyn Williams (Wigan).

Northern Command

The Northern Command Sports Board (NCSB) arranged an extensive rugby union fixture list during the conflict, its teams regularly containing a large number of rugby league players. Rugby league grounds such as Belle Vue, Fartown (in Huddersfield) and Headingley were regularly made available for Northern Command matches and brought increased proceeds, which in many cases went to the Northern Command Welfare Funds.

In addition, the NCSB organised a sevens tournament, which was first played at Odsal Stadium on 15 April 1944. Eight teams, six of which were mixed between League and Union took part in the tournament. The two non-mixed teams were both of Scottish origin. The Rugby League seven defeated the Rugby Union seven in front of 18,000 spectators. The NCSB held another sevens tournament at Headingley on 12 May 1945.

There was a particular significance to the meeting of Northern Command and a Yorkshire Services XV, a team mostly drawn from the Catterick Garrison, at Odsal Stadium on Saturday 15 February 1941 besides the fact that 22 of the 30 players on the pitch were attached to NRL clubs. In the programme for a match that Northern Command won 17–5, it was stated that the two teams had issued a joint challenge to Bradford Northern to meet if the latter retained the Rugby League Championship.

Northern duly did its bit by beating Wigan in mid-April to set up a meeting with a military team under Rugby League rules. The first indication that the challenge would be honoured came on Monday 26 May when it was announced that Bradford Northern would play an Army XIII on Saturday 7 June. Even though a team had been named, that match did not go ahead. However, it was finally played as an opener for the third wartime season. On Saturday 30 August, Bradford Northern took on and beat an Army XIII 24-21 in front of 4,000 spectators. The Army XIII, which on the day was all Army except for a stand-in Welsh RAF scrum half, had the honour of being the first ever representative service rugby league team.

John Wilson had a good working relationship with Northern Command and he used it to try and help the beleaguered members of the War Emergency League. At the start of 1942–43, he secured a concession from Northern Command that no rugby league players would be called upon for rugby union matches. Initially, this concession only applied to representative matches, but was later in the season extended to cover local unit matches.

As the war situation eased, there were indications that Northern Command was still prepared to slip the occasional rugby league match into its busy schedule. Northern Command issued a challenge to the Yorkshire Cup holders, Dewsbury, and a match was approved by a meeting of the RFL's emergency committee on Wednesday 9 December 1942. Eddie Waring's men were well prepared but proved no match for a strong Army team, who won 21–10 on 2 January 1943. The proceeds of the match, £180, went to the Red Cross Prisoners of War Relief Fund.

That was probably enough for the Rugby League authorities at the time. Setting up an official Army Rugby League would certainly have created some conflict. Some of that conflict would have been with the ARU, which would not have wanted to lose its primacy or its access to all rugby players. There would also probably have been conflicts between the military selectors and those clubs that were still functioning in the wartime emergency leagues, which at a time when player availability was a major problem, would have been extremely unwilling to lose players to more service matches.

Army Rugby League

However, there were signs that a more open, enlightened approach to rugby league might be on the way. Yet despite much lobbying in 1941, the RFL was unable to set up an official fixture and its officials became extremely frustrated by the failure of the ASCB to assemble a representative Army XIII. Northern Command took it upon itself to approach the RFL and reached agreement for a match to be played between teams selected by them under Rugby League rules. The results, attendances and members of those teams, which in 1943–44 was described as an Army XIII, are listed below.

21 March 1942: RL XIII 18 Northern Command 22 at Halifax (crowd: 6,000)
Northern Command: E. Ward (Bradford N), D. Case (Bradford N), G.R. Pepperell (Huddersfield), A. Langley (Featherstone R), R.W. Lloyd (Castleford); R.L. Francis (Barrow), T.N. Walsh (Castleford); D.R. Prosser (Leeds), L.L. White (Hunslet), L. White (York), T. Foster (Bradford N), K. Jubb (Leeds), E. Tattersfield (Leeds).
Scorers: Tries: Case, Pepperell, Francis, Walsh. *Goals:* Ward 5.

10 October 1942: RL XIII 10 Northern Command 14 at Hull (5,000)
Northern Command: E. Ward (Bradford N), H. Mills (York), G.R. Pepperell (Huddersfield), R.L. Francis (Barrow), R.W. Lloyd (Castleford), O. Morris (Leeds), W. Thornton (Hunslet), K. Jubb (Leeds), L.L. White (Hunslet), L. Garner (St Helens), T. Foster (Bradford N), E. Tattersfield (Leeds), W.G. Chapman (Warrington).
Scorers: Tries: Lloyd, Chapman, Foster 2. *Goal:* Ward

18 December 1943: RL XIII 11 Army 4 at Halifax (2,500)
Army: L. Davies (Featherstone R); W. Dockar (Hull), E. Ward (Bradford N), G. Price (Leeds), K. Davies (Keighley); W.T. Davies (Huddersfield), L. Garbutt (Castleford); D.R. Prosser (Leeds), G.S. Brown (Batley), J. Rhodes (Batley), T. Foster (Bradford N), S. Newbound (Hunslet), E. Tattersfield (Leeds).
Substitute: L.L. White (Hunslet) for Brown. Brown retired after 15 minutes to allow White, who had been delayed, to take the field as selected. Len Garbutt replaced Reg Lloyd who was still 15 miles from Thrum Hall when the match ended.
Goals: Ward 2.

7 October 1944:RL XIII 27 Northern Command 23 at Huddersfield (3,500)
Northern Command: H. Lockwood (Halifax); O. Peake (Warrington), E. Ward (Bradford N), S. Brogden (Hull), N. Guest (Castleford); W.T. Davies (Huddersfield), T.N. Walsh (Castleford); J.H. Fox (Castleford), W.E. Colbert (Batley), L. Rees (Oldham), T. Foster (Bradford N), G.S. Brown (Batley), E. Tattersfield (Leeds).
Scorers: Tries: Brogden 2, Guest, Brown, Tattersfield. *Goals:* Davies 3, Lockwood.

Western Command

Over in Western Command's area, where there was much less senior rugby league being played, a similar pattern was followed of selecting rugby league professionals and using rugby league grounds. Watersheddings, where former Lieutenant Jimmy Parkinson was now club President, was made available for a match against Northern Command on 14 November 1942 and an Army XIII met St Helens on 13 February 1943. However, this was on a smaller scale than Northern Command which did more and as a result drew more attention.

Cross-code match

However, it was the NCSB's decision to organise a ground-breaking match at the Headingley Grounds, Leeds on Saturday 23 January 1943 between a Rugby Union XV and a Rugby League XV that is most remembered from those wartime years.

A luncheon was held prior to the match and it allowed a number of those involved with the match to air their views. Captain Stanley Wilson, who had organised the match for the NCSB, expressed his personal sentiments when he called "for the playing of an annual fixture between the Union and the League in the hope of eventually healing the breach". Responding, Bob Oakes, by now the Yorkshire Rugby Union President, stressed that while the two games would probably go their own separate ways after the war there could be no line of demarcation between men in uniform. Once more, he repeated his view that if a man was good enough to wear the King's uniform there should be no barrier to stop him playing any game he liked. John Wilson, while regretting the past, tacitly agreed with Oakes, but kept his options partially open by saying that he saw no reason why such a match should not become an annual event. The Union team's captain for this match, Captain N.M. Walford

(Oxford University), expressed plainly his own personal sentiments, saying "we are concerned solely with playing rugby and not whom we are playing with or against".

There was a crowd of 8,000 in the ground to see the League XV struggle to hold their opponents early on. According to Ken Dalby, despite half of the League pack being former Welsh Union players, the League XV were, as a result of their adaptation to the 'play-the-ball' rules, disadvantaged in the rucks and wanting practice at the line-outs. At half-back, the League XV had problems in the first-half, kicking far too infrequently to touch in defence. This was only to be expected when it is realised that their scrum-half, Billy Thornton (Hunslet) was playing only his second game of union. Unfortunately for the Union XV, Cowe had to leave the field in the second-half and that provided the League team with sufficient advantage to secure victory. The match was played in a good spirit and the play was good enough to ensure that future meetings would draw a crowd. Dalby recognised that among the players there was something extra about this match. It was more than an exhibition match and the League XV raised their game in the second-half to pull off a famous victory.

However, a note of discord was struck on the day when a message received from the Scottish RFU Secretary was made public. It raised concerns regarding Northern Command's next scheduled match against an Edinburgh University XV, the Scottish Secretary demanded assurances from Northern Command that no member of their chosen team would have played rugby league. When no such assurance was forthcoming the fixture was cancelled.

Although most team line-ups from the war do not give each player's rank the cross-code matches do and provide an intriguing insight into the nature of the two games at the time.

Rugby League XV (3) 18 Rugby Union XV (8) 11.

League: Cpl G.R. Pepperell (Huddersfield); Sgt-I R.L. Francis (Dewsbury), Trpr H. Mills (Hull), Pte J. Stott (St Helens), Cpl E.W. Lloyd (Castleford); L-Bdr H. Royal (Dewsbury), Sgm W. Thornton (Hunslet); Sgt-I D.R. Prosser (Leeds), L-Cpl L.L. White (Hunslet), Gnr L. White (York), Cpl K. Jubb (Leeds), Cpl E. Tattersfield (Leeds), Pte W. Chapman (Warrington), Cpl H. Bedford (Hull), Sgt-I T. Foster (Bradford Northern)
Tries: Jubb (2), Mills (2), Chapman, Tattersfield.
Union: Cpl J. Bond (Cumberland); Lt T.G.H. Jackson (Army), Capt N.M. Walford (Oxford University), Lt D.R. MacGregor (Rosslyn Park), Sgt-I D.F. Mitchell (Galashiels); -Lt L.B. Lockhart (Cambridge University), O-Cdt H. Tanner (Swansea); Major R.O. Murray (London Scottish), Sgm J.D.H. Hastie (Melrose), Cpl J. Maltman (Hawick), Cadet R.C.V. Stewart (Waterloo), Cpl R. Cowe (Melrose), -Lt R.A. Huskisson (Oxford University), Pte R.A. Crawford (Melrose), -Lt R.G. Furbank (Bedford).
Try: Walford. *Conversion:* Cowe. *Penalty Goals:* Cowe 2.

Combined Services teams
Rugby League Combined Services 15 Rugby Union Combined Services 10.

Saturday 29 April 1944 – organised by the Inter-Service Rugby Football Committee at Odsal Stadium, Bradford. Attendance: 18,000.

This was not strictly an Army match as all sections of the home-based Armed Forces were eligible for selection, which should have meant the teams were stronger, but they turned out weaker due to late withdrawals through injury. After initially struggling to cope with the union pack's open dribbling play and conceding two early tries, the league team mounted a fight back and eventually brought the scores level. It was the skill and artistry of the league team's backs which in the end determined the outcome of a close match. With three minutes remaining, the league men worked a memorable score for Brogden. For a second time victory had gone to the League's representatives.

The teams were:

League: L-Cpl E. Ward (Bradford Northern); Sgt-I R.L. Francis (Barrow), Cpl J. Stott (St Helens), LAC J. Lawrenson (Wigan), Cpl A. Edwards (Salford); Sgt S. Brogden (Hull), Bdr H. Royal (Dewsbury); Sgt-I D.R. Prosser (Leeds), Dvr L. White (Hunslet), LAC C. Brereton (Halifax), Dvr D. Murphy (Bramley), Flt-Sgt E. Watkins (Wigan), Sgt I.A. Owens (Leeds), Sgt W. Chapman (Warrington), Sgt-I T. Foster (Bradford Northern).

Union: CSM I. Trott (Penarth); Lt G. Hollis (Sale), Cpl T. Sullivan (Swansea), Lt H. Tanner (Swansea), Sub-Lt E.S. Simpson (Bradford); Lt T. Gray (Heriot's F.P.), Sqdn-Ldr J. Parsons (Leicester); Cpl R.J. Longland (Northampton), Sgt G.T. Dancer (Bedford), Capt R.E. Prescott (Harlequins), Lt P.M. Walker (Gloucester), Cpl D.V. Phillips (Swansea), Capt G.D. Shaw (Galashiels), Capt J.A. Waters (Selkirk), Flt-Lt R.G. Weighell (Waterloo).

When posted overseas, servicemen took whatever opportunities presented themselves to enjoy sport. For rugby league most of that activity was informally organised. However, in Egypt a Rugby League XV was organised to take part in local rugby union fixtures. Details of some of the more extraordinary informal matches can be found in the diary of Battery Sergeant Hawarden who recorded that two England versus Wales matches and a Lancashire versus Yorkshire match had been played by rugby league enthusiasts who were prisoners of war in Stalag 383 in Bavaria.

Offers of assistance from Northern Command, no matter how useful they might have been at the time, did not in themselves make up for a lack of official national recognition. If anything those offers tended to reinforce the idea that the game was limited to the northern counties of England. That situation in no way reflected the reality of Army life, which saw units regularly sent on tours of duty far away from home. Once away from the north, a rugby league player in one of those units had no chance to enjoy the concessions of Northern Command.

Being unrecognised did not mean that servicemen who had strayed outside the north could not play the game. If the soldiers of a particular unit wanted a game they could organise a team and with the permission of their commanding officer arrange matches. Outside the northern counties, that was not always straightforward, but many determined units persevered and arranged matches, although records are practically non-existent of their endeavours.

Top: Many professional sportsmen were Physical Training Instructors in the Second World War. This photo taken at the Army School of Physical Training at Aldershot in 1944 includes Sergeant-Instructor Trevor Foster MBE in the back row, one in from the right. Trevor went on to play for Great Britain and Wales, and was a stalwart of Rugby League in Bradford. He won the MBE for service to the community.
(Photo: Courtesy Simon Foster)

Left: The cover of the programme from the 1944 inter-code rugby union match at Odsal.
(Courtesy Peter Lush)

251

Although the full-scale global conflict had just about ended when the 1945–46 season began, the Army was still involved in a number of smaller, more local operations. The spirit of wartime unity prevailed for a little while longer, although player availability became more of an issue once the NRL restarted in August 1945. Northern Command continued to use Rugby League grounds, fielding a team containing several Rugby League players against a team drawn from the Second New Zealand Expeditionary Force at Headingley in mid-November and meeting Western Command at Fartown three weeks later.

Five members of the ARU party that had toured the continent, playing two matches against the new British Army of the Rhine (BAOR), returned just in time to play in the England versus Wales Rugby League international held at Swansea on Saturday 24 November 1945. While there was pressure for a return to peacetime operations, the military continued to organise its activities in 1945–46 largely as it had in wartime with one significant difference; for whatever reason there were no rugby league fixtures arranged by Northern Command.

A changing national situation did not mean that the ARU was keen to release all of its Rugby League players. Corporal Doug Phillips (Oldham and RAC) and Lance Corporal Ernest Ward (Bradford Northern and Lancashire Fusiliers) were still serving His Majesty in early 1946 when the selection process began for the hastily arranged Rugby League tour of Australasia. Neither Phillips nor Ward were released to take part in either of the two tour trials, but both were included when the names of the tour party were announced on Monday 11 March.

Both soldiers had played for the Army against the Royal Navy on 4 March and both would also be required to turn out against the RAF on 23 March. By the time the latter match was played, the RFL was urgently requesting information on the expected release date of the two players. When news was forthcoming on Monday 25 March, it was not good – the War Office announced that leave for Phillips had been refused while making no mention of Ward.

The following day, a group of Yorkshire MPs got together and put pressure on the War Office. But Services' rugby had not finished with either man yet and both were required to join a few of their fellow professionals in a Great Britain Services XV that met a Dominions' Services team at Leicester on Saturday 31 March. Finally, parliamentary pressure had the desired effect and Phillips and Ward were granted leave just in time for them to join the rest of the party on board HMS Indomitable before it set sail on the following Wednesday.

As war readiness was wound down, it immediately produced signs of the old absurdity returning into Army sport. For one of the Army XV, who had played alongside Phillips and Ward in the 1946 Inter-Service Competition, there were to be less welcome problems with officialdom. J.A. Gregory (RAMC) had taken the opportunity to experience rugby league at first hand by assisting the Huddersfield RLFC side while stationed near the town immediately after the war. Once this was known, and Gregory was open about it, he was banned by the RFU. Educated at a public school, Rydal in north Wales, Gregory, who had been a member of the RAMC depot team, based at Crookham Camp, Aldershot that had won the Army Cup in 1946–47 was an unlikely dissident, but it cut little ice when he applied, unsuccessfully, for re-instatement.

Spurred on by his commanding officer, a further application was made on Gregory's behalf by the ARU. Gregory's application was referred to a three-man sub-committee, which initially decided to confirm the player's expulsion before a more liberal view prevailed. Finally, it was decided that Gregory would be suspended for one season, the sentence running until the end of April 1948. After that, he was free to resume playing rugby union, which he did with Blackheath. An England 'cap' finally came his way when he was chosen on the wing for the match against Wales at Cardiff on 15 January 1949. It proved to be his only international appearance, but it was significant as the first awarded to a reinstated player.

The Grenadier Guards

In October 1949, a Rugby League team was raised from the Battalion of the Grenadier Guards, based at the Wellington Barracks. Corporal Hayes, who acted as the team's secretary, wrote to the fledgling London Amateur Rugby League requesting a match against Mitcham. Arrangements were quickly put in place and 10 days later, on Saturday 8 October, the Guards' team turned out at Mitcham Stadium. Permission to play had been requested and granted and the team travelled to Mitcham in an official Army truck and played in official Army kit.

The Grenadier Guards team

Three days after the match, the wider Army authorities took an interest. The players were called in and suspended from playing rugby union. In addition, warning notices were posted at various barracks and further games were banned. By the end of the year, the suspensions had been removed and the players 'pardoned' – this ensured that the Battalion's rugby union team would not be crippled by their loss – but were warned not to play rugby league again.

Articles in the rugby league press carried details of what it described as the 'Mitcham Incident' and speculated as to where the blame lay for the decision – was it with the ARU, the ASCB or the RFU? The press also mentioned that negotiations were on-going for an all-Army match at Mitcham. To ensure that it would be played, the article indicated that no details would be announced until the teams were on the field! Such clandestine manoeuvres hardly helped in getting commitment from any units that were wary of getting similarly involved.

However, according to the rugby league press there was clear evidence that there were several regiments containing men who were keen to play rugby league. The question was why did the ASCB, whose job it was to organise and supervise facilities for all games, not take steps to provide an official outlet for their enthusiasm? Or did the Board have its own agenda, which saw it favouring only certain sports at the expense of others?

James Audsley, writing in the *Rugby League Gazette*, strongly suggested the RFL should take up the matter with the War Office and if necessary raise the matter in the House of Commons, but instead of building momentum around the issue the game's leaders appeared to happy to leave it alone. There was some movement and the ASCB, keen to exonerate itself from any part in this shameful episode, issued a statement in mid-year confirming that soldiers were at liberty to play Rugby League if they so wished, but stopping well short of officially sanctioning the game.

The story from the *Rugby League Gazette*, February 1950.
The *Gazette* was the official journal of the RFL at this time.

National Service

To cope with the onset of the Cold War and the retreat from Empire, an increased military presence was needed and Clement Atlee's Labour Government reluctantly agreed in May 1947 to retain conscription. As a result, legislation was passed requiring all the country's young men to spend time serving His Majesty. National Service, as it was known, came into force on 1 January 1949 and covered all young men between the ages of 18 and 26. Initially, conscription lasted for 18 months, but this was increased to two years once the Korean War began.

A conscript could apply to defer his enlistment until he was older if he had a good reason, such as if he was following an apprenticeship or attending university, but most chose to join up at 18 and get it over and done with. The vast majority of those young men found themselves directed to the Army, the rest going almost totally to the RAF as the Royal Navy chose not to become too reliant on conscripts.

The RFU amended its regulations to include the following stipulations while conscription was in force:

c. A rugby union player is permitted whilst in HM Forces, to play for a Services team in a rugby league game but may not play for any civilian team.

d. A rugby league player is permitted whilst in HM Forces to play in a Rugby Union game for a team composed entirely of serving members of HM Forces against an English or Welsh Rugby Union team only.

e. A rugby league player who has played under the above may continue to play Rugby League Football for other than a Service team but cannot play Rugby Union Football except for a Service team.

While rugby league remained unrecognised, the only handling game generally open to those young conscripts was rugby union. Some Army units were only too pleased to recruit and harness the talent available in the absence of organised rugby league.

Major Gordon Fraser was with the Royal Corps of Signals' Training Regiment based at Catterick Camp. Being in a training regiment had advantages; the chance to learn technical skills that could lead to better employment prospects when they returned to civilian life was a significant attraction for many conscripts. Kept well informed by his many contacts, Fraser was able to attract and marshal some of the best young talent in the Army. A youthful Signals' side, combining the best of Union and League skills, proved capable of winning the ARU Cup on six occasions – 1948–49, 1949–50, 1950–51, 1952–53, 1953–54 and 1956–57.

The Signallers unprecedented success in the ARU Cup led to an unprecedented wave of resentment, which focused on the unfair advantage that training regiments apparently enjoyed. Not wishing to increase tensions further, the Signallers decided not to defend the trophy in 1954–55 while an investigation went ahead and possible changes to the competition were discussed. At the end of that process, all was found to be above board, the competition was left unchanged and the Signallers returned to the Cup in 1955–56.

The Signallers also entered the Yorkshire Rugby Union Cup, winning it twice, in 1951–52 and 1953–54. However, their success in the Cup caused problems and led to the County Union banning league servicemen from taking part in the competition. Among the Signals' squad were the likes of Billy Boston, Phil Jackson, Brian Gabbitas and Jimmy Dunn all future leading players in rugby league plus Russell Robbins, Phil Horrocks-Taylor and Reg Higgins all of whom went on to receive international rugby union honours.

While requiring their conscripts to be available for unit and regimental matches, commanding officers were often sympathetic towards a young player's professional ambitions. It was an arrangement that meant that a highly promising young professional like Gunner Ike Southward could, in spring 1956, enjoy being the toast of the crowd at both at the Military Stadium, Aldershot and Borough Park, Workington.

Southward was not the first to combine both roles. Syd Lowdon signed for Whitehaven RLFC, having previously played with Whitehaven RUFC, Cumberland and Westmorland RU and for the Army against the Royal Navy, in August 1954, halfway through his National Service with the Royal Artillery. Lowdon's switch to the professional ranks did not prevent him from regaining his place in the Army XV for the match against the RAF in March 1955.

If a player fancied giving Rugby League a try, but was unable to do that close to their home, then National Service offered a welcome opportunity as one young Welshman, Stan Owen, showed. Posted to the REME workshops at Burscough, near Ormskirk, Owen contacted Leigh to ask for a trial. Owen impressed and was signed on in December 1951, to begin a professional career that would last for nearly 15 years.

In some cases, commanding officers could be a bit difficult as another young Welshman found. Billy Boston signed for Wigan on Friday 13 March 1953, but the news was suppressed. Boston's signing was only officially announced after details appeared in the press. He did not play his first rugby league – an 'A' team match – until 31 October. A change of status did not prevent Boston from appearing in the Army XV.

As mentioned above those selecting ARU representative teams were also very keen to incorporate that professional talent, even if its rugby union experience was very limited. Among the many young servicemen who had already signed professional contracts, the following got the chance to tread Twickenham's lush turf while playing for the Army XV in the Inter-Service matches:

Jack Broome, RAOC and Wigan (1951–52, 1952–53)
Stan Owen, REME and Leigh (1952–53)
Billy Boston, Royal Signals and Wigan (1953–54)
Brian Gabbitas, Royal Signals and Hunslet (1953–54, 1954–55)
Phil Jackson, Royal Signals and Barrow (1953–54, 1954–55)
Ike Southward, Royal Artillery and Workington (1955–56, 1956–57)
Bobby Chisnall, Royal Artillery and Widnes (1956–57, 1957–58)
Jack Scroby, Duke of Wellington's Regiment and Bradford Northern (1957–58, 1958–59)
Brian Saville, Duke of Wellington's Regiment and Hull (1957–58)
Charlie Renilson, Duke of Wellington's Regiment and Halifax (1960–61)

Matches against the French Services

With the co-operation of Northern Command, which allowed leave, among other things, it was also possible for conscripts, selected by the RFL, to play for a Combined Services XIII against a French Combined Services League team. It had been intended that these matches would become an annual event to raise funds for service charities, but the teams only met on two occasions. Although these teams were described as Combined Services, they were composed primarily of national servicemen in the Army plus a couple of RAF personnel. The teams and results were

13 April 1955: English Services 15 French Services 7
at Leeds (3,453)
D. Metcalfe (Wakefield T); H.B. Howard (St Helens), P. Jackson (Barrow), M. Sullivan (Huddersfield), R. Bleasby (Keighley); B. Gabbitas (Hunslet), D. Rees (Belle Vue Rangers); J. Porritt (Dewsbury Celtic), L. Brookfield (Hull K.R.), C. Cooper (Hunslet), R.S. de Witt (Widnes), L. Gilfedder (Warrington), M. Bell (Keighley).
Tries: Howard, Jackson, Brookfield. *Goals:* Gilfedder 3.

15 April 1956   French Services 18 English Services 10
at Marseilles (6,000)
B.C. Critchley (Swinton); I. Southward (Workington T.), J. Challinor (Warrington), D. Hallas (Keighley), M. Sullivan (Huddersfield); G. Parkinson (Swinton), K. Gowers (Swinton); A. Key (Workington T.), L. Brookfield (Hull K.R.), T. Freeman (Leigh), R.S. de Witt (Widnes), B. Culley (Hunslet), D. Wilson (Barrow).
Tries: Challinor, Hallas. *Goals:* Southward 2.
(Programme cover Courtesy Peter Lush)

Speaking at a meeting of the RL Council in December 1956, the chairman, Hector Rawson (Hunslet), warned that there was a possibility that the inter-service matches would be discontinued. This was because the British Services, unlike the French Services, gave "little or no assistance". Rawson expressed the hope that the meetings would continue and that the British Services might be urged to promote the matches themselves. This proved to be a forlorn hope.

While sympathy for professional ambitions was good news for those good enough to secure a professional contract, it brought no real benefits to those serving regular soldiers who were only interested in playing amateur rugby league. Rugby union held sway, but occasionally there was news of soldiers being prepared to break the mould. The programme for the match at Leeds above makes reference to matches being played over the past two seasons by a unit of the Coldstream Guards stationed in the south. Obviously, it was possible to play regular rugby league matches, but this became much more difficult for southern based Army units when the Southern Amateur Rugby League (SARL) went into abeyance in 1955.

It should have been easier in the north of England, but even there only a couple of teams played regularly in the mid-1950s – one associated with Royal Tank Regiment's headquarters in Oldham and the other one with a unit of the Army Pay Corps which was housed in Halifax.

National service ends

A changing perception of the external threat and growing unpopularity at home after the Suez debacle led to National Service being scaled down from the late 1950s onwards. Numbers fell as deferments increased until finally the call-up was ended at the start of 1961, what remained of that last intake being demobbed in May 1963. After that, the Army returned to being a regulars' only outfit.

Clive Sullivan was probably the most successful regular to leave the Army to take up a professional contract. Having signed on with the Royal Signals, the Cardiff born winger was based at Catterick when he appeared as an 18-year-old trialist at the Boulevard in December 1961. Hull liked what they saw and the following day Sullivan signed professional forms. When Sullivan approached the Regiment to buy himself out, he was told that because of the expensive training he had received he would have to wait three years. Finally, in spring 1964, Sullivan secured his discharge. Over a professional career that would stretch to 1985, Clive Sullivan would make 17 appearances for Great Britain between 1967 and 1973 and 15 appearances for Wales RL between 1968 and 1979.

Interest was still present in the all-regular Army. The February 1968 issue of the *Rugby League Magazine* carried a report from Tony Smith on the activities in London which stated that two new clubs had been formed at the start of the year – one was the Coldstream Guards, Chelsea and the other was a team from the Parachute Regiment based at Aldershot – and joined the recently re-launched SARL. The Battalion of the Parachute Regiment was listed as a member of the SARL from 1969–70 to 1973–74 and Corporal N. Moore, based at the Rhine Barracks, was listed as the team's secretary. Although the Paras probably only played occasional fixtures, they did, according to the *John Player Rugby League Yearbook 1973–74*, win the SARL Sevens on at least one occasion.

Despite the obvious anomalies in the situation, nothing much appeared to have changed by the end of the 1980s. Sporting opportunity might be seen as a valuable recruiting tool in important areas of the country, but that was not enough to convince the Army to recognise rugby league. In the absence of formal recognition of the game, some units were still playing occasionally. Pressure to get Rugby League added to the 32 sports that were officially recognised by the Combined Services Sports Board had been applied, much of it in the Houses of Parliament by the All-Party Parliamentary Rugby League Group.

The RFL and the British Amateur Rugby League Association (BARLA) tried to help the process along on the field of play by staging the first inter-service match. An RAF XIII, representing the RAF Amateur Rugby League Association, which had been formed the previous month, met an Army team as a curtain-raiser to the opening match of the Kiwi tour at St Helens on Sunday 1 October 1989. A number of senior officers were present to see the scratch Army team, which was drawn from the ranks of the Royal Regiment of Fusiliers, the amalgamated successor to the old Lancashire Fusiliers, lose 22–14.

Once again, the match demonstrated that there was significant interest within the Army, but crucially not how much. Hopes that the incentive of a regular match against the French Army's Battalion Joinville would lead to a groundswell of interest proved unfounded. Discovering how much interest there was seemed to present at times an insurmountable problem and led BARLA's national secretary, Tom Keaveney, to comment rather ruefully in his 1991 report that "the ground swell of demand from within the Armed Forces for the playing of Rugby League is yet to materialise".

That continued to be a major stumbling block and when a delegation from the All-Party Parliamentary Rugby League Group met the Armed Forces Minister, Archie Hamilton, in March 1992 they were met with scepticism about the demand. A full and frank discussion at that meeting was probably instrumental in ending the impasse and led to officials of the Ministry of Defence being assigned to try and find ways for BARLA to coordinate interest and organise Rugby League in the Armed Forces.

Appendix 1: Statistics and records

Army Rugby League 1st XIII

Inter Services tournament

Season	Winners	Notes
1994	Army	Two matches, Army won both
1995	Army	
1996	Army	Retain trophy as holders after draw with RAF
1997	Army	
1998	Army	
1999	Army	
2000	Army	
2001	RAF	
2002	Army	
2003	Army	
2004	Royal Navy	
2005	RAF	Won on points difference
2006	RAF	Won on points difference
2007	RAF	
2008	Royal Navy	
2009	RAF	Won on points difference
2010	Army	
2011	Army	
2012	RAF	

Army versus Royal Navy: Since 2000, this match has been for the Jack Harrison VC Memorial Trophy. To 2012, the Army have won 6 times.

Army versus RAF: Since 2004, this match has been for the Nick Mawston Trophy. To 2012, the Army have won 5 times.

Inter-services tournament tables

1998	W	D	L	F	A	Pts
Army	2	0	0	70	26	4
RAF	1	0	1	41	52	2
Royal Navy	0	0	2	36	69	0

1999	W	D	L	F	A	Pts
Army	2	0	0	62	18	4
RAF	1	0	1	36	48	2
Royal Navy	0	0	2	34	66	0

2000	W	D	L	F	A	Pts
Army	2	0	0	50	24	4
Royal Navy	1	0	1	44	40	2
RAF	0	0	2	18	48	0

2001	W	D	L	F	A	Pts
RAF	2	0	0	51	28	4
Army	1	0	1	27	42	2
Royal Navy	0	0	2	22	30	0

2002	W	D	L	F	A	Pts
Army	2	0	0	74	31	4
Royal Navy	1	0	1	40	53	2
RAF	0	0	2	34	64	0

2003	W	D	L	F	A	Pts
Army	2	0	0	56	42	4
RAF	1	0	1	44	53	2
Royal Navy	0	0	2	41	46	0

2004	W	D	L	F	A	Pts
Royal Navy	2	0	0	45	26	4
RAF	1	0	1	32	44	2
Army	0	0	2	28	35	0

2005	W	D	L	F	A	Pts
RAF	1	0	1	55	42	2
Army	1	0	1	45	45	2
Royal Navy	1	0	1	44	66	2

2006	W	D	L	F	A	Pts
RAF	1	0	1	26	24	2
Army	1	0	1	29	27	2
Royal Navy	1	0	1	26	30	2

2007	W	D	L	F	A	Pts
RAF	2	0	0	39	20	4
Army	1	0	1	32	23	2
Royal Navy	0	0	2	14	42	0

2008	W	D	L	F	A	Pts
Royal Navy	2	0	0	60	22	4
Army	1	0	1	32	50	2
RAF	0	0	2	14	34	0

2009	W	D	L	F	A	Pts
RAF	1	0	1	54	38	2
Army	1	0	1	26	25	2
Royal Navy	1	0	1	33	50	2

2010	W	D	L	F	A	Pts
Army	2	0	0	52	18	4
Royal Navy	1	0	1	18	20	2
RAF	0	0	2	12	44	0

2011	W	D	L	F	A	Pts
Army	1	1	0	59	26	3
RAF	1	0	1	34	65	2
Royal Navy	0	1	1	30	32	1

2012	W	D	L	F	A	Pts
RAF	1	1	0	41	32	3
Royal Navy	1	0	1	42	25	2
Army	0	1	1	28	54	0

2013	W	D	L	F	A	Pts
Army	2	0	0	36	10	4
RAF	1	0	1	26	38	2
Royal Navy	0	0	2	26	40	0

Champions (to 2013)
Army: 12 (one retained by Army as holders in 1996 after draw)
RAF: 6 (2 on points difference)
Royal Navy: 2

Matches

Date	Opponents	Venue	Result (Army score first)
11 May 1994	RAF	Leigh	26–22
13 Dec 1994	RAF	Chatham	18–12
28 Apr 1995	RAF	Uxbridge	20–18
26 Apr 1996	RAF	Uxbridge	26–26
2 May 1997	RAF	Uxbridge	25–18
1 May 1998	RAF	Uxbridge	28–14
9 May 1998	Royal Navy	Aldershot	42–12
16 Sep 1999	Royal Navy	Portsmouth	32–16
22 Sep 1999	RAF	Chatham	30–2
13 Sep 2000	Royal Navy	Hull	28–18
20 Sep 2000	RAF	Uxbridge	22–6

7 Sep 2001	RAF	York	14–34
21 Sep 2001	Royal Navy	Portsmouth	13–8
Sep 2002	RAF	Dewsbury	42–13
Sep 2002	Royal Navy	Leigh	32–16
5 Sep 2003	RAF	Portsmouth	32–22
10 Sep 2003	Royal Navy	Portsmouth	24–20
10 Sep 2004	RAF	Uxbridge	16–18
29 Sep 2004	Royal Navy	Richmond	10–17
9 Sep 2005	Royal Navy	Portsmouth	23–24
21 Sep 2005	RAF	Richmond	22–12
13 Sep 2006	Royal Navy	Richmond	13–18
29 Sep 2006	RAF	Uxbridge	16–9
7 Sep 2007	Royal Navy	Portsmouth	18–8
19 Sep 2007	RAF	Aldershot	14–15
5 Sep 2008	RAF	Uxbridge	14–10
17 Sep 2008	Royal Navy	Aldershot	18–40
9 Sep 2009	RAF	Aldershot	16–14
25 Sep 2009	Royal Navy	Portsmouth	10–11
2 Sep 2010	Royal Navy	Aldershot	16–10
16 Sep 2010	RAF	Cranwell	36–8
1 Sep 2011	RAF	Aldershot	47–14
16 Sep 2011	Royal Navy	Portsmouth	12–12
21 Sep 2012	RAF	Cranwell	22–22
28 Sep 2012	Royal Navy	Aldershot	6–32
13 Sep 2013	RAF	Aldershot	18–4
20 Sep 2013	Royal Navy	Portsmouth	18–6

Army in all Inter-Services tournament matches:
Played: 37; Won: 25; Draw: 3; Lost: 9.
Against RAF: Played 22; Won 17; Draw: 2; Lost: 3
Against Royal Navy: Played: 16; Won: 9; Draw: 1; Lost 6.

Development team matches

2004
Royal Navy 36 RAF 14
RAF 16 Army 21
Army 25 Royal Navy 19

2005
Royal Navy 14 Army 35
RAF 20 Royal Navy 8
Army beat RAF

2006
Army 6 Royal Navy 28

Royal Navy 24 RAF 4
RAF lost to Army

2007
Royal Navy lost to Army
Army beat RAF
Royal Navy beat RAF

2008
Army 22 Royal Navy 22
RAF 6 Army 56
Royal Navy 56 RAF 6

2009
Army 100 RAF 0
RAF 34 Royal Navy 8
Royal Navy 4 Army 46

2010
Army 36 Royal Navy 12
RAF 16 Army 40
Royal Navy 16 RAF 12

2011
Army 40 RAF 8
Royal Navy 14 Army 4
RAF 0 Royal Navy 48

2012
Royal Navy 22 RAF 0
RAF 11 Army 4
Army 14 Royal Navy 26

2013
Army 16 RAF 14
Royal Navy 30 Army 40
RAF 38 Royal Navy 16

Ladies' matches

2008
Army 52 Royal Navy 0
RAF 0 Army 42
Royal Navy 34 RAF 6

2009
Army 52 RAF 4
Royal Navy 0 Army 72
RAF 18 Royal Navy 22

2010
Army 70 Royal Navy 8
Royal Navy 14 RAF 10

2011
Army 44 RAF 0
Royal Navy 14 Army 36
RAF 4 Royal Navy 28

2012
Army 64 Royal Navy 0

2013
Army 64 RAF 0
Royal Navy 4 Army 66

Veterans team matches

2009
Army beat RAF
RAF 35 Royal Navy 20
RN 22 Army 24

2010
Army 40 Royal Navy 18
RAF 6 Army 58
Royal Navy 12 RAF 32

2011
Royal Navy 12 Army 24

2012 and 2013
No matches played

Challenge Cup

(Professional opposition in **bold**)

Season	Rd	Date	H/A	Opponents	Result (Army score first)
2000	1	4 Dec 1999	H	Dewsbury Celtic	54–7
	2	18 Dec 1999	H	Oulton Raiders	24–10
	3	16 Jan 2000	A	**Rochdale Hornets**	6–66
2001	1	16 Dec 2000	A	Wath Brow Hornets	6–41
2001–2	1	1 Dec 2001	A	Saddleworth Rangers	15–6
	2	15 Dec 2001	A	Halton Simms Cross	10–34
2002–3	1	1 Dec 2002	A	Hunslet Warriors	10–22
2003–4	1	27 Nov 03	A	East Hull	12–22
2005	1	5 Feb 2005	A	West Hull	38–8
	2	19 Feb 2005	A	Waterhead	12–15
2006	1	4 Feb 2006	H	West Hull	38–18
	2	18 Feb 2006	H	West Bowling	14–20
2007	1	3 Feb 2007	H	Leigh Miners Rangers	20–28
2008	1	3 Feb 2008	H	Thatto Heath	34–12
	2	24 Feb 2008	A	Ince Rose Bridge	26–25
	3	11 Mar 2008	H	**Oldham Roughyeds**	10–56
2009	P	18 Jan 2009	A	West London Sharks	22–10
	1	24 Jan 2009	H	Northumbria University	72–0
	2	14 Feb 2009	A	Featherstone Lions	30–12
	3	8 Mar 2009	A	**Featherstone Rovers**	2–94
2010	1	23 Jan 2010	A	Featherstone Lions	24–14
	2	14 Feb 2010	A	Warrington Wizards	20–28
2011	1	23 Jan 2011	A	Valley Cougars	30–24
	2	5 Feb 2011	H	RAF	27–16
	3	5 Mar 2011	A	**Featherstone Rovers**	0–86

| 2012 | 2 | 10 Mar 2012 | A | Oulton Raiders | 5–19 |
| 2013 | 2 | 9 Mar 2013 | A | Leigh East | 24–28 |

Army in Challenge Cup summary (to end 2013)

| | | | | | | Round Achieved | | | |
Played	Won	Draw	Lost	Home	Away	Rd 1	Rd 2	Rd 3	Rd 4
27	13	0	14	9	18	4	5	4	0

Public Services Cup

(N.B. This competition has had various sponsors, including Scottish Courage, Skanska and Steeden). It usually had two groups, then a semi-final and final.

Season	Rd	Date	H/A	Opponents	Result (Army score first)
1998	QF	22 July 1998		British Students	10–35
1999	SF	30 Jun 1999	A	Royal Navy	36–18
	F	25 Aug 1999	St Helens	British Students	28–22
2000	Gr	Mar 2000	Leigh MR	Civil Service	
2000		29 Jun 2000	A	RAF	37–4
2000	F	28 Jul 2000	Castleford LL	British Students	16–36
2001	Gr		H	Royal Navy	20–8
	Gr		A	Civil Service & Prison Service	36–30
	Gr		A	BARLA GB under-21	10–40
2002	F	19 Mar 2003	Leigh MR	BARLA GB under-21	6–62
	Gr	5 May 2004	A	BARLA GB under-21	
2004	Gr	28 July 2004	A	Civil Service	
2005	Gr	5 Jul 2005	A	Scottish Students	
2006	Gr	5 Apr 2006	Shaw Cross	British Police	18–26
2006	Gr		H	Prison Service	26–18
2006	Gr		A	British Students	30–18
	SF			British Police	W
2006	F	4 Oct 2006	Batley	BARLA GB	16–40
2007	Gr	18 Apr 2007	A	BARLA GB	14–26
2009	Gr	25 Mar 2009	A	Prison Service	34–26
	Gr	1 Apr 2009	A	British Police	22–20
	Gr	13 May 2009	H	British Students	6–28

International series or tours:

New Zealand 2001
New Zealand 2002
Australia 2004
South Africa 2009

Other matches
(Army score first)

3 Jul 2010	GB Community Lions	A	4–26
14 Jul 2010	Blackwood Bulldogs	A	38–22
1 Aug 2010	Castleford Panthers	A	40–0
4 Aug 2010	Myton Warriors	A	40–20
7 Aug 2010	BARLA	A	18–42
16 Jul 2011	East Hull	A	20–12
20 Jul 2011	GB Police	A	16–16
30 Jul 2011	Castleford Panthers	A	42–12
2 Aug 2011	Myton Warriors	A	18–18
6 Aug 2011	BARLA	A	22–23
23 May 2012	England Students	A	30–32
13 Jun 2012	GB Police	A	24–4
31 Jul 2012	Fryston	A	18–26
5 Aug 2012	London Skolars 'A'	A	42–10
2 Sep 2012	BARLA	A	16–48

Army Rugby League competitions

Army Rugby League Lawson Cup (Corps Championship)

Season	Winners	Runners Up
1995	Royal Engineers	Royal Electrical & Mechanical Engineers
1996	Royal Engineers	Royal Signals
1997	Royal Engineers	Royal Signals
1998	Royal Engineers	Infantry
1999	Royal Engineers	Royal Electrical & Mechanical Engineers
2000	Royal Electrical & Mechanical Engineers	Royal Engineers
2001	Royal Engineers	Royal Electrical & Mechanical Engineers

Year			
2002	Adjutant General's Corps	Royal Engineers	
2003	Royal Engineers	Royal Electrical & Mechanical Engineers	AGC ⁻ RLC 4th
2004	Royal Engineers	Royal Electrical & Mechanical Engineers	RAC – R Sigs
2005	Royal Engineers	Royal Logistic Corps	R Sigs – Inf
2006	Royal Engineers	Royal Armoured Corps	RAC – R Sigs
2007	Royal Engineers	Royal Armoured Corps	RA – RLC
2008	Royal Engineers	Royal Electrical & Mechanical Engineers	RLC – R Sigs
2009	Royal Engineers		
2010	Royal Artillery (42–4 in final)	Royal Electrical & Mechanical Engineers	
2011	Royal Engineers (22–10 in final at The Stoop)	Royal Electrical & Mechanical Engineers	
2012	Royal Artillery (36–22 in final)	Royal Electrical & Mechanical Engineers	League 2: R Sigs 40 AGC 34

Army Rugby League Yeoman Cup Competition (Club Competition)

Season	Date	Venue	Cup Winners	Shield Winners
1995	Apr	Chatham	1 RSME Regt	NA
1996	Apr	Arborfield	1 PARA	NA
1996	Nov	Chatham	7 PARA RHA	NA
1997	Sep	Uxbridge	1 RSME Regt	1 QLR
1998	30 Sep 98	Chatham	38 Engr Regt	2 PARA
1999	29 Sep 99	Chatham	38 Engr Regt	SEME
2000	19 Nov 00	Arborfield	38 Engr Regt	39 Engr Regt
2001	10 Oct 01	Aldershot	SEAE	
2002	25 Jul 03	Aldershot	1 RSME Regt	11 Sigs Regt
2003	24 Sep 03	Aldershot	1 RSME Regt	Not played
2004	29 Sep 04	Aldershot	2 RGJ	1 RSME Regt
2005	28 Sep 05	Aldershot	1 RGJ	3 RSME Regt
2006	20 Sep 06	Aldershot	3 YORKS (Dukes)	2 LANCS
2007	26 Sep 07	Aldershot	3 YORKS (Dukes)	Not played
2008	16 Jul 08	Aldershot	12 (Air Sp) Engr Gp	42 Engr Regt
2009	22 Jul 09	Aldershot	3 YORKS (44–14 in final)	RSME
2010				
2011	20 Jul 2011	Aldershot	29 Regt RLC	Plate: 4 Med Regt Bowl: 1 Gren Guards

2012	20 Jun 2012	Borden	3 YORKS	
2013	24 July 2013	Aldershot	3 YORKS	Plate: 33 Engr Regt Bowl: ASPT

Army Rugby League Corps 9s

Season	Date	Venue	Cup Winners	Shield Winners
2004	Mar	Bordon	Royal Engineers	
2005	Jul	Harrogate	Royal Engineers	Infantry
2006	6 Sep	Aldershot	Royal Engineers	RLC

Army Rugby League (Club Competition)
Champions Challenge Trophy

Season	Date	Venue	Cup Winners	Runners Up	Remarks
1998	5 Jul 08	Chatham	1 RSME Regt	2 RRF	(48 – 18)
2003	01 Oct 03	Aldershot	1 DWR	1 RSME Regt	(15 – 13)
2005	5 Oct 05	Aldershot	1 DWR	1 RGJ	(50 – 16)

Army Rugby League Unit 9s: Naivalurua Cup from 2013

Season	Date	Venue	Cup Winners	Shield Winners
1994	Apr	Chepstow	12 RSME Regt (7's)	NA
1995	Sep	Ripon	1 PARA	NA
1996	Sep	Arborfield	1 PARA	NA
1997	Mar	Chatham	Royal Navy	NA
1998	28 Feb 1998	Chatham	1 RSME Regt	HMS Collingwood
1999	Apr	Chester	25 Engr Regt	1 RWF
2000	04 Mar 2000	Chatham	25 Engr Regt	RDG
2001	Mar 2001	Deepcut		
2002	Mar 2002	Aldershot	1 RRW	
2003	12 Mar 2003	Bordon	SEAE	HMS Sultan
2004	Mar 2004	Deepcut	1 RSME Regt	2 Sig Regt
2005	Mar 2005	Aldershot	16 AA Regt RLC	11 Sig Regt
2006	15 Mar 2006	Aldershot	1 RSME Regt	38 Engr Regt
2007	4 Jul 2007	Aldershot	1 SCOTS	1 RSME Regt
2008	5 Jul 2008	Aldershot	2 LANCS	
2011	6 May 2011	Aldershot	3 YORKS	Plate: 21 Engr Regt Bowl: 39 Engr Regt
2013	22 May 2013	Aldershot	Paras	Plate: ASPT

Trafalgar Cup

2000: Paras 0 Royal Marines 36
2001:
2002: Not played
2003: Not played
2004: Paras 16 Royal Marines 6
2005: Paras 6 Royal Marines 20
2006:

2007: Not played
2008: Not played
2009: Royal Marines 26 Paras 26
2010: Paras 25 Royal Marines 14
2011: Paras 4 Royal Marines 28
2012: Royal Marines 16 Paras 30

Nines competitions

York 9s
Carnegie 9s 2010 & qualifying tournament
All Golds Cup 2009
Middlesex 9s (RE): Winners: 2003, 2005, runners-up: 2004

International Players:

Lee Innes   British Amateur Rugby League Association
Darrell Cooper   British Amateur Rugby League Association
Dave Goddard   British Amateur Rugby League Association
Rob Smart   Great Britain Community Lions & Scotland
Ben Taylor   Great Britain Community Lions
Marc Donnelly   Great Britain / England Community Lions
Tom Howley   Great Britain Community Lions
Colin Maragon   Great Britain Community Lions

Lee Innes and Darrell Cooper both played for Great Britain & Ireland in the 2000 Emerging Nations World Cup.

Appendix 2: The Army ranks and structure

Ranks (in order of seniority):

Officer ranks

General
Lieutenant-General
Major-General
Brigadier
Colonel
Lieutenant-Colonel
Major

Captain
Lieutenant
Second Lieutenant
Officer Cadet (This rank is held only during initial officer training at the Royal Military Academy Sandhurst)

Non Commissioned ranks

Warrant Officer Class 1
Warrant Officer Class 2
Staff/Colour Sergeant
Sergeant

Corporal
Lance Corporal
Private

All new soldiers start as Privates although the title may be Trooper, Gunner, Signaller, Sapper, Guardsman, Craftsman, Rifleman or even Kingsman, depending on the Corps/Regiment joined after completion of initial training. There are also different names for some other ranks, e.g. Bombardier for Corporal in the Royal Regiment of Artillery.

All ranks within the British Army (but excluding the Army Reserve) are eligible for selection to represent the Army at Rugby League. They can be drawn from any part of the Army, which is organised into the following Corps and Regiments (only Regiments with different cap badges are listed):

Royal Armoured Corps, made up of:
Household Cavalry
Queen's Dragoon Guards
Royal Scots Dragoon Guards
Royal Dragoon Guards
Queen's Royal Hussars
/ Lancers
King's Royal Hussars
Light Dragoons
Queen's Royal Lancers
 Royal Tank Regiment
 Royal Tank Regiment
Army Air Corps
Royal Regiment of Artillery
Royal Corps of Signals
Corps of Royal Engineers
Corps of Royal Electrical & Mechanical Engineers
Royal Logistic Corps
Intelligence Corps
Royal Army Chaplains Department
Infantry, made up of:
Grenadier Guards
Coldstream Guards
Scots Guards

Irish Guards
Welsh Guards
Royal Regiment of Scotland
Princess of Wales's Royal Regiment
Duke of Lancaster's Regiment
Royal Regiment of Fusiliers
Royal Anglian Regiment
Yorkshire Regiment
Mercian Regiment
Royal Welsh
Royal Irish Regiment
Parachute Regiment
Royal Gurkha Rifles
Rifles
Adjutant General's Corps
Army Medical Services, made up of:
Royal Army Medical Corps
Royal Army Veterinary Corps
Royal Army Dental Corps
Royal Army Nursing Corps
Corps of Army Music
Royal Army Physical Training Corps
Small Arms School Corps

As at date of publication, with acknowledgement to www.army.mod.uk

Bibliography

BARLA handbooks	1990–91, 1991–92, 1992–93 (Huddersfield)
Billot, John	*The All Blacks in Wales* (Ferndale, 1972)
Collins, Tony	*A Social History of English Rugby Union* (London, 2009)
Cooper, Stephen	*The Final Whistle: The Great War in Fifteen Players* (Stroud, 2012)
Dalby, Ken	*The Headingley Story 1890-1955 Volume 1: Rugby* (Leeds, n.d.)
Evans, Craig (compiler)	*A History of Millom RLFC From 1873* (Millom, 2010)
Foster, Simon, Gate Robert & Lush, Peter	*Trevor Foster* (London, 2005)
Fox, Dave & Hoskins, Mark	*100 Greats: Bristol FC (RFU)* (Stroud, 2002)
Heyman, Charles	*The British Army Guide 2012–13* (Barnsley, 2011)
Hickman, Tom	*The Call-Up* (London, 2004)
Hinchliffe, David	*Rugby's Class War* (London, 2000)
Hoyer Millar, C.C.	*Fifty Years of Rosslyn Park* (London, 1929)
Huxley, John	*The Rugby League Challenge Cup* (Enfield, 1992)
Latus, Joe	*Hard Road to the Top* (Hull, 1973)
Mace, John	*The History of RAF Rugby* (2000)
Mather, Tom	*Missing In Action* (Lytham, 2005)
Mason, Tony & Riedi, Eliza	*Sport and the Military* (Cambridge, 2010)
McLaren, John	*The History of Army Rugby* (Aldershot, 1986)
Moorhouse, Geoffrey	*Hell's Foundations* (Sevenoaks, 1993)
	A People's Game (London, 1995)
Oldham RL Heritage Trust	*Watersheddings Memories* (Oldham, 2010)
Riddoch, Andrew & Kemp, John	*When the Whistle Blows* (Yeovil, 2011)
Schleppi, Dr John R	*Rugby League in Wartime* (Code 13 Numbers 2, 10, 12)
Sheard, Stuart	*Let Them Play By All Means* (2012)
Smith, David & Williams, Gareth	*Fields of Praise* (Cardiff, 1980)
Turner, Michael	*Oldham RLFC: The Complete History* (Oldham, 1997)
Wilkinson, Tim & Gent, Ray	*Rugby League In Its Own Words* (Halifax, 2004)
Willacy, Gavin	*Rugby League Bravehearts* (London, 2002)
Williams, Nigel	*Bradford Northern* (Bradford, 1989)
Winstanley, Jack (ed.)	*John Player Rugby League Yearbook* (London, 1973)
BARLA / RFL Bulletin	Various issues
Daily Telegraph	12 May 1994
League Express	Various issues
League Weekly	Various issues
Rugby League Gazette	February 1950, Volume 4 Number 7
Rugby League Journal	Number 5 (Winter 2003)
Rugby League Magazine	Volume 3, Number 26 (February 1968)
Rugby League World	Various issues
Rugby Leaguer	Various issues
RFL	Programme for Services International 13 April 1955
Open Rugby	Number 119 – November 1989
Yorkshire Post	Friday 22 December 2006

Various websites, including Army RL, RAF RL, Royal Navy RL, Royal Engineers RL and Soldiers' League
Various Army RL publications, including match programmes, handbooks and annual reports.

Other books from London League Publications Ltd:

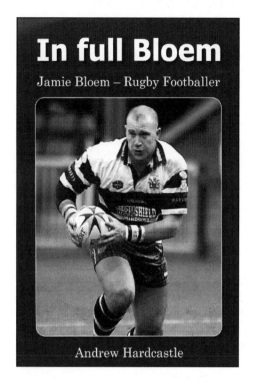

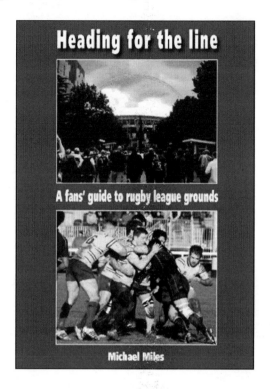

In full Bloem: The explosive biography of Jamie Bloem, current referee and former Halifax, South Africa and Scotland player.
Published in February 2013 @ £14.95 (hardback), just £12.00 post free in the UK direct from London League Publications Ltd.

Heading for the line: Great new guidebook for rugby league grounds, published in April 2013 @ £7.95 (paperback), just £7.50 post free in the UK direct from London League Publications Ltd.

All our books can be ordered from any bookshop @ full price. To order direct from London League Publications Ltd visit our website: www.llpshop.co.uk or write to LLP, PO Box 65784, London NW2 9NS (cheques payable to London League Publications Ltd).

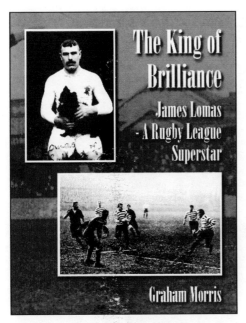

Great new book about one of the sport's genuine legends. James Lomas played for Bramley, Salford, Oldham and York, and won representative honours for Lancashire, Cumberland, England and Great Britain. He captained the first Lions team to tour Australia and New Zealand in 1910. This is the first biography of him.

Published in October 2011 at £16.95 (hardback). Copies available for jut £13.95 post-free in the United Kingdom direct from London League Publications Ltd, PO Box 65784, London NW2 9NS (cheques payable to London League Publications Ltd); credit card orders via our website: www.llpshop.co.uk or from any bookshop. Available as an E-Book for Kindle from www.Amazon.co.uk

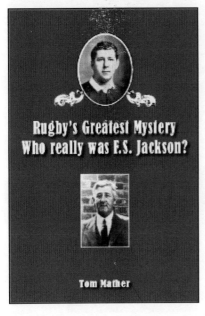

Rugby's Greatest Mystery
Who really was F.S. Jackson?

A true life rugby detective story

This is the story of a man whose life was made up of mystery, intrigue and deception, but was also a Rugby Union star before the First World War. He played for Leicester and Cornwall when they won the 1908 County Championship. He was selected for the Anglo-Welsh Rugby Union tour to New Zealand and Australia in 1908. However, the RFU recalled him from the tour and banned him from the sport over allegations that he was a professional player, and had played for Swinton in the Northern Union. The scandal around his suspension from rugby union caused great problems for the RFU and almost saw a further split in the game.

He then played Rugby League for New Zealand, against the British Lions in 1910. After the First World War he was reinstated by the New Zealand RU, became an East Coast selector and saw his son play for the All Blacks. For around 60 years he used the name Frederick Stanley Jackson, even though it was not his given name. When he died in 1957 he took to the grave his true identity. Even his family knew little about his early years in England, or even where he came from. **It was a mystery that remained unresolved until now.** The book also includes an analysis of the development of Leicester Tigers RFC up to the First World War.

Published in March 2012 at £12.95. Copies available for just £9.95 post-free in the United Kingdom direct from London League Publications Ltd, PO Box 65784, London NW2 9NS (cheques payable to London League Publications Ltd); credit card orders via our website: www.llpshop.co.uk or from any bookshop. Available as an E-Book for Kindle from www.Amazon.co.uk

Best in the Northern Union

The pioneering 1910 Rugby League Lions tour of Australia and New Zealand

Tom Mather

Fascinating account of the first Great Britain Lions tour of Australia and New Zealand. Published in 2010 at £12.95, special offer £10.00 post-free in the United Kingdom direct from London League Publications Ltd. Credit card orders via www.llpshop.co.uk , orders by cheque to LLP, PO Box 65784, London NW2 9NS
Available as an E-Book for Kindle on www.Amazon.co.uk

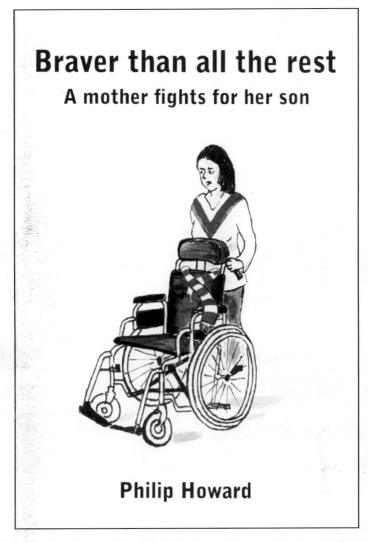

Braver than all the rest

A mother fights for her son

Philip Howard

Dave and Sarah Burgess are devastated when their young son Karl is found to have muscular dystrophy. Then another tragedy hits the family hard. But the family are committed to do the best they can for Karl, who has a passion for rugby league. Based in Castleton, a Yorkshire town near the border with Lancashire, Karl's determination to get the most out of life, despite his disability, inspires those around him, in particular Chris Anderton, one of the Castleton Rugby League Club players, who is coming to the end of his career in the game. A moving novel of family life and rugby league.

Published in 2010 at £9.95, special offer £9.00 direct from London League Publications Ltd.
Credit card orders via www.llpshop.co.uk ,
orders by cheque to LLP, PO Box 65784, London NW2 9NS
Available as an E-Book for Kindle from Amazon.co.uk

"Come on Northern"

The fall and rise of
Bradford Northern RLFC 1954 to 1965

Trevor Delaney

The collapse of Bradford Northern RLFC in December 1963 sent shock waves throughout rugby league in Great Britain. Northern were the first team to appear in three successive Wembley Cup finals, from 1947 to 1949, and were top of the league at the start of the 1954–55 season.

However, by December 1963, this once proud club had sunk to the bottom of the league table and withdrew from the competition in mid-season. It was the first time since the 1920s that a team had pulled out of the league without completing their fixtures. Their membership of the Rugby Football League was terminated and that season's record was expunged.

No club in the game's history had fallen from the heights quite like the old Northern. Their subsequent re-entry to the league was a great achievement for two men of vision – former Odsal greats, Trevor Foster and Joe Phillips.

The acclaimed rugby league historian, Trevor Delaney, recalls this period in the club's turbulent history. *"Come on Northern"* is an essential read for everyone interested in rugby league.

Available for just £13.00 post free in the UK direct from London League Publications Ltd. Credit card orders via .llpshop.co.uk; payment by cheque to PO Box 65784, London NW2 9NS. Available in bookshops at £13.95.

Available as an E-Book for Kindle at www.Amazon.co.uk